THE RECURSIVE BOOK OF RECURSION

T0266406

THE RECURSIVE BOOK OF RECURSION

Ace the Coding Interview with Python and JavaScript

by Al Sweigart

**no starch
press**

San Francisco

Printed in the United States of America

First printing

26 25 24 23 22   1 2 3 4 5

ISBN-13: 978-1-7185-0202-4 (print)
ISBN-13: 978-1-7185-0203-1 (ebook)

Publisher: William Pollock
Production Manager: Rachel Monaghan
Production Editor: Miles Bond
Developmental Editor: Frances Saux
Cover Illustrator: James L. Barry
Interior Design: Octopod Studios
Technical Reviewer: Sarah Kuchinsky
Copyeditor: Sharon Wilkey
Compositor: Maureen Forys, Happenstance Type-O-Rama
Proofreader: Audrey Doyle

For information on distribution, bulk sales, corporate sales, or translations, please contact No Starch Press, Inc. directly at info@nostarch.com or:

No Starch Press, Inc.
245 8th Street, San Francisco, CA 94103
phone: 1.415.863.9900
www.nostarch.com

Library of Congress Cataloging-in-Publication Data

Library of Congress Control Number: 2022932456

[S]

To Jack, who held up a mirror
in front of my mirror

About the Author

Al Sweigart is a software developer, fellow of the Python Software Foundation, and author of several programming books with No Starch Press, including the worldwide bestseller *Automate the Boring Stuff with Python*. His Creative Commons licensed works are available at *https://www.inventwithpython.com*.

About the Technical Reviewer

Sarah Kuchinsky, MS, is a corporate trainer and consultant. She uses Python for a variety of applications, including health systems modeling, game development, and task automation. Sarah is a co-founder of the North Bay Python conference, tutorials chair for PyCon US, and lead organizer for PyLadies Silicon Valley. She holds degrees in management science as well as in engineering and mathematics.

BRIEF CONTENTS

CONTENTS IN DETAIL

6
PERMUTATIONS AND COMBINATIONS

7
MEMOIZATION AND DYNAMIC PROGRAMMING

8
TAIL CALL OPTIMIZATION

9
DRAWING FRACTALS

PART II: PROJECTS   201

10
FILE FINDER   203

11
MAZE GENERATOR   215

12
SLIDING-TILE SOLVER   231

FOREWORD

When I was approached by Al to write the foreword to this book, I was pretty excited about the prospect. A book on recursion! Now, that's something you just don't see every day. Considered by many to be one of the more mysterious topics in programming, recursion is often discouraged. Oddly, this stands in stark contrast to its storied use in weird job interview questions.

However, there are all sorts of practical reasons to learn about recursion. Recursive thinking is very much a mindset about problem-solving. At its core, larger problems get broken into smaller problems. And sometimes along the way, hard problems are rewritten into equivalent but easier-to-solve simple problems. This sort of thinking can be a useful tool when applied to software design—even when recursion is not being used. Thus, it's a worthy topic of study for programmers of all skill levels.

In my unbridled excitement to say more about recursion, I originally wrote this foreword in the form of a few short stories involving friends who'd applied recursive thinking in different ways but achieved a similar result. First there was the story of Ben, who learned about recursion, took it too far, and somehow managed to disappear off the face of the earth under mysterious circumstances after committing the following Python code into production:

```
result = [(lambda r: lambda n: 1 if n < 2 else r(r)(n-1) + r(r)(n-2))(
          (lambda r: lambda n: 1 if n < 2 else r(r)(n-1) + r(r)(n-2)))(n)
          for n in range(37)]
```

Then there was the story of Chelsea, who became so effective at real-world problem-solving that she was promptly fired! Oh, you wouldn't believe how much all the fine editors at No Starch (bless their hearts) hated these stories. "You can't start a book by telling people stories like that. It's just going to scare everyone away!" To be fair, they probably have a point. In fact, they *even* made me move a more reassuring paragraph about recursion from later in this foreword up to the second paragraph just so you wouldn't first read about the stories of Ben and Chelsea and run away in a screaming horror to read a book about design patterns instead.

Clearly, writing the foreword to a book is serious business. So, regrettably, I'll have to share the true stories of Ben and Chelsea with you another time. But, getting back to the book, it's true that recursion is not a technique that gets applied to the vast majority of problems in day-to-day programming. As such, it often carries an aura of magic about it. This book hopes to dispel much of that. This is a good thing.

Finally, as you set off on your recursion journey, be prepared to have your brain bent in new directions. Not to worry—this is normal! However, it's also important to stress that recursion is supposed to be a bit of fun. Well, at least a little bit. So, enjoy the ride!

—David Beazley
Author of *Python Cookbook* and *Python Distilled*
Teacher of aspiring problem solvers
https://www.dabeaz.com

ACKNOWLEDGMENTS

It's misleading to have only my name on the cover. I'd like to thank my publisher, Bill Pollock; my editor, Frances Saux; my technical reviewer, Sarah Kuchinsky; my production editor, Miles Bond; the production manager, Rachel Monaghan; and the rest of the staff at No Starch Press for their invaluable help.

Finally, I would like to thank my family, friends, and readers for all their suggestions and support.

INTRODUCTION

The programming technique of recursion can produce elegant code solutions. More often, however, it produces confused programmers. This doesn't mean programmers can (or should) ignore recursion. Despite its reputation for being challenging, recursion is an important computer science topic and can yield keen insights into programming itself. At the very least, knowing recursion can help you nail a coding job interview.

If you're a student with an interest in computer science, recursion is a necessary hurdle you'll have to overcome to understand many popular algorithms. If you're a programming bootcamp graduate or self-taught programmer who managed to bypass the more theoretical computer science topics, recursion problems are still sure to come up during whiteboard coding interviews. And if you're an experienced software engineer who has never touched a recursive algorithm before, you might find recursion to be an embarrassing gap in your knowledge.

There's no need to worry. Recursion isn't as hard to understand as it is to teach. As I'll explain in Chapter 1, I attribute the widespread misunderstanding of recursion to poor instruction rather than any inherent difficulty. And since recursive functions aren't commonly used in day-to-day programming, many folks get along just fine without them.

But a certain conceptual beauty lies behind recursive algorithms that can aid your understanding of programming even if you don't often apply them. Recursion has a visual beauty as well. The technique is behind the amazing mathematical art of *fractals*, the self-similar shapes shown in Figure 1.

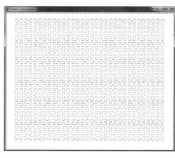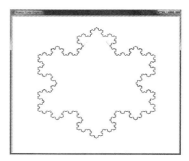

Figure 1: These examples of fractals include a Sierpiński triangle (left), a Hilbert curve (center), and a Koch snowflake (right).

However, this book is not entirely in praise of recursion. I include some sharp criticisms of this technique. Recursion is overused in cases where a simpler solution exists. Recursive algorithms can be hard to understand, have worse performance, and are susceptible to crash-causing stack overflow errors. And a certain kind of programmer may use recursion not because it's the right technique for a given problem, but simply because they feel smarter when they write code that other programmers struggle to understand. Computer scientist Dr. John Wilander once said, "When you finish a PhD in computer science, they take you to a special room and explain that you must never use recursion in real life. Its only purpose is to make programming hard for undergrads."

So, whether you want to get an edge in coding interviews, you want to create beautiful mathematical art, or you stubbornly seek to finally understand the intriguing properties of this concept, this book will be your guide down the rabbit hole that is recursion (and the rabbit holes within that rabbit hole). Recursion is one of the computer science topics that separates the professionals from the beginners. By reading this book, you'll master a great skill and learn its dark secret: recursion isn't as complicated as people think it is.

Who Is This Book For?

This book is for those who are intimidated or intrigued by recursive algorithms. Recursion is one of those topics that seems like black magic to beginner programmers or freshman computer science students. Most recursion lessons are hard to follow and make the subject seem frustrating, even fearsome. For these readers, I hope this book's direct explanations and ample examples can help make the topic finally click.

The only prerequisite for this book is basic programming experience with either the Python or JavaScript programming languages, which the chapters' code examples use. The book's programs have been stripped down to their essences; if you know how to call and create functions and the difference between global and local variables, you know enough to work through the programming examples.

About This Book

This book has 14 chapters:

Part I: Understanding Recursion

Chapter 1: What Is Recursion?   Explains recursion and how it is the natural result of the way programming languages implement functions and function calls. This chapter also argues that recursion isn't nearly the elegant, mystical concept many claim it is.

Chapter 2: Recursion vs. Iteration   Dives into the differences (and many similarities) between recursive and iterative techniques.

Chapter 3: Classic Recursion Algorithms   Covers famous recursive programs such as the Tower of Hanoi, the flood fill algorithm, and others.

Chapter 4: Backtracking and Tree Traversal Algorithms   Discusses a problem for which recursion is particularly suited: traversing tree data structures, such as when solving mazes and navigating a directory.

Chapter 5: Divide-and-Conquer Algorithms   Discusses how recursion is useful for splitting large problems into smaller subproblems and covers several common divide-and-conquer algorithms.

Chapter 6: Permutations and Combinations   Covers recursive algorithms involving ordering and matching, as well as the common programming problems to which these techniques are applied.

Chapter 7: Memoization and Dynamic Programming   Explains some simple tricks to improve code efficiency when applying recursion in the real world.

Chapter 8: Tail Call Optimization   Covers tail call optimization, a common technique used to improve the performance of recursive algorithms, and how it works.

Chapter 9: Drawing Fractals Tours the intriguing art that can be programmatically produced by recursive algorithms. This chapter makes use of turtle graphics for generating its images.

Part II: Projects

Chapter 10: File Finder Covers a project that searches through the files on your computer according to custom search parameters you provide.

Chapter 11: Maze Generator Covers a project that automatically generates mazes of any size using the recursive backtracker algorithm.

Chapter 12: Sliding-Tile Solver Covers a project that solves sliding-tile puzzles, also called 15-puzzles.

Chapter 13: Fractal Art Maker Explores a project that can produce custom fractal art of your own design.

Chapter 14: Droste Maker Explores a project that produces recursive, picture-in-picture images using the Pillow image-manipulation module.

Hands-On, Experimental Computer Science

Reading about recursion won't teach you how to implement it on its own. This book includes many recursive code examples in both the Python and JavaScript programming languages for you to experiment with. If you're new to programming, you can read my book *Automate the Boring Stuff with Python,* 2nd edition (No Starch Press, 2019), or *Python Crash Course,* 2nd edition, by Eric Matthes (No Starch Press, 2019) for an introduction to both programming and the Python programming language.

I recommend stepping through these programs with a debugger. A *debugger* lets you execute programs one line at a time and inspect the state of the program along the way, allowing you to pinpoint where bugs occur. Chapter 11 of *Automate the Boring Stuff with Python,* 2nd edition, covers how to use the Python debugger and is free to read online at *https://automatetheboringstuff.com/2e/chapter11.*

The chapters in this book display the Python and JavaScript code examples together. The Python code is saved in a *.py* file, and the JavaScript code in an *.html* file (not a *.js* file). For example, take the following *hello.py* file:

```
print('Hello, world!')
```

And the following *hello.html* file:

```
<script type="text/javascript">
document.write("Hello, world!<br />");
</script>
```

The two code listings act as a Rosetta stone, describing programs that produce the same results in two different languages.

NOTE *The `<br />` HTML tag in* hello.html *is a* break return, *also called a* newline, *which prevents all the output from appearing on a single line. Python's* `print()` *function automatically adds break returns to the end of the text, while JavaScript's* `document.write()` *function doesn't.*

I encourage you to manually copy these programs by using your keyboard, rather than simply copying and pasting their source code into a new file. This helps your "muscle memory" of the programs and forces you to consider each line as you type it.

The *.html* files are technically not valid because they're missing several necessary HTML tags, such as `<html>` and `<body>`, but your browser will still be able to display the output. These tags have been left out on purpose. The programs in this book are written for simplicity and readability, not to demonstrate web development best practices.

Installing Python

While every computer has a web browser that can view the *.html* files in this book, you must install Python separately if you wish to run the book's Python code. You can download Python for Microsoft Windows, Apple macOS, and Ubuntu Linux for free from *https://python.org/downloads*. Be sure to download a version of Python 3 (such as 3.10) and not Python 2. Python 3 made a few backward-incompatible changes to the language, and the programs in this book may not run correctly, if at all, on Python 2.

Running IDLE and the Python Code Examples

You can use the IDLE editor that comes with Python to write your Python code or install a free editor, such as the Mu Editor from *https://codewith.mu*, PyCharm Community Edition from *https://www.jetbrains.com/pycharm/download*, or Microsoft Visual Studio Code from *https://code.visualstudio.com/Download*.

To open IDLE on Windows, open the Start menu in the lower-left corner of your screen, enter **IDLE** in the search box, and select **IDLE (Python 3.10 64-bit)**.

On macOS, open the Finder window and click **Applications ▸ Python 3.10**, and then the IDLE icon.

On Ubuntu, select **Applications ▸ Accessories ▸ Terminal** and then enter **IDLE 3**. You may also be able to click **Applications** at the top of the screen, select **Programming**, and then click **IDLE 3**.

IDLE has two types of windows. The interactive shell window has the >>> prompt and is used for running Python instructions one at a time. This is useful when you want to experiment with bits of Python code. The file editor window is where you can enter full Python programs and save them as *.py* files. This is how you'll enter the source code for the Python programs in this book. To open a new file editor window, click **File ▸ New File**. You can run the programs by clicking **Run ▸ Run Module** or pressing **F5**.

Running the JavaScript Code Examples in the Browser

Your computer's web browser can run the JavaScript programs and display their output, but to write JavaScript code, you'll need a text editor. A simple program like Notepad or TextMate will do, but you can also install text editors specifically for writing code, such as IDLE or Sublime Text from *https://www.sublimetext.com*.

After typing the code for your JavaScript programs, save the files as *.html* files, not *.js* files. Open them in a web browser to view the results. Any modern web browser works for this purpose.

PART I

UNDERSTANDING RECURSION

1

WHAT IS RECURSION?

Recursion has an intimidating reputation. It's considered hard to understand, but at its core, it depends on only two things: function calls and stack data structures.

Most new programmers trace through what a program does by following the execution. It's an easy way to read code: you just put your finger on the line of code at the top of the program and move down. Sometimes your finger will loop back; other times, it will jump into a function and later return. This makes it easy to visualize what a program does and in what order.

But to understand recursion, you need to become familiar with a less obvious data structure, called the *call stack*, that controls the program's flow of execution. Most programming beginners don't know about stacks, because programming tutorials often don't even mention them when discussing function calls. Furthermore, the call stack that automatically manages function calls doesn't appear anywhere in the source code.

It's hard to understand something when you can't see it and don't know it exists! In this chapter, we'll pull back the curtain to dispel the overblown notion that recursion is hard, and you'll be able to appreciate the elegance underneath.

The Definition of Recursion

Before we begin, let's get the clichéd recursion jokes out of the way, starting with this: "To understand recursion, you must first understand recursion."

During the months I've spent writing this book, I can assure you that this joke gets funnier the more you hear it.

Another joke is that if you search Google for *recursion*, the results page asks if you mean *recursion*. Following the link, as shown in Figure 1-1, takes you to . . . the search results for *recursion*.

Figure 1-1: The Google search results for recursion link to the Google search results for recursion.

Figure 1-2 shows a recursion joke from the webcomic xkcd.

Figure 1-2: I'm So Meta, Even This Acronym (I.S. M.E.T.A.) (xkcd.com/917 by Randall Munroe)

Most jokes about the 2010 science fiction action movie *Inception* are recursion jokes. The film features characters having dreams within dreams within dreams.

And finally, what computer scientist could forget that monster from Greek mythology, the recursive centaur? As you can see in Figure 1-3, it is half horse, half recursive centaur.

Figure 1-3: The recursive centaur. Image by Joseph Parker.

Based on these jokes, you might conclude that recursion is a sort of meta, self-referencing, dream-within-a-dream, infinite mirror-into-mirror sort of thing. Let's establish a concrete definition: a *recursive* thing is something whose definition includes itself. That is, it has a self-referential definition.

The Sierpiński triangle in Figure 1-4 is defined as an equilateral triangle with an upside-down triangle in the middle that forms three new equilateral triangles, each of which contains a Sierpiński triangle. The definition of Sierpiński triangles includes Sierpiński triangles.

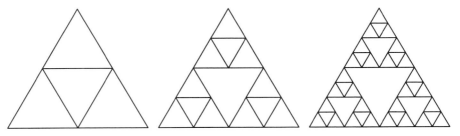

Figure 1-4: Sierpiński triangles are fractals (recursive shapes) that include Sierpiński triangles.

In a programming context, a *recursive function* is a function that calls itself. Before we explore recursive functions, let's take a step back and understand how regular functions work. Programmers tend to take function calls for granted, but even experienced programmers will find it worthwhile to review functions in the next section.

What Are Functions?

Functions can be described as mini-programs inside your program. They're a feature of nearly every programming language. If you need to run identical instructions at three different places in a program, instead of copying and pasting the source code three times you can write the code in a function once and call the function three times. The beneficial result is a shorter and more readable program. The program is also easier to change: if you need to fix a bug or add features, you need to change your program in only one place instead of three.

All programming languages implement four features in their functions:

1. Functions have code that is run when the function is called.
2. *Arguments* (that is, values) are passed to the function when it's called. This is the input to the function, and functions can have zero or more arguments.
3. Functions return a *return value*. This is the output of the function, though some programming languages allow functions not to return anything or to return null values like undefined or None.
4. The program remembers which line of code called the function and returns to it when the function finishes its execution.

Different programming languages might have additional features, or different options for how to call functions, but they all have these four general elements. You can visually see the first three of these elements because you write them in the source code, but how does a program keep track of where the execution should return to when the function returns?

To get a better sense of the problem, create a *functionCalls.py* program that has three functions: a(), which calls b(), which calls c():

Python
```python
def a():
    print('a() was called.')
    b()
    print('a() is returning.')

def b():
    print('b() was called.')
    c()
    print('b() is returning.')

def c():
    print('c() was called.')
    print('c() is returning.')

a()
```

This code is equivalent to the following *functionCalls.html* program:

JavaScript
```javascript
<script type="text/javascript">
function a() {
    document.write("a() was called.<br />");
    b();
    document.write("a() is returning.<br />");
}
```

```
function b() {
    document.write("b() was called.<br />");
    c();
    document.write("b() is returning.<br />");
}

function c() {
    document.write("c() was called.<br />");
    document.write("c() is returning.<br />");
}

a();
</script>
```

When you run this code, the output looks like this:

```
a() was called.
b() was called.
c() was called.
c() is returning.
b() is returning.
a() is returning.
```

The output shows the start of functions a(), b(), and c(). Then, when the functions return, the output appears in reverse order: c(), b(), and then a(). Notice the pattern to the text output: each time a function returns, it remembers which line of code originally called it. When the c() function call ends, the program returns to the b() function and displays b() is returning. Then the b() function call ends, and the program returns to the a() function and displays a() is returning. Finally, the program returns to the original a() function call at the end of the program. In other words, function calls don't send the execution of the program on a one-way trip.

But how does the program remember if it was a() or b() that called c()? This detail is handled by the program implicitly with a call stack. To understand how call stacks remember where the execution returns at the end of a function call, we need to first understand what a stack is.

What Are Stacks?

Earlier I mentioned the clichéd wisecrack, "To understand recursion, you must first understand recursion." But this is actually wrong: to really understand recursion, you must first understand stacks.

A *stack* is one of the simplest data structures in computer science. It stores multiple values like a list does—but unlike lists, it limits you to adding to or removing values from the "top" of the stack only. For stacks implemented with lists or arrays, the "top" is the last item, at the right end of the list or array. Adding values is called *pushing* values onto the stack, while removing values is called *popping* values off the stack.

Imagine that you're engaged in a meandering conversation with someone. You're talking about your friend Alice, which then reminds you of a story about your co-worker Bob, but for that story to make sense, you first have to explain something about your cousin Carol. You finish your story about Carol and go back to talking about Bob, and when you finish your story about Bob, you go back to talking about Alice. Then you are reminded about your brother David, so you tell a story about him. Eventually, you get around to finishing your original story about Alice.

Your conversation follows a stack-like structure, as in Figure 1-5. The conversation is stack-like because the current topic is always at the top of the stack.

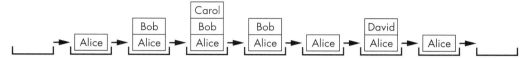

Figure 1-5: Your meandering conversation stack

In our conversation stack, the new topics are added to the top of the stack and taken off as they are completed. The previous topics are "remembered" underneath the current topic in the stack.

We can use Python lists as stacks if, to amend the list's contents, we limit ourselves to the append() and pop() methods to perform pushing and popping. JavaScript arrays can also be used as stacks through their push() and pop() methods.

NOTE *Python uses the terms* list *and* item, *while JavaScript uses the terms* array *and element, but they are respectively identical for our purposes. In this book, I use the terms* list *and* item *for both languages.*

For example, consider this *cardStack.py* program, which pushes and pops string values of playing cards to the end of a list named cardStack:

Python
```
cardStack = ❶ []
❷ cardStack.append('5 of diamonds')
print(','.join(cardStack))
cardStack.append('3 of clubs')
print(','.join(cardStack))
cardStack.append('ace of hearts')
print(','.join(cardStack))
❸ cardStack.pop()
print(','.join(cardStack))
```

The following *cardStack.html* program contains the equivalent code in JavaScript:

JavaScript
```
<script type="text/javascript">
let cardStack = ❶ [];
❷ cardStack.push("5 of diamonds");
document.write(cardStack + "<br />");
cardStack.push("3 of clubs");
document.write(cardStack + "<br />");
```

```
cardStack.push("ace of hearts");
document.write(cardStack + "<br />");
❸ cardStack.pop()
document.write(cardStack + "<br />");
</script>
```

When you run this code, the output looks like this:

```
5 of diamonds
5 of diamonds,3 of clubs
5 of diamonds,3 of clubs,ace of hearts
5 of diamonds,3 of clubs
```

The stack starts off as empty ❶. Three strings representing cards are pushed onto the stack ❷. Then the stack is popped ❸, which removes the ace of hearts and leaves the three of clubs at the top of the stack again. The state of the cardStack stack is tracked in Figure 1-6, going from left to right.

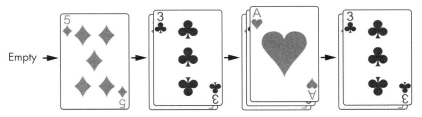

Figure 1-6: The stack starts empty. Cards are then pushed onto and popped off the stack.

You can see only the topmost card in the card stack, or, in our program's stacks, the topmost value. In the simplest stack implementations, you can't see how many cards (or values) are in the stack. You can see only whether the stack is empty or not.

Stacks are a *LIFO* data structure, which stands for *last in, first out*, since the last value pushed onto the stack is the first value popped out of it. This behavior is similar to your web browser's Back button. Your browser tab's history functions like a stack that contains all the pages you've visited in the order that you visited them. The browser is always displaying the web page at the "top" of the history's "stack." Clicking a link pushes a new web page onto the history stack, while clicking the Back button pops the top web page off and reveals the one "underneath."

What Is the Call Stack?

Programs use stacks too. The program's *call stack*, also simply called *the stack*, is a stack of frame objects. *Frame objects*, also simply called *frames*, contain information about a single function call, including which line of code called the function, so the execution can move back there when the function returns.

Frame objects are created and pushed onto the stack when a function is called. When the function returns, that frame object is popped off the stack. If we call a function that calls a function that calls a function, the call stack will have three frame objects on the stack. When all these functions return, the call stack will have zero frame objects on the stack.

Programmers don't have to write code dealing with frame objects, since the programming language handles them automatically. Different programming languages have different ways of implementing frame objects, but in general they contain the following:

- The return address, or the spot in the program where the execution should move when the function returns
- The arguments passed to the function call
- A set of local variables created during the function call

For example, take a look at the following *localVariables.py* program, which has three functions, just as our previous *functionCalls.py* and *functionCalls.html* programs did:

Python
```
def a():
❶ spam = 'Ant'
❷ print('spam is ' + spam)
❸ b()
   print('spam is ' + spam)

def b():
❹ spam = 'Bobcat'
   print('spam is ' + spam)
❺ c()
   print('spam is ' + spam)

def c():
❻ spam = 'Coyote'
   print('spam is ' + spam)

❼ a()
```

This *localVariables.html* is the equivalent JavaScript program:

JavaScript
```
<script type="text/javascript">
function a() {
❶ let spam = "Ant";
❷ document.write("spam is " + spam + "<br />");
❸ b();
   document.write("spam is " + spam + "<br />");
}

function b() {
❹ let spam = "Bobcat";
   document.write("spam is " + spam + "<br />");
❺ c();
```

```
      document.write("spam is " + spam + "<br />");
  }

  function c() {
    ❻ let spam = "Coyote";
      document.write("spam is " + spam + "<br />");
  }

❼ a();
  </script>
```

When you run this code, the output looks like this:

```
spam is Ant
spam is Bobcat
spam is Coyote
spam is Bobcat
spam is Ant
```

When the program calls function a() ❼, a frame object is created and placed on the top of the call stack. This frame stores any arguments passed to a() (in this case, there are none), along with the local variable spam ❶ and the place where the execution should go when the a() function returns.

When a() is called, it displays the contents of its local spam variable, which is Ant ❷. When the code in a() calls function b() ❸, a new frame object is created and placed on the call stack above the frame object for a(). The b() function has its own local spam variable ❹, and calls c() ❺. A new frame object for the c() call is created and placed on the call stack, and it contains c()'s local spam variable ❻. As these functions return, the frame objects pop off the call stack. The program execution knows where to return to, because that return information is stored in the frame object. When the execution has returned from all function calls, the call stack is empty.

Figure 1-7 shows the state of the call stack as each function is called and returns. Notice that all the local variables have the same name: spam. I did this to highlight the fact that local variables are always separate variables with distinct values, even if they have the same name as local variables in other functions.

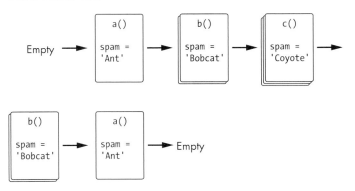

Figure 1-7: The state of the call stack as the localVariables program runs

As you can see, programming languages can have separate local variables with the same name (spam) because they are kept in separate frame objects. When a local variable is used in the source code, the variable with that name in the topmost frame object is used.

Every running program has a call stack, and multithreaded programs have one call stack for each thread. But when you look at the source code for a program, you can't see the call stack in the code. The call stack isn't stored in a variable as other data structures are; it's automatically handled in the background.

The fact that the call stack doesn't exist in source code is the main reason recursion is so confusing to beginners: recursion relies on something the programmer can't even see! Revealing how stack data structures and the call stack work removes much of the mystery behind recursion. Functions and stacks are both simple concepts, and we can use them together to understand how recursion works.

What Are Recursive Functions and Stack Overflows?

A *recursive function* is a function that calls itself. This *shortest.py* program is the shortest possible example of a recursive function:

Python
```
def shortest():
    shortest()

shortest()
```

The preceding program is equivalent to this *shortest.html* program:

JavaScript
```
<script type="text/javascript">
function shortest() {
    shortest();
}

shortest();
</script>
```

The shortest() function does nothing but call the shortest() function. When this happens, it calls the shortest() function again, and that will call shortest(), and so on, seemingly forever. It is similar to the mythological idea that the crust of the Earth rests on the back of a giant space turtle, which rests on the back of another turtle. Beneath that turtle: another turtle. And so on, forever.

But this "turtles all the way down" theory doesn't do a good job of explaining cosmology, nor recursive functions. Since the call stack uses the computer's finite memory, this program cannot continue forever, the way an infinite loop does. The only thing this program does is crash and display an error message.

NOTE   *To view the JavaScript error, you must open the* browser developer tools. *On most browsers, this is done by pressing F12 and then selecting the Console tab.*

The Python output of *shortest.py* looks like this:

```
Traceback (most recent call last):
  File "shortest.py", line 4, in <module>
    shortest()
  File "shortest.py", line 2, in shortest
    shortest()
  File "shortest.py", line 2, in shortest
    shortest()
  File "shortest.py", line 2, in shortest
    shortest()
  [Previous line repeated 996 more times]
RecursionError: maximum recursion depth exceeded
```

The JavaScript output of *shortest.html* looks like this in the Google Chrome web browser (other browsers will have similar error messages):

```
Uncaught RangeError: Maximum call stack size exceeded
    at shortest (shortest.html:2)
    at shortest (shortest.html:3)
    at shortest (shortest.html:3)
    at shortest (shortest.html:3)
    at shortest (shortest.html:3)
    at shortest (shortest.html:3)
    at shortest (shortest.html:3)
    at shortest (shortest.html:3)
    at shortest (shortest.html:3)
    at shortest (shortest.html:3)
```

This kind of bug is called a *stack overflow*. (This is where the popular website *https://stackoverflow.com* got its name.) The constant function calls with no returns grow the call stack until all the computer's memory allocated for the call stack is used up. To prevent this, the Python and JavaScript interpreters crash the program after a certain limit of function calls that don't return a value.

This limit is called the *maximum recursion depth* or *maximum call stack size*. For Python, this is set to 1,000 function calls. For JavaScript, the maximum call stack size depends on the browser running the code but is generally at least 10,000 or so. Think of a stack overflow as happening when the call stack gets "too high" (that is, consumes too much computer memory), as in Figure 1-8.

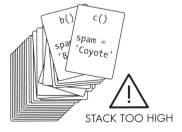

STACK TOO HIGH

Figure 1-8: A stack overflow happens when the call stack becomes too high, with too many frame objects taking up the computer's memory.

Stack overflows don't damage the computer. The computer just detects that the limit of function calls without returns has been reached and terminates the program. At worst, you'll lose any unsaved work the program had. Stack overflows can be prevented by having something called a *base case*, which is explained next.

Base Cases and Recursive Cases

The stack overflow example has a shortest() function that calls shortest() but never returns. To avoid a crash, there needs to be a case, or set of circumstances, where the function stops calling itself and instead just returns. This is called a *base case*. By contrast, a case where the function recursively calls itself is called a *recursive case*.

All recursive functions require at least one base case and at least one recursive case. If there is no base case, the function never stops making recursive calls and eventually causes a stack overflow. If there is no recursive case, the function never calls itself and is an ordinary function, not a recursive one. When you start writing your own recursive functions, a good first step is to figure out what the base case and recursive case should be.

Take a look at this *shortestWithBaseCase.py* program, which defines the shortest recursive function that won't crash from a stack overflow:

Python
```python
def shortestWithBaseCase(makeRecursiveCall):
    print('shortestWithBaseCase(%s) called.' % makeRecursiveCall)
    if not makeRecursiveCall:
        # BASE CASE
        print('Returning from base case.')
      ❶ return
    else:
        # RECURSIVE CASE
      ❷ shortestWithBaseCase(False)
        print('Returning from recursive case.')
        return

print('Calling shortestWithBaseCase(False):')
❸ shortestWithBaseCase(False)
print()
print('Calling shortestWithBaseCase(True):')
❹ shortestWithBaseCase(True)
```

This code is equivalent to the following *shortestWithBaseCase.html* program:

JavaScript
```javascript
<script type="text/javascript">
function shortestWithBaseCase(makeRecursiveCall) {
    document.write("shortestWithBaseCase(" + makeRecursiveCall +
    ") called.<br />");
    if (makeRecursiveCall === false) {
        // BASE CASE
        document.write("Returning from base case.<br />");
      ❶ return;
```

```
        } else {
            // RECURSIVE CASE
        ❷ shortestWithBaseCase(false);
            document.write("Returning from recursive case.<br />");
            return;
        }
    }

    document.write("Calling shortestWithBaseCase(false):<br />");
❸ shortestWithBaseCase(false);
    document.write("<br />");
    document.write("Calling shortestWithBaseCase(true):<br />");
❹ shortestWithBaseCase(true);
    </script>
```

When you run this code, the output looks like this:

```
Calling shortestWithBaseCase(False):
shortestWithBaseCase(False) called.
Returning from base case.

Calling shortestWithBaseCase(True):
shortestWithBaseCase(True) called.
shortestWithBaseCase(False) called.
Returning from base case.
Returning from recursive case.
```

This function doesn't do anything useful except provide a short example of recursion (and it could be made shorter by removing the text output, but the text is useful for our explanation). When shortestWithBaseCase(False) is called ❸, the base case is executed and the function merely returns ❶. However, when shortestWithBaseCase(True) is called ❹, the recursive case is executed and shortestWithBaseCase(False) is called ❷.

It's important to note that when shortestWithBaseCase(False) is recursively called from ❷ and then returns, the execution doesn't immediately move back to the original function call at ❹. The rest of the code in the recursive case after the recursive call still runs, which is why Returning from recursive case. appears in the output. Returning from the base case doesn't immediately return from all the recursive calls that happened before it. This will be important to keep in mind in the countDownAndUp() example in the next section.

Code Before and After the Recursive Call

The code in a recursive case can be split into two parts: the code before the recursive call and the code after the recursive call. (If there are two recursive calls in the recursive case, such as with the Fibonacci sequence example in Chapter 2, there will be a before, a between, and an after. But let's keep it simple for now.)

The important thing to know is that reaching the base case doesn't necessarily mean reaching the end of the recursive algorithm. It only means the base case won't continue to make recursive calls.

For example, consider this *countDownAndUp.py* program whose recursive function counts from any number down to zero, and then back up to the number:

Python
```python
def countDownAndUp(number):
  ❶ print(number)
    if number == 0:
        # BASE CASE
      ❷ print('Reached the base case.')
        return
    else:
        # RECURSIVE CASE
      ❸ countDownAndUp(number - 1)
      ❹ print(number, 'returning')
        return

❺ countDownAndUp(3)
```

Here is the equivalent *countDownAndUp.html* program:

JavaScript
```javascript
<script type="text/javascript">
function countDownAndUp(number) {
  ❶ document.write(number + "<br />");
    if (number === 0) {
        // BASE CASE
      ❷ document.write("Reached the base case.<br />");
        return;
    } else {
        // RECURSIVE CASE
      ❸ countDownAndUp(number - 1);
      ❹ document.write(number + " returning<br />");
        return;
    }
}

❺ countDownAndUp(3);
</script>
```

When you run this code, the output looks like this:

```
3
2
1
0
Reached the base case.
1 returning
2 returning
3 returning
```

Remember that every time a function is called, a new frame is created and pushed onto the call stack. This frame is where all the local variables and parameters (such as number) are stored. So, there is a separate

number variable for each frame on the call stack. This is another often confusing point about recursion: even though, from the source code, it looks
like there is only one number variable, remember that because it is a local
variable, there is actually a different number variable for each function call.

When countDownAndUp(3) is called ❺, a frame is created, and that frame's
local number variable is set to 3. The function prints the number variable to the
screen ❶. As long as number isn't 0, countDownAndUp() is recursively called with
number - 1 ❸. When it calls countDownAndUp(2), a new frame is pushed onto
the stack, and that frame's local number variable is set to 2. Again, the recursive case is reached and calls countDownAndUp(1), which again reaches the
recursive case and calls countDownAndUp(0).

This pattern of making consecutive recursive function calls and then
returning from the recursive function calls is what causes the countdown
of numbers to appear. Once countDownAndUp(0) is called, the base case is
reached ❷, and no more recursive calls are made. However, this isn't the
end of our program! When the base case is reached, the local number variable is 0. But when that base case returns, and the frame is popped off
the call stack, the frame under it has its own local number variable, with the
same 1 value it's always had. As the execution returns back to the previous
frames in the call stack, the code *after* the recursive call is executed ❹.
This is what causes the count up of numbers to appear. Figure 1-9 shows
the state of the call stack as countDownAndUp() is recursively called and then
returns.

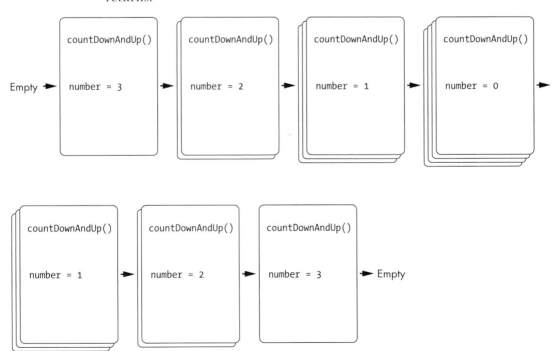

Figure 1-9: The call stack keeping track of the values in the number local variable for each function call

The fact that the code doesn't stop immediately when the base case is reached will be important to keep in mind for the factorial calculation in the next chapter. Remember, any code after the recursive case will still have to run.

At this point, you might be thinking that the recursive `countDownAndUp()` function is overengineered and difficult to follow. Why not, instead, use an iterative solution to print numbers? An *iterative* approach, which uses loops to repeat a task until it's done, is usually thought of as the opposite of recursion.

Whenever you find yourself asking, "Wouldn't using a loop be easier?" the answer is almost certainly "Yes," and you should avoid the recursive solution. Recursion can be tricky for both beginner and experienced programmers, and recursive code isn't automatically "better" or "more elegant" than iterative code. Readable, easy-to-understand code is more important than any supposed elegance that recursion provides. However, on some occasions an algorithm cleanly maps to a recursive approach. Algorithms that involve tree-like data structures and require backtracking are especially suited for recursion. These ideas are further explored in Chapters 2 and 4.

Summary

Recursion often confuses new programmers, but it is built on the simple idea that a function can call itself. Every time a function call is made, a new frame object with information related to the call (such as local variables and a return address for the execution to move to when the function returns) is added to the call stack. The call stack, being a stack data structure, can be altered only by having data added to or removed from its "top." This is called *pushing to* and *popping from* the stack, respectively.

The call stack is handled by the program implicitly, so there is no call stack variable. Calling a function pushes a frame object to the call stack, and returning from a function pops a frame object from the call stack.

Recursive functions have recursive cases, those in which a recursive call is made, and base cases, those where the function simply returns. If there is no base case or a bug prevents a base case from being run, the execution causes a stack overflow that crashes the program.

Recursion is a useful technique, but recursion doesn't automatically make code "better" or more "elegant." This idea is explored more in the next chapter.

Further Reading

You can find other introductions to recursion in my 2018 North Bay Python conference talk, "Recursion for Beginners: A Beginner's Guide to Recursion," at *https://youtu.be/AfBqVVKg4GE*. The YouTube channel Computerphile also introduces recursion in its video "What on Earth is Recursion?" at *https://youtu.be/Mv9NEXX1VHc*. Finally, V. Anton Spraul talks about recursion in his book *Think Like a Programmer* (No Starch Press, 2012) and in his video

"Recursion (Think Like a Programmer)" at *https://youtu.be/oKndim5-G94*. Wikipedia's article on recursion goes into great detail at *https://en.wikipedia .org/wiki/Recursion*.

You can install the ShowCallStack module for Python. This module adds a showcallstack() function that you can place anywhere in your code to see the state of the call stack at that particular point in your program. You can download the module and find instructions for it at *https://pypi.org/project/ ShowCallStack*.

Practice Questions

Test your comprehension by answering the following questions:

1. In general, what is a recursive thing?
2. In programming, what is a recursive function?
3. What four features do functions have?
4. What is a stack?
5. What are the terms for adding and removing values to and from the top of a stack?
6. Say you push the letter *J* to a stack, then push the letter *Q*, then pop the stack, then push the letter *K*, then pop the stack again. What does the stack look like?
7. What is pushed and popped onto the call stack?
8. What causes a stack overflow to happen?
9. What is a base case?
10. What is a recursive case?
11. How many base cases and recursive cases do recursive functions have?
12. What happens if a recursive function has zero base cases?
13. What happens if a recursive function has zero recursive cases?

2

RECURSION VS. ITERATION

Neither recursion nor iteration is a superior technique in general. In fact, any recursive code can be written as iterative code with a loop and a stack. Recursion doesn't have some special power enabling it to perform calculations that an iterative algorithm cannot. And any iterative loop can be rewritten as a recursive function.

This chapter compares and contrasts recursion and iteration. We'll look at the classic Fibonacci and factorial functions and see why their recursive algorithms have critical weaknesses. We'll also explore the insights a recursive approach can yield by considering an exponent algorithm. Altogether this chapter shines light on the supposed elegance of recursive algorithms and shows when a recursive solution is useful and when it is not.

Calculating Factorials

Many computer science courses use factorial calculation as a classic example of a recursive function. The factorial of an integer (let's call it n) is the product of all integers from 1 to n. For example, the factorial of 4 is $4 \times 3 \times 2 \times 1$, or 24. An exclamation mark is the math notation for factorials, as in 4!, which means *the factorial of 4*. Table 2-1 shows the first few factorials.

Table 2-1: Factorials of the First Few Integers

n!		Expanded form		Product
1!	=	1	=	1
2!	=	1 × 2	=	2
3!	=	1 × 2 × 3	=	6
4!	=	1 × 2 × 3 × 4	=	24
5!	=	1 × 2 × 3 × 4 × 5	=	120
6!	=	1 × 2 × 3 × 4 × 5 × 6	=	720
7!	=	1 × 2 × 3 × 4 × 5 × 6 × 7	=	5,040
8!	=	1 × 2 × 3 × 4 × 5 × 6 × 7 × 8	=	40,320

Factorials are used in all sorts of calculations—for example, finding the number of permutations for something. If you want to know the number of ways that exist to order four people—Alice, Bob, Carol, and David—in a line, the answer is the factorial of 4. Four possible people can be first in line (4); then for each of those four options, three remaining people can be second in line (4×3); then two people can be third in line ($4 \times 3 \times 2$); and the last person left will be fourth in line ($4 \times 3 \times 2 \times 1$). The number of ways people can be ordered in line—that is, the number of permutations—is the factorial of the number of people.

Now let's examine both an iterative and a recursive approach to calculating factorials.

The Iterative Factorial Algorithm

Calculating factorials iteratively is fairly straightforward: multiply the integers 1 up to and including n in a loop. *Iterative* algorithms always use a loop. A *factorialByIteration.py* program looks like this:

Python
```python
def factorial(number):
    product = 1
    for i in range(1, number + 1):
        product = product * i
    return product
print(factorial(5))
```

And a *factorialByIteration.html* program looks like this:

```javascript
<script type="text/javascript">
function factorial(number) {
    let product = 1;
    for (let i = 1; i <= number; i++) {
        product = product * i;
    }
    return product;
}
document.write(factorial(5));
</script>
```

When you run this code, the output displays the calculation for 5! like this:

```
120
```

There's nothing wrong with the iterative solution for calculating factorials; it's straightforward and gets the job done. But let's also take a look at the recursive algorithm for insights into the nature of factorials and recursion itself.

The Recursive Factorial Algorithm

Notice that the factorial of 4 is $4 \times 3 \times 2 \times 1$, and the factorial of 5 is $5 \times 4 \times 3 \times 2 \times 1$. So you could say that $5! = 5 \times 4!$. This is *recursive* because the definition of the factorial of 5 (or any number n) includes the definition of the factorial of 4 (the number $n - 1$). In turn, $4! = 4 \times 3!$, and so on, until you must calculate $1!$, the base case, which is simply 1.

The *factorialByRecursion.py* Python program uses a recursive factorial algorithm:

```python
def factorial(number):
    if number == 1:
        # BASE CASE
        return 1
    else:
        # RECURSIVE CASE
      ❶ return number * factorial(number - 1)
print(factorial(5))
```

And the *factorialByRecursion.html* JavaScript program with equivalent code looks like this:

```javascript
<script type="text/javascript">
function factorial(number) {
    if (number == 1) {
        // BASE CASE
        return 1;
```

```
    } else {
        // RECURSIVE CASE
      ❶ return number * factorial(number - 1);
    }
}
document.write(factorial(5));
</script>
```

When you run this code to calculate 5! recursively, the output matches the iterative program's output:

```
120
```

To many programmers, this recursive code looks strange. You know that factorial(5) must compute $5 \times 4 \times 3 \times 2 \times 1$, but it's hard to point to the line of code where this multiplication is taking place.

The confusion arises because the recursive case has one line ❶, half of which is executed before the recursive call and half of which takes place after the recursive call returns. We aren't used to the idea of only half of a line of code executing at a time.

The first half is factorial(number - 1). This involves calculating number - 1 and making a recursive function, causing a new frame object to be pushed to the call stack. This happens before the recursive call is made.

The next time the code runs with the old frame object is after factorial (number - 1) has returned. When factorial(5) is called, factorial(number - 1) will be factorial(4), which returns 24. This is when the second half of the line runs. The return number * factorial(number - 1) now looks like return 5 * 24, which is why factorial(5) returns 120.

Figure 2-1 tracks the state of the call stack as frame objects are pushed (which happens as recursive function calls are made) and frame objects are popped (as recursive function calls return). Notice that the multiplication happens after the recursive calls are made, not before.

When the original function call to factorial() returns, it returns the calculated factorial.

Why the Recursive Factorial Algorithm Is Terrible

The recursive implementation for calculating factorials has a critical weakness. Calculating the factorial of 5 requires five recursive function calls. This means five frame objects are placed on the call stack before the base case is reached. This doesn't scale.

If you want to calculate the factorial of 1,001, the recursive factorial() function must make 1,001 recursive function calls. However, your program is likely to cause a stack overflow before it can finish, because making so many function calls without returning would exceed the maximum call stack size of the interpreter. This is terrible; you would never want to use a recursive factorial function in real-world code.

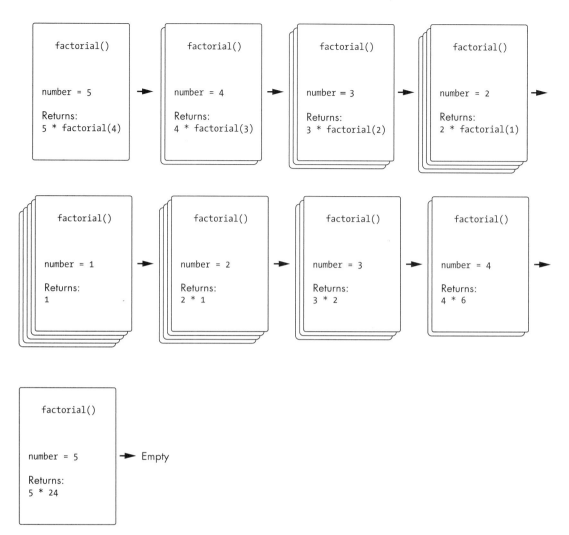

Figure 2-1: The state of the call stack as the recursive calls to factorial() are called and then return

The iterative factorial algorithm, on the other hand, will complete the calculation quickly and efficiently. The stack overflow can be avoided using a technique available in some programming languages called *tail call optimization*. Chapter 8 covers this topic. However, this technique further complicates the implementation of the recursive function. For calculating factorials, the iterative approach is the simplest and most direct.

Calculating the Fibonacci Sequence

The *Fibonacci sequence* is another classic example for introducing recursion. Mathematically, the Fibonacci sequence of integers begins with the numbers 1 and 1 (or sometimes, 0 and 1). The next number in the sequence is the sum of the previous two numbers. This creates the sequence 1, 1, 2, 3, 5, 8, 13, 21, 34, 55, 89, 144, and so on, forever.

If we call the latest two numbers in the sequence *a* and *b*, you can see in Figure 2-2 how the sequence grows.

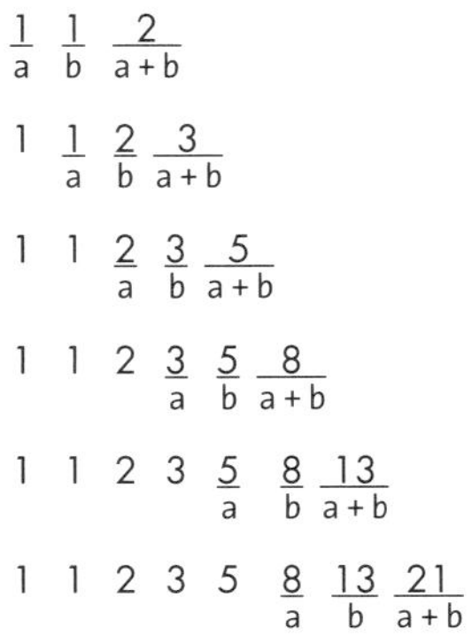

$$\underbrace{1}_{a} \; \underbrace{1}_{b} \; \underbrace{2}_{a+b}$$

$$1 \; \underbrace{1}_{a} \; \underbrace{2}_{b} \; \underbrace{3}_{a+b}$$

$$1 \; 1 \; \underbrace{2}_{a} \; \underbrace{3}_{b} \; \underbrace{5}_{a+b}$$

$$1 \; 1 \; 2 \; \underbrace{3}_{a} \; \underbrace{5}_{b} \; \underbrace{8}_{a+b}$$

$$1 \; 1 \; 2 \; 3 \; \underbrace{5}_{a} \; \underbrace{8}_{b} \; \underbrace{13}_{a+b}$$

$$1 \; 1 \; 2 \; 3 \; 5 \; \underbrace{8}_{a} \; \underbrace{13}_{b} \; \underbrace{21}_{a+b}$$

Figure 2-2: Each number of the Fibonacci sequence is the sum of the previous two numbers.

Let's explore some code examples of both the iterative and recursive solutions for generating Fibonacci numbers.

The Iterative Fibonacci Algorithm

The iterative Fibonacci example is straightforward, consisting of a simple for loop and two variables, a and b. This *fibonacciByIteration.py* Python program implements the iterative Fibonacci algorithm:

Python
```python
def fibonacci(nthNumber):
❶  a, b = 1, 1
    print('a = %s, b = %s' % (a, b))
    for i in range(1, nthNumber):
❷      a, b = b, a + b # Get the next Fibonacci number.
        print('a = %s, b = %s' % (a, b))
    return a

print(fibonacci(10))
```

This *fibonacciByIteration.html* program has the equivalent JavaScript code:

JavaScript
```javascript
<script type="text/javascript">
function fibonacci(nthNumber) {
❶  let a = 1, b = 1;
    let nextNum;
    document.write('a = ' + a + ', b = ' + b + '<br />');
    for (let i = 1; i < nthNumber; i++) {
❷      nextNum = a + b; // Get the next Fibonacci number.
        a = b;
        b = nextNum;
```

```
            document.write('a = ' + a + ', b = ' + b + '<br />');
        }
        return a;
    };

    document.write(fibonacci(10));
</script>
```

When you run this code to calculate the 10th Fibonacci number, the output looks like this:

```
a = 1, b = 1
a = 1, b = 2
a = 2, b = 3
--snip--
a = 34, b = 55
55
```

The program needs to track only the latest two numbers of the sequence at a time. Since the first two numbers in the Fibonacci sequence are defined as 1, we store 1 in variables a and b ❶. Inside the for loop, the next number in the sequence is calculated by adding a and b ❷, which becomes the next value of b, while a obtains the previous value of b. By the time the loop is finished, b contains the nth Fibonacci number, so it is returned.

The Recursive Fibonacci Algorithm

Calculating Fibonacci numbers involves a recursive property. For example, if you want to calculate the 10th Fibonacci number, you add the ninth and eighth Fibonacci numbers together. To calculate those Fibonacci numbers, you add the eighth and seventh, then the seventh and sixth Fibonacci numbers. A lot of repeat calculations occur: notice that adding the ninth and eighth Fibonacci numbers involves calculating the eighth Fibonacci number again. You continue this recursion until you reach the base case of the first or second Fibonacci number, which is always 1.

The recursive Fibonacci function is in this *fibonacciByRecursion.py* Python program:

```
def fibonacci(nthNumber):
    print('fibonacci(%s) called.' % (nthNumber))
    if nthNumber == 1 or nthNumber == 2: ❶
        # BASE CASE
        print('Call to fibonacci(%s) returning 1.' % (nthNumber))
        return 1
    else:
        # RECURSIVE CASE
        print('Calling fibonacci(%s) and fibonacci(%s).' % (nthNumber - 1, nthNumber - 2))
        result = fibonacci(nthNumber - 1) + fibonacci(nthNumber - 2)
        print('Call to fibonacci(%s) returning %s.' % (nthNumber, result))
        return result

print(fibonacci(10))
```

This *fibonacciByRecursion.html* file has the equivalent JavaScript program:

```
<script type="text/javascript">
function fibonacci(nthNumber) {
    document.write('fibonacci(' + nthNumber + ') called.<br />');
    if (nthNumber === 1 || nthNumber === 2) { ❶
        // BASE CASE
        document.write('Call to fibonacci(' + nthNumber + ') returning 1.<br />');
        return 1;
    }
    else {
        // RECURSIVE CASE
        document.write('Calling fibonacci(' + (nthNumber - 1) + ') and fibonacci(' + (nthNumber
- 2) + ').<br />');
        let result = fibonacci(nthNumber - 1) + fibonacci(nthNumber - 2);
        document.write('Call to fibonacci(' + nthNumber + ') returning ' + result + '.<br />');
        return result;
    }
}

document.write(fibonacci(10) + '<br />');
</script>
```

When you run this code to calculate the 10th Fibonacci number, the output looks like this:

```
fibonacci(10) called.
Calling fibonacci(9) and fibonacci(8).
fibonacci(9) called.
Calling fibonacci(8) and fibonacci(7).
fibonacci(8) called.
Calling fibonacci(7) and fibonacci(6).
fibonacci(7) called.
--snip--
Call to fibonacci(6) returning 8.
Call to fibonacci(8) returning 21.
Call to fibonacci(10) returning 55.
55
```

Much of the code is for displaying this output, but the fibonacci() function itself is simple. The base case—the circumstances where recursive calls are no longer made—occurs when nthNumber is 1 or 2 ❶. In this case, the function returns 1 since the first and second Fibonacci numbers are always 1. Any other case is a recursive case, so the value that is returned is the sum of fibonacci(nthNumber - 1) and fibonacci(nthNumber - 2). As long as the original nthNumber argument is an integer greater than 0, these recursive calls will eventually reach the base case and stop making more recursive calls.

Remember how the recursive factorial example had a "before the recursive call" and "after the recursive call" part? Because the recursive Fibonacci algorithm makes two recursive calls in its recursive case, you should keep in mind that it has three parts: "before the first recursive call," "after the first recursive call but before the second recursive call," and "after the second recursive call." But the same principles apply. And don't think that because a base case is reached, no more code remains to run after either recursive call. The recursive algorithm is finished only after the original function call has returned.

You might ask, "Isn't the iterative Fibonacci solution simpler than the recursive Fibonacci solution?" The answer is "Yes." Even worse, the recursive solution has a critical inefficiency that is explained in the next section.

Why the Recursive Fibonacci Algorithm Is Terrible

Like the recursive factorial algorithm, the recursive Fibonacci algorithm also suffers from a critical weakness: it repeats the same calculations over and over. Figure 2-3 shows how calling fibonacci(6), marked in the tree diagram as fib(6) for brevity, calls fibonacci(5) and fibonacci(4).

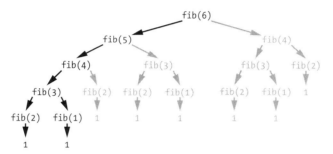

Figure 2-3: A tree diagram of the recursive function calls made starting with fibonacci(6). The redundant function calls are in gray.

This causes a cascade of other function calls until they reach the base cases of fibonacci(2) and fibonacci(1), which return 1. But notice that fibonacci(4) is called twice, and fibonacci(3) is called three times, and so on. This slows the overall algorithm with unnecessarily repeated calculations. This inefficiency gets worse as the Fibonacci number you want to calculate gets larger. While the iterative Fibonacci algorithm can complete fibonacci(100) in less than a second, the recursive algorithm would take over a million years to complete.

Converting a Recursive Algorithm into an Iterative Algorithm

Converting a recursive algorithm into an iterative algorithm is always possible. While recursive functions repeat a calculation by calling themselves, this repetition can be performed instead by a loop. Recursive functions also make use of the call stack; however, an iterative algorithm can replace this with a stack data structure. Thus, any recursive algorithm can be performed iteratively by using a loop and a stack.

To demonstrate this, here is *factorialEmulateRecursion.py*, a Python program that implements an iterative algorithm to emulate a recursive algorithm:

```python
callStack = [] # The explicit call stack, which holds "frame objects". ❶
callStack.append({'returnAddr': 'start', 'number': 5}) # "Call" the "factorial() function". ❷
returnValue = None

while len(callStack) > 0:
    # The body of the "factorial() function":

    number = callStack[-1]['number'] # Set number parameter.
    returnAddr = callStack[-1]['returnAddr']

    if returnAddr == 'start':
        if number == 1:
            # BASE CASE
            returnValue = 1
            callStack.pop() # "Return" from "function call". ❸
            continue
        else:
            # RECURSIVE CASE
            callStack[-1]['returnAddr'] = 'after recursive call'
            # "Call" the "factorial() function":
            callStack.append({'returnAddr': 'start', 'number': number - 1}) ❹
            continue
    elif returnAddr == 'after recursive call':
        returnValue = number * returnValue
        callStack.pop() # "Return from function call". ❺
        continue

print(returnValue)
```

The *factorialEmulateRecursion.html* program holds the equivalent JavaScript:

```html
<script type="text/javascript">
let callStack = []; // The explicit call stack, which holds "frame objects". ❶
callStack.push({"returnAddr": "start", "number": 5}); // "Call" the "factorial() function". ❷
let returnValue;

while (callStack.length > 0) {
// The body of the "factorial() function":
    let number = callStack[callStack.length - 1]["number"]; // Set number parameter.
    let returnAddr = callStack[callStack.length - 1]["returnAddr"];

    if (returnAddr == "start") {
        if (number === 1) {
            // BASE CASE
            returnValue = 1;
            callStack.pop(); // "Return" from "function call". ❸
            continue;
        } else {
            // RECURSIVE CASE
```

```
            callStack[callStack.length - 1]["returnAddr"] = "after recursive call";
            // "Call" the "factorial() function":
            callStack.push({"returnAddr": "start", "number": number - 1}); ❹
            continue;
        }
    } else if (returnAddr == "after recursive call") {
        returnValue = number * returnValue;
        callStack.pop(); // "Return from function call". ❺
        continue;
    }
}

document.write(returnValue + "<br />");
</script>
```

Notice that this program doesn't have a recursive function; it doesn't have any functions at all! The program emulates recursive function calls by using a list as a stack data structure (stored in the callStack variable ❶) to mimic the call stack. A dictionary storing the return address information and nthNumber local variable emulates a frame object ❷. The program emulates function calls by pushing these frame objects onto the call stack ❹, and it emulates returning from a function call by popping frame objects off the call stack ❸ ❺.

Any recursive function can be written iteratively this way. Although this code is incredibly difficult to understand and you'd never write a real-world factorial algorithm this way, it does demonstrate that recursion has no innate capability that iterative code does not have.

Converting an Iterative Algorithm into a Recursive Algorithm

Likewise, converting an iterative algorithm into a recursive algorithm is always possible. An iterative algorithm is simply code that uses a loop. The code that is repeatedly executed (the loop's body) can be placed in a recursive function's body. And just as the code in the loop's body is executed repeatedly, we need to repeatedly call the function to execute its code. We can do this by calling the function from the function itself, creating a recursive function.

The Python code in *hello.py* demonstrates printing Hello, world! five times by using a loop and then also using a recursive function:

Python
```
print('Code in a loop:')
i = 0
while i < 5:
    print(i, 'Hello, world!')
    i = i + 1

print('Code in a function:')
def hello(i=0):
    print(i, 'Hello, world!')
    i = i + 1
    if i < 5:
        hello(i) # RECURSIVE CASE
```

```
        else:
            return # BASE CASE
    hello()
```

The equivalent JavaScript code is in *hello.html*:

JavaScript
```
<script type="text/javascript">
document.write("Code in a loop:<br />");
let i = 0;
while (i < 5) {
    document.write(i + " Hello, world!<br />");
    i = i + 1;
}

document.write("Code in a function:<br />");
function hello(i) {
    if (i === undefined) {
        i = 0; // i defaults to 0 if unspecified.
    }

    document.write(i + " Hello, world!<br />");
    i = i + 1;
    if (i < 5) {
        hello(i); // RECURSIVE CASE
    }
    else {
        return; // BASE CASE
    }
}
hello();
</script>
```

The output of these programs looks like this:

```
Code in a loop:
0 Hello, world!
1 Hello, world!
2 Hello, world!
3 Hello, world!
4 Hello, world!
Code in a function:
0 Hello, world!
1 Hello, world!
2 Hello, world!
3 Hello, world!
4 Hello, world!
```

The while loop has a condition, i < 5, that determines whether the program keeps looping. Similarly, the recursive function uses this condition for its recursive case, which causes the function to call itself and execute the Hello, world! to display its code again.

For a more real-world example, the following are iterative and recursive functions that return the index of a substring, needle, in a string, haystack. The functions return -1 if the substring isn't found. This is similar to Python's find() string method and JavaScript's indexOf() string method. This *findSubstring.py* program has a Python version:

Python

```python
def findSubstringIterative(needle, haystack):
    i = 0
    while i < len(haystack):
        if haystack[i:i + len(needle)] == needle:
            return i # Needle found.
        i = i + 1
    return -1 # Needle not found.

def findSubstringRecursive(needle, haystack, i=0):
    if i >= len(haystack):
        return -1 # BASE CASE (Needle not found.)

    if haystack[i:i + len(needle)] == needle:
        return i # BASE CASE (Needle found.)
    else:
        # RECURSIVE CASE
        return findSubstringRecursive(needle, haystack, i + 1)

print(findSubstringIterative('cat', 'My cat Zophie'))
print(findSubstringRecursive('cat', 'My cat Zophie'))
```

This *findSubstring.html* program has the equivalent JavaScript version:

JavaScript

```javascript
<script type="text/javascript">
function findSubstringIterative(needle, haystack) {
    let i = 0;
    while (i < haystack.length) {
        if (haystack.substring(i, i + needle.length) == needle) {
            return i; // Needle found.
        }
        i = i + 1
    }
    return -1; // Needle not found.
}

function findSubstringRecursive(needle, haystack, i) {
    if (i === undefined) {
        i = 0;
    }

    if (i >= haystack.length) {
        return -1; // # BASE CASE (Needle not found.)
    }

    if (haystack.substring(i, i + needle.length) == needle) {
        return i; // # BASE CASE (Needle found.)
    } else {
        // RECURSIVE CASE
        return findSubstringRecursive(needle, haystack, i + 1);
    }
```

```
        }
        document.write(findSubstringIterative("cat", "My cat Zophie") + "<br />");
        document.write(findSubstringRecursive("cat", "My cat Zophie") + "<br />");
        </script>
```

These programs make a call to findSubstringIterative() and findSubstring
Recursive(), which return 3 because that is the index where cat is found in My
cat Zophie:

```
3
3
```

The programs in this section demonstrate that it is always possible to
turn any loop into an equivalent recursive function. While replacing a loop
with recursion is possible, I advise against it. This is doing recursion for
recursion's sake, and since recursion is often harder to understand than
iterative code, code readability deteriorates.

Case Study: Calculating Exponents

Although recursion doesn't necessarily produce better code, taking a recursive approach can give you new insights into your programming problem.
As a case study, let's examine how to calculate exponents.

Exponents are calculated by multiplying a number by itself. For example,
the exponent "three raised to the sixth power," or 3^6, is equal to multiply-
ing 3 by itself six times: $3 \times 3 \times 3 \times 3 \times 3 \times 3 = 729$. This is such a common
operation that Python has the ** operator and JavaScript has the built-in
Math.pow() function to perform exponentiation. We can calculate 3^6 with the
Python code 3 ** 6 and with the JavaScript code Math.pow(3, 6).

But let's write our own exponent-calculating code. The solution is
straightforward: create a loop that repeatedly multiplies a number by itself
and returns the final product. Here is an iterative *exponentByIteration.py*
Python program:

Python
```
def exponentByIteration(a, n):
    result = 1
    for i in range(n):
        result *= a
    return result

print(exponentByIteration(3, 6))
print(exponentByIteration(10, 3))
print(exponentByIteration(17, 10))
```

And here is an equivalent JavaScript *exponentByIteration.html* program:

JavaScript
```
<script type="text/javascript">
function exponentByIteration(a, n) {
    let result = 1;
    for (let i = 0; i < n; i++) {
```

```
        result *= a;
    }
    return result;
}

document.write(exponentByIteration(3, 6) + "<br />");
document.write(exponentByIteration(10, 3) + "<br />");
document.write(exponentByIteration(17, 10) + "<br />");
</script>
```

When you run these programs, the output looks like this:

```
729
1000
2015993900449
```

This is a straightforward calculation that we can easily write with a loop. The downside to using a loop is that the function slows as the exponents get larger: calculating 3^{12} takes twice as long as 3^6, and 3^{600} takes one hundred times as long as 3^6. In the next section, we address this by thinking recursively.

Creating a Recursive Exponents Function

Let's think of what a recursive solution for the exponentiation of, say, 3^6 would be. Because of the associative property of multiplication, $3 \times 3 \times 3 \times 3 \times 3 \times 3$ is the same as $(3 \times 3 \times 3) \times (3 \times 3 \times 3)$, which is the same as $(3 \times 3 \times 3)^2$. And since $(3 \times 3 \times 3)$ is the same as 3^3, we can determine that 3^6 is the same as $(3^3)^2$. This is an example of what mathematics calls the *power rule*: $(a^m)^n = a^{mn}$. Mathematics also gives us the *product rule*: $a^n \times a^m = a^{n+m}$, including $a^n \times a = a^{n+1}$.

We can use these mathematical rules to make an exponentByRecursion() function. If exponentByRecursion(3, 6) is called, it's the same as exponentByRecursion(3, 3) * exponentByRecursion(3, 3). Of course, we don't actually have to make both exponentByRecursion(3, 3) calls: we could just save the return value to a variable and multiply it by itself.

That works for even-numbered exponents, but what about for odd-numbered exponents? If we had to calculate 3^7, or $3 \times 3 \times 3 \times 3 \times 3 \times 3 \times 3$, this is the same as $(3 \times 3 \times 3 \times 3 \times 3 \times 3) \times 3$, or $(3^6) \times 3$. Then we can make the same recursive call to calculate 3^6.

NOTE *A simple programming trick for determining whether an integer is odd or even uses the modulus operator (%). Any even integer mod 2 results in 0, and any odd integer mod 2 results in 1.*

Those are the recursive cases, but what are the base cases? Mathematically speaking, any number to the zeroth power is defined as 1, while any number to the first power is the number itself. So for any function call exponentByRecursion(a, n), if n is 0 or 1, we can simply return 1 or a, respectively, because a^0 is always 1 and a^1 is always a.

Using all this information, we can write code for the exponentBy
Recursion() function. Here is an *exponentByRecursion.py* file with the
Python code:

```python
def exponentByRecursion(a, n):
    if n == 1:
        # BASE CASE
        return a
    elif n % 2 == 0:
        # RECURSIVE CASE (When n is even.)
        result = exponentByRecursion(a, n // 2)
        return result * result
    elif n % 2 == 1:
        # RECURSIVE CASE (When n is odd.)
        result = exponentByRecursion(a, n // 2)
        return result * result * a

print(exponentByRecursion(3, 6))
print(exponentByRecursion(10, 3))
print(exponentByRecursion(17, 10))
```

And here is the equivalent JavaScript code in *exponentByRecursion.html*:

```javascript
<script type="text/javascript">
function exponentByRecursion(a, n) {
    if (n === 1) {
        // BASE CASE
        return a;
    } else if (n % 2 === 0) {
        // RECURSIVE CASE (When n is even.)
        result = exponentByRecursion(a, n / 2);
        return result * result;
    } else if (n % 2 === 1) {
        // RECURSIVE CASE (When n is odd.)
        result = exponentByRecursion(a, Math.floor(n / 2));
        return result * result * a;
    }
}

document.write(exponentByRecursion(3, 6));
document.write(exponentByRecursion(10, 3));
document.write(exponentByRecursion(17, 10));
</script>
```

When you run this code, the output is identical to the iterative version:

```
729
1000
2015993900449
```

Each recursive call effectively cuts the problem size in half. This is what
makes our recursive exponent algorithm faster than the iterative version;
calculating 3^{1000} iteratively entails 1,000 multiplication operations, while

doing it recursively requires only 23 multiplications and divisions. When running the Python code under a performance profiler, calculating 3^{1000} iteratively 100,000 times takes 10.633 seconds, but the recursive calculation takes only 0.406 seconds. That is a huge improvement!

Creating an Iterative Exponents Function Based on Recursive Insights

Our original iterative exponents function took a straightforward approach: loop the same number of times as the exponent power. However, this doesn't scale well for larger powers. Our recursive implementation forced us to think about how to break this problem into smaller subproblems. This approach turns out to be much more efficient.

Because every recursive algorithm has an equivalent iterative algorithm, we could make a new iterative exponents function based on the power rule that the recursive algorithm uses. The following *exponentWith PowerRule.py* program has such a function:

Python
```python
def exponentWithPowerRule(a, n):
    # Step 1: Determine the operations to be performed.
    opStack = []
    while n > 1:
        if n % 2 == 0:
            # n is even.
            opStack.append('square')
            n = n // 2
        elif n % 2 == 1:
            # n is odd.
            n -= 1
            opStack.append('multiply')

    # Step 2: Perform the operations in reverse order.
    result = a # Start result at `a`.
    while opStack:
        op = opStack.pop()

        if op == 'multiply':
            result *= a
        elif op == 'square':
            result *= result

    return result

print(exponentWithPowerRule(3, 6))
print(exponentWithPowerRule(10, 3))
print(exponentWithPowerRule(17, 10))
```

Here is the equivalent JavaScript program in *exponentWithPowerRule.html*:

JavaScript
```javascript
<script type="text/javascript">
function exponentWithPowerRule(a, n) {
    // Step 1: Determine the operations to be performed.
    let opStack = [];
    while (n > 1) {
```

```
            if (n % 2 === 0) {
                // n is even.
                opStack.push("square");
                n = Math.floor(n / 2);
            } else if (n % 2 === 1) {
                // n is odd.
                n -= 1;
                opStack.push("multiply");
            }
        }

        // Step 2: Perform the operations in reverse order.
        let result = a; // Start result at `a`.
        while (opStack.length > 0) {
            let op = opStack.pop();

            if (op === "multiply") {
                result = result * a;
            } else if (op === "square") {
                result = result * result;
            }
        }

        return result;
    }

    document.write(exponentWithPowerRule(3, 6) + "<br />");
    document.write(exponentWithPowerRule(10, 3) + "<br />");
    document.write(exponentWithPowerRule(17, 10) + "<br />");
</script>
```

Our algorithm keeps reducing n by dividing it in half (if it's even) or subtracting 1 (if it's odd) until it is 1. This gives us the squaring or multiply-by-a operations we have to perform. After finishing this step, we perform these operations in reverse order. A generic stack data structure (separate from the call stack) is useful for reversing the order of these operations since it's a first-in, last-out data structure. The first step pushes squaring or multiply-by-a operations to a stack in the opStack variable. In the second step, it performs these operations as it pops them off the stack.

For example, calling exponentWithPowerRule(6, 5) to calculate 6^5 sets a as 6 and n as 5. The function notes that n is odd. This means we should subtract 1 from n to get 4 and push a multiply-by-a operation to opStack. Now that n is 4 (even), we divide it by 2 to get 2 and push a squaring operation to opStack. Since n is now 2 and even again, we divide it by 2 to get 1 and push another squaring operation to opStack. Now that n is 1, we are finished with this first step.

To perform the second step, we start the result as a (which is 6). We pop the opStack stack to get a squaring operation, telling the program to set result to result * result (that is, $result^2$) or 36. We pop the next operation off opStack, and it is another squaring operation, so the program changes the 36 in result to 36 * 36, or 1296. We pop the last operation off opStack, and it is a multiply-by-a operation, so we multiply the 1296 in result by a (which is 6) to get 7776. There are no more operations on opStack, so the function is now finished. When we double-check our math, we find that 6^5 is indeed 7,776.

The stack in opStack looks like Figure 2-4 as the function call exponentWithPowerRule(6, 5) executes.

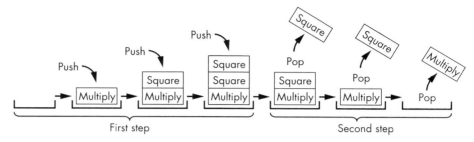

Figure 2-4: The stack in opStack during the exponentWithPowerRule(6, 5) function call

When you run this code, the output is identical to the other exponent programs:

```
729
1000
2015993900449
```

The iterative exponents function that uses the power rule has the improved performance of the recursive algorithm, while not suffering from the risk of a stack overflow. We might not have thought of this new, improved iterative algorithm without the insights of recursive thinking.

When Do You Need to Use Recursion?

You never *need* to use recursion. No programming problem *requires* recursion. This chapter has shown that recursion has no magical power to do things that iterative code in a loop with a stack data structure cannot do. In fact, a recursive function might be an overcomplicated solution for what you're trying to achieve.

However, as the exponent functions we created in the previous section show, recursion can provide new insights into how to think about our programming problem. Three features of a programming problem, when present, make it especially suitable to a recursive approach:

- It involves a tree-like structure.
- It involves backtracking.
- It isn't so deeply recursive as to potentially cause a stack overflow.

A tree has a *self-similar* structure: the branching points look similar to the root of a smaller subtree. Recursion often deals with self-similarity and problems that can be divided into smaller, similar subproblems. The root of the tree is analogous to the first call to a recursive function, the branching points are analogous to recursive cases, and the leaves are analogous to the base cases where no more recursive calls are made.

A maze is also a good example of a problem that has a tree-like structure and requires backtracking. In a maze, the branching points occur wherever you must pick one of many paths to follow. If you reach a dead end, you've encountered the base case. You must then backtrack to a previous branching point to select a different path to follow.

Figure 2-5 shows a maze's path visually morphed to look like a biological tree. Despite the visual difference between the maze paths and the tree-shaped paths, their branching points are related to each other in the same way. Mathematically, these graphs are equivalent.

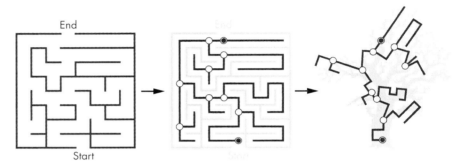

Figure 2-5: A maze (left) along with its interior paths (center) morphed to match a biological tree's shape (right)

Many programming problems have this tree-like structure at their core. For example, a filesystem has a tree-like structure; the subfolders look like the root folders of a smaller filesystem. Figure 2-6 compares a filesystem to a tree.

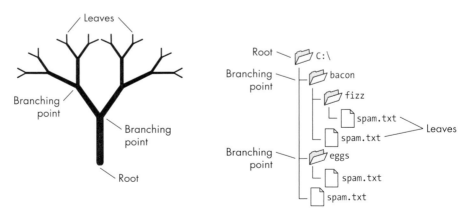

Figure 2-6: A filesystem is similar to a tree structure.

Searching for a specific filename in a folder is a recursive problem: you search the folder and then recursively search the folder's subfolders. Folders with no subfolders are the base cases that cause the recursive searching to stop. If your recursive algorithm doesn't find the filename it's looking for, it backtracks to a previous parent folder and continues searching from there.

The third point is a matter of practicality. If your tree structure has so many levels of branches that a recursive function would cause a stack overflow before it can reach the leaves, then recursion isn't a suitable solution.

On the other hand, recursion is the best approach for creating programming language compilers. Compiler design is its own expansive subject and beyond the scope of this book. But programming languages have a set of grammar rules that can break source code into a tree structure similar to the way grammar rules can break English sentences into a tree diagram. Recursion is an ideal technique to apply to compilers.

We'll identify many recursive algorithms in this book, and they often have the tree-like structure or backtracking features that lend themselves to recursion well.

Coming Up with Recursive Algorithms

Hopefully, this chapter has given you a firm idea of how recursive functions compare to the iterative algorithms you're likely more familiar with. The rest of this book dives into the details of various recursive algorithms. But how should you go about writing your own recursive functions?

The first step is always to identify the recursive case and the base case. You can take a top-down approach by breaking the problem into subproblems that are similar to the original problem but smaller; this is your *recursive case*. Then consider when the subproblems are small enough to have a trivial answer; this is your *base case*. Your recursive function may have more than one recursive case or base case, but all recursive functions will always have at least one recursive case and at least one base case.

The recursive Fibonacci algorithm is an example. A Fibonacci number is the sum of the previous two Fibonacci numbers. We can break the problem of finding a Fibonacci number into the subproblems of finding two smaller Fibonacci numbers. We know the first two Fibonacci numbers are both 1, so that provides the base case answer once the subproblems are small enough.

Sometimes it helps to take a bottom-up approach and consider the base case first, and then see how larger and larger problems are constructed and solved from there. The recursive factorial problem is an example. The factorial of 1! is 1. This forms the base case. The next factorial is 2!, and you create it by multiplying 1! by 2. The factorial after that, 3!, is created by multiplying 2! by 3, and so on. From this general pattern, we can figure out what the recursive case for our algorithm will be.

Summary

In this chapter, we covered calculating factorials and the Fibonacci sequence, two classic recursive programming problems. This chapter featured both iterative and recursive implementations for these algorithms. Despite being classic examples of recursion, their recursive algorithms suffer from critical flaws. The recursive factorial function can cause stack overflows, while the recursive Fibonacci function performs so many redundant calculations that it's far too slow to be effective in the real world.

We explored how to create recursive algorithms from iterative algorithms and how to create iterative algorithms from recursive algorithms. Iterative algorithms use a loop, and any recursive algorithm can be performed iteratively by using a loop and a stack data structure. Recursion is often an overly complicated solution, but programming problems that involve a tree-like structure and backtracking are particularly suitable for recursive implementations.

Writing recursive functions is a skill that improves with practice and experience. The rest of this book covers several well-known recursion examples and explores their strengths and limitations.

Further Reading

You can find more information about comparing iteration and recursion in the Computerphile YouTube channel's video "Programming Loops vs. Recursion" at *https://youtu.be/HXNhEYqFo0o*. If you want to compare the performance of iterative and recursive functions, you need to learn how to use a profiler. Python profilers are explained in Chapter 13 of my book *Beyond the Basic Stuff with Python* (No Starch Press, 2020), which can be read at *https://inventwithpython.com/beyond/chapter13.html*. The official Python documentation also covers profilers at *https://docs.python.org/3/library/profile.html*. The Firefox profiler for JavaScript is explained on Mozilla's website at *https://developer.mozilla.org/en-US/docs/Tools/Performance*. Other browsers have profilers similar to Firefox's.

Practice Questions

Test your comprehension by answering the following questions:

1. What is 4! (that is, the factorial of 4)?
2. How can you use the factorial of $(n - 1)$ to calculate the factorial of n?
3. What is the critical weakness of the recursive factorial function?
4. What are the first five numbers of the Fibonacci sequence?
5. What two numbers do you add to get the nth Fibonacci number?
6. What is the critical weakness of the recursive Fibonacci function?
7. What does an iterative algorithm always use?
8. Is it always possible to convert an iterative algorithm into a recursive one?

9. Is it always possible to convert a recursive algorithm into an iterative one?

10. Any recursive algorithm can be performed iteratively by using what two things?

11. What three features do programming problems that are suitable to recursive solutions have?

12. When is recursion required to solve a programming problem?

Practice Projects

For practice, write a function for each of the following tasks:

1. Iteratively calculate the sum of the integer series from 1 to n. This is similar to the factorial() function, except it performs addition instead of multiplication. For example, sumSeries(1) returns 1, sumSeries(2) returns 3 (that is, 1 + 2), sumSeries(3) returns 6 (that is, 1 + 2 + 3), and so on. This function should use a loop instead of recursion. Take a look at the *factorialByIteration.py* program in this chapter for guidance.

2. Write the recursive form of sumSeries(). This function should use recursive function calls instead of a loop. Look at the *factorialByRecursion.py* program in this chapter for guidance.

3. Iteratively calculate the sum of the first n powers of 2 in a function named sumPowersOf2(). The powers of 2 are 2, 4, 8, 16, 32, and so on. In Python, these are calculated with 2 ** 1, 2 ** 2, 2 ** 3, 2 ** 4, 2 ** 5, and so on, respectively. In JavaScript, these are calculated with Math.pow(2, 1), Math.pow(2, 2), and so on. For example, sumPowersOf2(1) returns 2, sumPowersOf2(2) returns 6 (that is, 2 + 4), sumPowersOf2(3) returns 14 (that is, 2 + 4 + 8), and so on.

4. Write the recursive form of sumPowersOf2(). This function should use recursive function calls instead of a loop.

3

CLASSIC RECURSION
ALGORITHMS

If you take a computer science course, the unit on recursion is sure to cover some of the classic algorithms presented in this chapter. Coding interviews (which, for lack of suitable ways to evaluate candidates, often crib notes from freshman computer science curricula) can touch upon them too. This chapter covers six classic problems in recursion, along with their solutions.

We begin with three simple algorithms: summing the numbers in an array, reversing a text string, and detecting whether a string is a palindrome. Then we explore an algorithm for solving the Tower of Hanoi puzzle, implement the flood fill drawing algorithm, and tackle the absurdly recursive Ackermann function.

In the process, you'll learn about the head-tail technique for splitting up the data in the recursive function arguments. We'll also ask ourselves three questions when trying to come up with recursive solutions: What is the base case? What argument is passed to the recursive function call? And how do the arguments passed to the recursive function calls become closer to the base case? As you gain more experience, answering these questions should come more naturally.

Summing Numbers in an Array

Our first example is simple: given a list (in Python) or an array (in JavaScript) of integers, return the total sum of all the integers. For example, a call such as sum([5, 2, 4, 8]) should return 19.

This is easy to solve with a loop, but solving it with recursion requires more thought. After reading Chapter 2, you might also notice that this algorithm doesn't map well enough to recursion's capabilities to justify recursion's added complexity. Still, summing numbers in an array (or some other calculation based on processing data in a linear data structure) is a common enough recursion problem in coding interviews that it deserves our attention.

To solve this problem, let's examine the *head-tail technique* for implementing recursive functions. This technique splits the recursive function's array argument into two parts: the *head* (the first element of the array) and the *tail* (a new array including everything after the first element). We define the recursive sum() function to find the sum of the array argument's integers by adding the head to the sum of the tail array. To find out the sum of the tail array, we recursively pass it as the array argument to sum().

Because the tail array is one element smaller than the original array argument, we'll eventually end up calling the recursive function and passing it an empty array. An empty array argument is trivial to sum and doesn't require more recursive calls; it is merely 0. From these facts, our answers to the three questions are as follows:

What is the base case?   An empty array, which has the sum of 0.

What argument is passed to the recursive function call?   The tail of the original number array, which has one less number than the original array argument.

How does this argument become closer to the base case?   The array argument shrinks by one element for each recursive call until it becomes a zero-length, or empty, array.

Here is *sumHeadTail.py*, a Python program to sum a list of numbers:

Python
```
def sum(numbers):
    if len(numbers) == 0: # BASE CASE
      ❶ return 0
    else: # RECURSIVE CASE
      ❷ head = numbers[0]
      ❸ tail = numbers[1:]
      ❹ return head + sum(tail)

nums = [1, 2, 3, 4, 5]
print('The sum of', nums, 'is', sum(nums))
nums = [5, 2, 4, 8]
```

```
print('The sum of', nums, 'is', sum(nums))
nums = [1, 10, 100, 1000]
print('The sum of', nums, 'is', sum(nums))
```

And here is the equivalent JavaScript program, *sumHeadTail.html*:

JavaScript
```
<script type="text/javascript">
function sum(numbers) {
    if (numbers.length === 0) { // BASE CASE
        ❶ return 0;
    } else { // RECURSIVE CASE
        ❷ let head = numbers[0];
        ❸ let tail = numbers.slice(1, numbers.length);
        ❹ return head + sum(tail);
    }
}

let nums = [1, 2, 3, 4, 5];
document.write('The sum of ' + nums + ' is ' + sum(nums) + "<br />");
nums = [5, 2, 4, 8];
document.write('The sum of ' + nums + ' is ' + sum(nums) + "<br />");
nums = [1, 10, 100, 1000];
document.write('The sum of ' + nums + ' is ' + sum(nums) + "<br />");
</script>
```

The output of these programs is shown here:

```
The sum of [1, 2, 3, 4, 5] is 15
The sum of [5, 2, 4, 8] is 19
The sum of [1, 10, 100, 1000] is 1111
```

When called with an empty array argument, the base case of our function simply returns 0 ❶. In the recursive case, we form the head ❷ and the tail ❸ from the original numbers argument. Keep in mind that the data type of tail is an array of numbers, just like the numbers argument. But the data type of head is just a single number value, and not an array with one number value. The return value of the sum() function is also a single number value and not an array of numbers; this is why we can add head and sum(tail) together in the recursive case ❹.

Each recursive call passes a smaller and smaller array to sum(), bringing it closer to the base case of an empty array. For example, Figure 3-1 shows the state of the call stack for sum([5, 2, 4, 8]).

In this figure, each card in the stack represents a function call. At the top of each card is the function name with the argument it was passed when called. Beneath that are the local variables: the numbers parameter, and the head and tail local variables created during the call. At the bottom of the card is the head + sum(tail) expression that the function call returns. When a new recursive function is made, a new card is pushed to the stack. When the function call returns, the top card is popped from the stack.

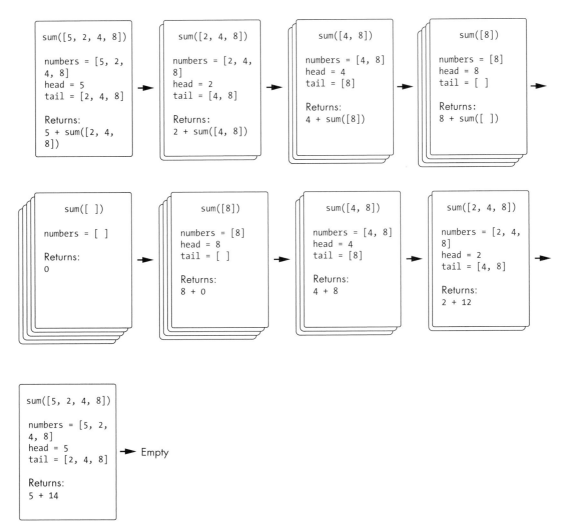

Figure 3-1: The state of the call stack when sum([5, 2, 4, 8]) runs

We can use the sum() function as a template for applying the head-tail technique to other recursive functions. For example, you can change the sum() function from one that sums an array of numbers to a concat() function that concatenates an array of strings together. The base case would return an empty string for an empty array argument, while the recursive case would return the head string joined with the return value of the recursive call that is passed the tail.

Recall from Chapter 2 that recursion is especially suited for problems that involve a tree-like structure and backtracking. An array, string, or other linear data structure can be considered a tree-like structure, albeit a tree that has only one branch at each node, as in Figure 3-2.

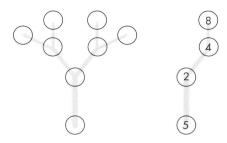

Figure 3-2: A [5, 2, 4, 8] array (right) is like a tree data structure (left) with only one branch at each node.

The key "tell" that our recursive function is unnecessary is that it never does any backtracking over the data it processes. It makes a single pass over each element in the array from beginning to end, which is something a basic loop can accomplish. Additionally, the Python recursive summation function is about 100 times slower than a straightforward iterative algorithm. Even if performance weren't an issue, the recursive sum() function would cause a stack overflow if passed a list with tens of thousands of numbers to sum. Recursion is an advanced technique, but it isn't always the best approach.

In Chapter 5, we'll examine a recursive summation function that uses a divide-and-conquer strategy, and in Chapter 8 we'll examine one that uses tail call optimization. These alternate recursive approaches work around some of the problems in the summation function in this chapter.

Reversing a String

Like summing the numbers in an array, reversing a string is another frequently cited recursive algorithm even though the iterative solution is straightforward. Because a string is essentially an array of single characters, we'll employ the head and tail approach for our rev() function just as we did for the summation algorithm.

Let's start with the smallest strings possible. A blank string and a single-character string are already the reverse of themselves. These naturally form our base cases: if the string argument is a string such as '' or 'A', our function should simply return the string argument.

For larger strings, let's try splitting the string into a head (just the first character) and tail (all characters after the first). For a two-character string like 'XY', 'X' is the head and 'Y' is the tail. To reverse the string, we need to place the head behind the tail: 'YX'.

Does this algorithm hold for longer strings? To reverse a string like 'CAT', we would break it into the head 'C' and the tail 'AT'. But placing the head behind the tail alone doesn't reverse the string; it gives us 'ATC'. What we actually want to do is put the head behind *the reverse of* the tail. In other words, 'AT' would reverse to 'TA', and then adding the head to the end of that would produce the reversed string, 'TAC'.

How can we reverse the tail? Well, we can recursively call rev() and pass it the tail. Forget about the implementation of our function for a moment and focus on its input and output: rev() takes one string argument and returns a string with the argument's characters reversed.

Thinking about how to implement a recursive function like rev() can be difficult because it involves a chicken-and-egg problem. In order to write rev()'s recursive case, we need to call a function that reverses a string—that is, rev(). As long as we have a solid understanding of what our recursive function's arguments and return value will be, we can use the *leap-of-faith* technique to get around this chicken-and-egg problem by writing our recursive case assuming the rev() function call returns the correct value even though we haven't finished writing it yet.

Taking a leap of faith in recursion is not a magical technique that guarantees your code works bug free. It is merely a perspective to hold to break past the mental programmer's block you can have when thinking about how to implement your recursive function. The leap of faith requires you to have a firm understanding of your recursive function's arguments and return value.

Note that the leap-of-faith technique only helps you write the recursive case. You must pass to the recursive call an argument that is closer to the base case. You can't simply pass the same argument that the recursive function received, like this:

```
def rev(theString):
    return rev(theString) # This won't magically work.
```

To continue our 'CAT' example, when we pass the tail 'AT' to rev(), the head is 'A' and the tail is 'T' in *that* function call. We already know that the reverse of a single-character string like 'T' is simply 'T'; that's our base case. So this second call to rev() will reverse 'AT' to 'TA', which is precisely what the previous call to rev() needs. Figure 3-3 shows the state of the call stack during all the recursive calls to rev().

Let's ask our three recursive algorithm questions about the rev() function:

What is the base case?   A zero- or one-character string.

What argument is passed to the recursive function call?   The tail of the original string argument, which has one less character than the original string argument.

How does this argument become closer to the base case?   The array argument shrinks by one element for each recursive call until it becomes a one- or zero-length array.

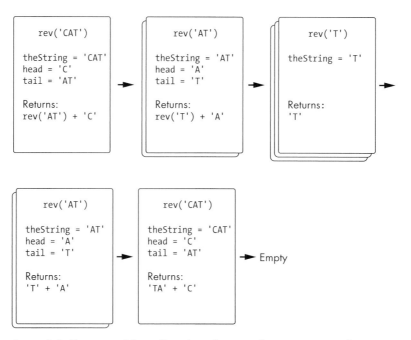

Figure 3-3: The state of the call stack as the rev() function reverses the CAT string

Here is *reverseString.py*, a Python program to reverse a string:

Python
```
def rev(theString):
❶   if len(theString) == 0 or len(theString) == 1:
        # BASE CASE
        return theString
    else:
        # RECURSIVE CASE
❷       head = theString[0]
❸       tail = theString[1:]
❹       return rev(tail) + head

print(rev('abcdef'))
print(rev('Hello, world!'))
print(rev(''))
print(rev('X'))
```

And here is the equivalent JavaScript code in *reverseString.html*:

JavaScript
```
<script type="text/javascript">
function rev(theString) {
❶   if (theString.length === 0 || theString.length === 1) {
        // BASE CASE
        return theString;
    } else {
        // RECURSIVE CASE
❷       var head = theString[0];
❸       var tail = theString.substring(1, theString.length);
```

```
❹  return rev(tail) + head;
    }
}

document.write(rev("abcdef") + "<br />");
document.write(rev("Hello, world!") + "<br />");
document.write(rev("") + "<br />");
document.write(rev("X") + "<br />");
</script>
```

Here is the output of these programs:

```
fedcba
!dlrow ,olleH

X
```

Our recursive function rev() returns the string that is the reverse of the argument, theString. Let's consider the simplest strings to reverse: the empty string and a single-character string would "reverse" to themselves. These are the two base cases with which we'll start (though we combine them with an or or || Boolean operator ❶). For the recursive case, we form head from the first character in theString ❷, and tail from every character after the first ❸. The recursive case then returns the reverse of tail followed by the head character ❹.

Detecting Palindromes

A *palindrome* is a word or phrase that is spelled the same when written forward and backward. *Level, race car, taco cat,* and *a man, a plan, a canal . . . Panama* are all examples of palindromes. If you would like to detect whether a string is a palindrome, you can write a recursive isPalindrome() function.

The base case is a zero- or one-character string, which by its nature is always the same, whether forward or backward. We'll use an approach similar to the head-tail technique, except that we'll split the string argument into head, middle, and last strings instead. If the head and last characters are the same and the middle characters also form a palindrome, the string is a palindrome. The recursion comes from passing the middle string to isPalindrome().

Let's ask the three recursive algorithm questions about the isPalindrome() function:

What is the base case?   A zero- or one-character string, which returns True because it is always a palindrome.

What argument is passed to the recursive function call?   The middle characters of the string argument.

How does this argument become closer to the base case?   The string argument shrinks by two characters for each recursive call until it becomes a zero- or one-character string.

Here is *palindrome.py*, a Python program to detect palindromes:

Python
```
def isPalindrome(theString):
    if len(theString) == 0 or len(theString) == 1:
        # BASE CASE
        return True
    else:
        # RECURSIVE CASE
     ❶ head = theString[0]
     ❷ middle = theString[1:-1]
     ❸ last = theString[-1]
     ❹ return head == last and isPalindrome(middle)

text = 'racecar'
print(text + ' is a palindrome: ' + str(isPalindrome(text)))
text = 'amanaplanacanalpanama'
print(text + ' is a palindrome: ' + str(isPalindrome(text)))
text = 'tacocat'
print(text + ' is a palindrome: ' + str(isPalindrome(text)))
text = 'zophie'
print(text + ' is a palindrome: ' + str(isPalindrome(text)))
```

Here is the equivalent JavaScript code in *palindrome.html*:

JavaScript
```
<script type="text/javascript">
function isPalindrome(theString) {
    if (theString.length === 0 || theString.length === 1) {
        // BASE CASE
        return true;
    } else {
        // RECURSIVE CASE
     ❶ var head = theString[0];
     ❷ var middle = theString.substring(1, theString.length -1);
     ❸ var last = theString[theString.length - 1];
     ❹ return head === last && isPalindrome(middle);
    }
}

text = "racecar";
document.write(text + " is a palindrome: " + isPalindrome(text) + "<br />");
text = "amanaplanacanalpanama";
document.write(text + " is a palindrome: " + isPalindrome(text) + "<br />");
text = "tacocat";
document.write(text + " is a palindrome: " + isPalindrome(text) + "<br />");
text = "zophie";
document.write(text + " is a palindrome: " + isPalindrome(text) + "<br />");
</script>
```

Here is the output of these programs:

```
racecar is a palindrome: True
amanaplanacanalpanama is a palindrome: True
tacocat is a palindrome: True
zophie is a palindrome: False
```

The base case returns True because a zero- or one-character string is always a palindrome. Otherwise, the string argument is broken into three pieces: the first character ❶, the last character ❸, and the middle characters between them ❷.

The return statement in the recursive case ❹ makes use of *Boolean short-circuiting*, a feature of almost every programming language. In an expression joined with the and or && Boolean operators, if the left-side expression is False, it doesn't matter if the right-side expression is True or False because the entire expression will be False. Boolean short-circuiting is an optimization that skips the evaluation of the right-side expression of an and operator if the left side is False. So, in the expression head == last and isPalindrome(middle), if head == last is False, the recursive call to isPalindrome() is skipped. This means that as soon as the head and last strings don't match, the recursion stops and simply returns False.

This recursive algorithm is still sequential, like the summation and reverse-string functions in the previous sections, except that instead of going from the start of the data to the end, it goes from both ends of the data toward the middle. The iterative version of this algorithm that uses a simple loop is more straightforward. We cover the recursive version in this book because it's a common coding interview problem.

Solving the Tower of Hanoi

The *Tower of Hanoi* is a puzzle involving a tower of stacked disks. The puzzle begins with the largest disk on the bottom, and the disk sizes decrease going up. Each disk has a hole in its center so that the disks can be stacked on top of one another on a pole. Figure 3-4 shows a wooden Tower of Hanoi puzzle.

Figure 3-4: A wooden Tower of Hanoi puzzle set

To solve the puzzle, the player must move the stack of disks from one pole to another while following three rules:

- The player can move only one disk at a time.
- The player can move disks only to and from the top of a tower.
- The player can never place a larger disk on top of a smaller disk.

Python's built-in `turtledemo` module has a Tower of Hanoi demonstration that you can see by running **python -m turtledemo** on Windows or **python3 -m turtledemo** on macOS/Linux, and then selecting **minimum_hanoi** from the Examples menu. Tower of Hanoi animations are readily found through an internet search as well.

The recursive algorithm for solving the Tower of Hanoi puzzle is not intuitive. Let's start with the smallest case: a Tower of Hanoi with one disk. The solution is trivial: move the disk to another pole and you're finished. Solving for two disks is slightly more complicated: move the smaller disk to one pole (we'll call it the *temporary pole*) and the larger disk to the other pole (we'll call it the *end pole*), and then finally move the smaller disk from the temporary pole to the end pole. Both disks are now on the end pole in the correct order.

Once you solve the three-disk tower, you'll notice that a pattern emerges. To solve a tower of n disks from the start pole to the end pole, you must do the following:

1. Solve the $n - 1$ disks puzzle by moving those disks from the start pole to the temporary pole.
2. Move the nth disk from the start pole to the end pole.
3. Solve the $n - 1$ disks puzzle by moving those disks from the temporary pole to the end pole.

Like the Fibonacci algorithm, the recursive case for the Tower of Hanoi algorithm makes two recursive calls instead of just one. If we draw a tree diagram of the operations for solving a four-disk Tower of Hanoi, it looks like Figure 3-6. Solving the four-disk puzzle requires the same steps as solving the three-disk puzzle, as well as moving the fourth disk and performing the steps of solving the three-disk puzzle again. Likewise, solving the three-disk puzzle requires the same steps as the two-disk puzzle plus moving the third disk, and so on. Solving the one-disk puzzle is the trivial base case: it involves only moving the disk.

The tree-like structure in Figure 3-5 hints that a recursive approach is ideal for solving the Tower of Hanoi puzzle. In this tree, the execution moves from top to bottom and from left to right.

While a three-disk or four-disk Tower of Hanoi is easy for a human to solve, increasing numbers of disks require an exponentially increasing number of operations to complete. For n disks, it takes a minimum of $2n - 1$ moves to solve. This means a 31-disk tower requires over a billion moves to complete!

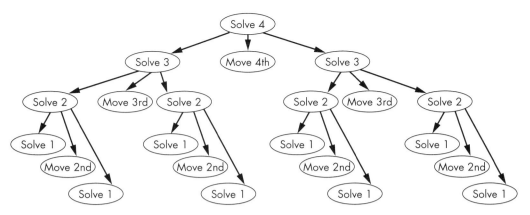

Figure 3-5: The series of operations for solving a four-disk Tower of Hanoi

Let's ask ourselves the three questions for creating a recursive solution:

What is the base case?   Solving a tower of one disk.

What argument is passed to the recursive function call?   Solving a tower of size one less than the current size.

How does this argument become closer to the base case?   The size of the tower to solve decreases by one disk for each recursive call until it is a one-disk tower.

The following *towerOfHanoiSolver.py* program solves the Tower of Hanoi puzzle and displays a visualization of each step:

```
import sys

# Set up towers A, B, and C. The end of the list is the top of the tower.
  TOTAL_DISKS = 6 ❶

# Populate Tower A:
  TOWERS = {'A': list(reversed(range(1, TOTAL_DISKS + 1))), ❷
           'B': [],
           'C': []}

def printDisk(diskNum):
    # Print a single disk of width diskNum.
    emptySpace = ' ' * (TOTAL_DISKS - diskNum)
    if diskNum == 0:
        # Just draw the pole.
        sys.stdout.write(emptySpace + '||' + emptySpace)
    else:
        # Draw the disk.
        diskSpace = '@' * diskNum
        diskNumLabel = str(diskNum).rjust(2, '_')
        sys.stdout.write(emptySpace + diskSpace + diskNumLabel + diskSpace + emptySpace)

def printTowers():
    # Print all three towers.
```

```
    for level in range(TOTAL_DISKS, -1, -1):
        for tower in (TOWERS['A'], TOWERS['B'], TOWERS['C']):
            if level >= len(tower):
                printDisk(0)
            else:
                printDisk(tower[level])
        sys.stdout.write('\n')
    # Print the tower labels A, B, and C.
    emptySpace = ' ' * (TOTAL_DISKS)
    print('%s A%s%s B%s%s C\n' % (emptySpace, emptySpace, emptySpace, emptySpace, emptySpace))

def moveOneDisk(startTower, endTower):
    # Move the top disk from startTower to endTower.
    disk = TOWERS[startTower].pop()
    TOWERS[endTower].append(disk)

def solve(numberOfDisks, startTower, endTower, tempTower):
    # Move the top numberOfDisks disks from startTower to endTower.
    if numberOfDisks == 1:
        # BASE CASE
        moveOneDisk(startTower, endTower) ❸
        printTowers()
        return
    else:
        # RECURSIVE CASE
        solve(numberOfDisks - 1, startTower, tempTower, endTower) ❹
        moveOneDisk(startTower, endTower) ❺
        printTowers()
        solve(numberOfDisks - 1, tempTower, endTower, startTower) ❻
        return

# Solve:
printTowers()
solve(TOTAL_DISKS, 'A', 'B', 'C')

# Uncomment to enable interactive mode:
#while True:
#    printTowers()
#    print('Enter letter of start tower and the end tower. (A, B, C) Or Q to quit.')
#    move = input().upper()
#    if move == 'Q':
#        sys.exit()
#    elif move[0] in 'ABC' and move[1] in 'ABC' and move[0] != move[1]:
#        moveOneDisk(move[0], move[1])
```

This *towerOfHanoiSolver.html* program contains the equivalent JavaScript code:

```
<script type="text/javascript">
// Set up towers A, B, and C. The end of the array is the top of the tower.
  var TOTAL_DISKS = 6; ❶
  var TOWERS = {"A": [], ❷
               "B": [],
               "C": []};
```

```
// Populate Tower A:
for (var i = TOTAL_DISKS; i > 0; i--) {
    TOWERS["A"].push(i);
}

function printDisk(diskNum) {
    // Print a single disk of width diskNum.
    var emptySpace = " ".repeat(TOTAL_DISKS - diskNum);
    if (diskNum === 0) {
        // Just draw the pole.
        document.write(emptySpace + "||" + emptySpace);
    } else {
        // Draw the disk.
        var diskSpace = "@".repeat(diskNum);
        var diskNumLabel = String("___" + diskNum).slice(-2);
        document.write(emptySpace + diskSpace + diskNumLabel + diskSpace + emptySpace);
    }
}

function printTowers() {
    // Print all three towers.
    var towerLetters = "ABC";
    for (var level = TOTAL_DISKS; level >= 0; level--) {
        for (var towerLetterIndex = 0; towerLetterIndex < 3; towerLetterIndex++) {
            var tower = TOWERS[towerLetters[towerLetterIndex]];
            if (level >= tower.length) {
                printDisk(0);
            } else {
                printDisk(tower[level]);
            }
        }
        document.write("<br />");
    }
    // Print the tower labels A, B, and C.
    var emptySpace = " ".repeat(TOTAL_DISKS);
    document.write(emptySpace + " A" + emptySpace + emptySpace +
" B" + emptySpace + emptySpace + " C<br /><br />");
}

function moveOneDisk(startTower, endTower) {
    // Move the top disk from startTower to endTower.
    var disk = TOWERS[startTower].pop();
    TOWERS[endTower].push(disk);
}

function solve(numberOfDisks, startTower, endTower, tempTower) {
    // Move the top numberOfDisks disks from startTower to endTower.
    if (numberOfDisks == 1) {
        // BASE CASE
        moveOneDisk(startTower, endTower); ❸
        printTowers();
        return;
    } else {
        // RECURSIVE CASE
        solve(numberOfDisks - 1, startTower, tempTower, endTower); ❹
```

```
        moveOneDisk(startTower, endTower); ❺
        printTowers();
        solve(numberOfDisks - 1, tempTower, endTower, startTower); ❻
        return;
    }
}

// Solve:
document.write("<pre>");
printTowers();
solve(TOTAL_DISKS, "A", "B", "C");
document.write("</pre>");
</script>
```

When you run this code, the output shows each move of the disks until the entire tower has moved from Tower A to Tower B:

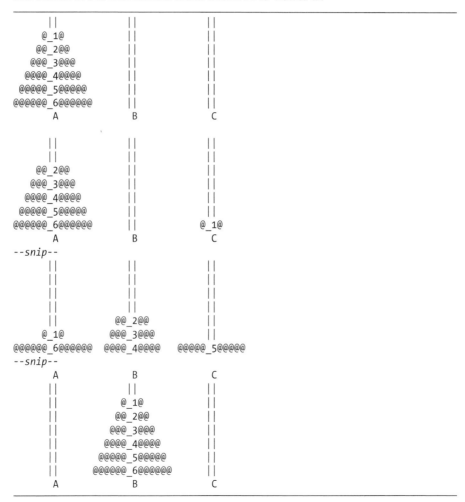

The Python version has an interactive mode too, where you can solve the puzzle yourself. Uncomment the lines of code at the end of *towerOf HanoiSolver.py* to play the interactive version.

You can start by running the program with the smaller cases by setting the TOTAL_DISKS constant ❶ at the top of the program to 1 or 2. In our program, a list of integers in Python and an array of integers in JavaScript represent a pole. The integer represents a disk, with larger integers representing larger disks. The integer at the start of the list or array is at the bottom of the pole, and the integer at the end is at the pole's top. For example, [6, 5, 4, 3, 2, 1] represents the starting pole with six disks with the largest on the bottom, while [] represents a pole with no disks. The TOWERS variable contains three of these lists ❷.

The base case merely moves the smallest disk from the start pole to the end pole ❸. The recursive case for a tower of *n* disks carries out three steps: solving the *n* – 1 case ❹, moving the *n*th disk ❺, and then solving the *n* – 1 case again ❻.

Using Flood Fill

Graphics programs commonly use the *flood fill algorithm* to fill an arbitrarily shaped area of the same color with another color. Figure 3-6 shows one such shape at the top left. The subsequent panels show three different sections of the shape flood-filled with a gray color. The flood fill begins on a white pixel and spreads until it meets a non-white pixel, filling the enclosed space.

The flood fill algorithm is recursive: it begins by changing a single pixel to a new color. The recursive function is then called on any neighbors of the pixel with its same old color. It then moves on to the neighbors of the neighbors, and so on, converting each pixel to the new color until the enclosed space is filled in.

The base case is a pixel whose color is the edge of the image or is not the old color. Since reaching the base case is the only way to stop the "spread" of recursive calls for every pixel in the image, this algorithm has the emergent behavior of changing all the contiguous pixels from the old color to the new color.

Let's ask the three recursive algorithm questions about our floodFill() function:

What is the base case?   When the x- and y-coordinates are for a pixel that is not the old color, or are at the edge of the image.

What arguments are passed to the recursive function call?   The x- and y-coordinates of the four neighboring pixels of the current pixel are the arguments to four recursive calls.

How do these arguments become closer to the base case?   The neighboring pixels run up to a different color than the old color or the edge of the image. Either way, eventually the algorithm runs out of pixels to check.

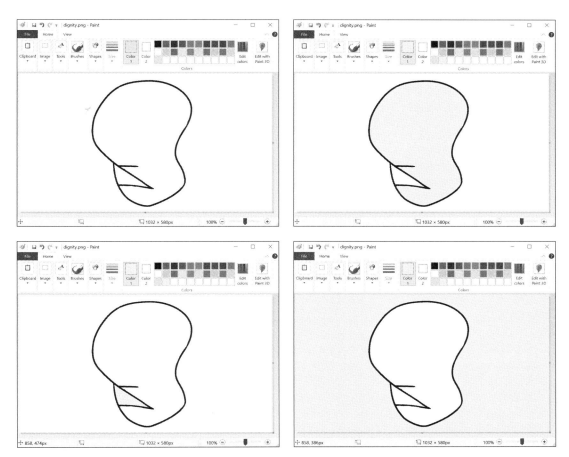

Figure 3-6: The original shape in a graphics editor (top left) and the same shape with three different areas flood-filled with a light gray color

Instead of an image for our sample program, we'll use a list of single-character strings to form a 2D grid of text characters to represent an "image." Each string represents a "pixel," and the specific character represents the "color." The *floodfill.py* Python program implements the flood fill algorithm, the image data, and a function to print the image on the screen:

Python

```
import sys

# Create the image (make sure it's rectangular!)
❶ im = [list('..#######################..........'),
       list('..#.....................#...#####...'),
       list('..#..........#######....#####...#...'),
       list('..#..........#......#...........#...'),
       list('..#..........#######.........####...'),
       list('..######.....................#......'),
       list('.......#..#####.....##########......'),
       list('.......####...#######...............')]

HEIGHT = len(im)
```

```
           WIDTH = len(im[0])

           def floodFill(image, x, y, newChar, oldChar=None):
               if oldChar == None:
                   # oldChar defaults to the character at x, y.
                 ❷ oldChar = image[y][x]
               if oldChar == newChar or image[y][x] != oldChar:
                   # BASE CASE
                   return

               image[y][x] = newChar # Change the character.

               # Uncomment to view each step:
               #printImage(image)

               # Change the neighboring characters.
               if y + 1 < HEIGHT and image[y + 1][x] == oldChar:
                   # RECURSIVE CASE
                 ❸ floodFill(image, x, y + 1, newChar, oldChar)
               if y - 1 >= 0 and image[y - 1][x] == oldChar:
                   # RECURSIVE CASE
                 ❹ floodFill(image, x, y - 1, newChar, oldChar)
               if x + 1 < WIDTH and image[y][x + 1] == oldChar:
                   # RECURSIVE CASE
                 ❺ floodFill(image, x + 1, y, newChar, oldChar)
               if x - 1 >= 0 and image[y][x - 1] == oldChar:
                   # RECURSIVE CASE
                 ❻ floodFill(image, x - 1, y, newChar, oldChar)
             ❼ return # BASE CASE

           def printImage(image):
               for y in range(HEIGHT):
                   # Print each row.
                   for x in range(WIDTH):
                       # Print each column.
                       sys.stdout.write(image[y][x])
                   sys.stdout.write('\n')
               sys.stdout.write('\n')

           printImage(im)
           floodFill(im, 3, 3, 'o')
           printImage(im)
```

The *floodfill.html* program contains the equivalent JavaScript code:

JavaScript
```
           <script type="text/javascript">
           // Create the image (make sure it's rectangular!)
         ❶ var im = ["..#######################...........".split(""),
                      "..#....................#...#####...".split(""),
                      "..#..........#######....#####...#...".split(""),
                      "..#..........#.......#............#...".split(""),
                      "..#..........#######........####...".split(""),
                      "..######................#.......".split(""),
                      ".......#..#####.....##########......".split(""),
                      ".......####...#######...............".split("")];
```

```javascript
var HEIGHT = im.length;
var WIDTH = im[0].length;

function floodFill(image, x, y, newChar, oldChar) {
    if (oldChar === undefined) {
        // oldChar defaults to the character at x, y.
      ❷ oldChar = image[y][x];
    }
    if ((oldChar == newChar) || (image[y][x] != oldChar)) {
        // BASE CASE
        return;
    }

    image[y][x] = newChar; // Change the character.

    // Uncomment to view each step:
    //printImage(image);

    // Change the neighboring characters.
    if ((y + 1 < HEIGHT) && (image[y + 1][x] == oldChar)) {
        // RECURSIVE CASE
      ❸ floodFill(image, x, y + 1, newChar, oldChar);
    }
    if ((y - 1 >= 0) && (image[y - 1][x] == oldChar)) {
        // RECURSIVE CASE
      ❹ floodFill(image, x, y - 1, newChar, oldChar);
    }
    if ((x + 1 < WIDTH) && (image[y][x + 1] == oldChar)) {
        // RECURSIVE CASE
      ❺ floodFill(image, x + 1, y, newChar, oldChar);
    }
    if ((x - 1 >= 0) && (image[y][x - 1] == oldChar)) {
        // RECURSIVE CASE
      ❻ floodFill(image, x - 1, y, newChar, oldChar);
    }
  ❼ return; // BASE CASE
}

function printImage(image) {
    document.write("<pre>");
    for (var y = 0; y < HEIGHT; y++) {
        // Print each row.
        for (var x = 0; x < WIDTH; x++) {
            // Print each column.
            document.write(image[y][x]);
        }
        document.write("\n");
    }
    document.write("\n</ pre>");
}

printImage(im);
floodFill(im, 3, 3, "o");
printImage(im);
</script>
```

When you run this code, the program fills the interior of the shape drawn by the # characters starting at coordinates 3, 3. It replaces all the period characters (.) with o characters. The following output shows the before and after images:

```
..#######################..........
..#.....................#...#####...
..#.........########....#####...#...
..#.........#......#............#...
..#.........########.........####...
..######.....................#......
.......#..#####.....##########......
.......####...#######...............

..#######################..........
..#ooooooooooooooooooooo#...#####...
..#oooooooooo########oooo####ooo#...
..#oooooooooo#......#ooooooooooo#...
..#oooooooooo########ooooooooo####...
..######ooooooooooooooooooooo#......
.......#oo#####ooooo##########......
.......####...#######...............
```

If you want to see every step of the flood fill algorithm as it fills in the new character, uncomment the printImage(image) line ❶ in the floodFill() function and run the program again.

The image is represented by a 2D array of string characters. We can pass this image data structure, an x coordinate and a y coordinate, and a new character to the floodFill() function. The function notes the character currently at the x and y coordinates and saves it to the oldChar variable ❷.

If the current characters at coordinates x and y in image are not the same as oldChar, this is our base case, and the function simply returns. Otherwise, the function continues on to its four recursive cases: passing the x- and y-coordinates of the bottom ❸, top ❹, right ❺, and left ❻ neighbors of the current coordinates. After these four potential recursive calls are made, the end of the function is an implicit base case, made explicit in our program with a return statement ❼.

The flood fill algorithm doesn't have to be recursive. For large images, a recursive function could cause stack overflows. If we were to implement flood fill with a loop and a stack instead, the stack would begin with the x- and y-coordinates of the starting pixel. The code in the loop would pop the coordinates off the top of the stack, and if that coordinate's pixel matches oldChar, it would push the coordinates of the four neighboring pixels. When the stack is empty because the base case is no longer pushing neighbors to the stack, the loop is finished.

However, the flood fill algorithm doesn't necessarily have to use a stack. The pushing and popping of a first-in, last-out stack is effective for backtracking behavior, but the order that the pixels are processed in the flood fill algorithm can be arbitrary. This means we could equally effectively use a set data structure that removes elements randomly. You can find these iterative flood fill algorithms implemented in *floodFillIterative.py* and *floodFillIterative.html* in the downloadable resources at *https://nostarch .com/recursive-book-recursion*.

Using the Ackermann Function

The *Ackermann function* is named after its discoverer, Wilhelm Ackermann. A student of mathematician David Hilbert (whose Hilbert curve fractal we discuss in Chapter 9), Ackermann published his function in 1928. Mathematicians Rózsa Péter and Raphael Robinson later developed the version of the function featured in this section.

While the Ackermann function has some application in advanced mathematics, it is mostly known for being an example of a highly recursive function. Even slight increases to its two integer arguments cause a large increase in the number of recursive calls it makes.

The Ackermann function takes two arguments, m and n, and has a base case of returning n + 1 when m is 0. There are two recursive cases: when n is 0, the function returns ackermann(m - 1, 1), and when n is greater than 0, the function returns ackermann(m - 1, ackermann(m, n - 1)). These cases likely aren't meaningful to you, but suffice it to say, the number of recursive calls the Ackermann function makes grows quickly. Calling ackermann(1, 1) results in three recursive function calls. Calling ackermann(2, 3) results in 43 recursive function calls. Calling ackermann(3, 5) results in 42,437 recursive function calls. And calling ackermann(5, 7) results in . . . well, actually I don't know how many recursive function calls, because it would take several times the age of the universe to calculate.

Let's answer the three questions we ask when constructing recursive algorithms:

What is the base case?　When m is 0.

What arguments are passed to the recursive function call?　Either m or m - 1 is passed for the next m parameter; and 1, n - 1, or the return value of ackermann(m, n - 1) is passed for the next n parameter.

How do these arguments become closer to the base case?　The m argument is always either decreasing or staying the same size, so it will eventually reach 0.

Here is an *ackermann.py* Python program:

```
def ackermann(m, n, indentation=None):
    if indentation is None:
        indentation = 0
    print('%sackermann(%s, %s)' % (' ' * indentation, m, n))

    if m == 0:
        # BASE CASE
        return n + 1
    elif m > 0 and n == 0:
        # RECURSIVE CASE
```

```
        return ackermann(m - 1, 1, indentation + 1)
    elif m > 0 and n > 0:
        # RECURSIVE CASE
        return ackermann(m - 1, ackermann(m, n - 1, indentation + 1), indentation + 1)

print('Starting with m = 1, n = 1:')
print(ackermann(1, 1))
print('Starting with m = 2, n = 3:')
print(ackermann(2, 3))
```

And here is the equivalent *ackermann.html* JavaScript program:

```
<script type="text/javascript">
function ackermann(m, n, indentation) {
    if (indentation === undefined) {
        indentation = 0;
    }
    document.write(" ".repeat(indentation) + "ackermann(" + m + ", " + n + ")\n");

    if (m === 0) {
        // BASE CASE
        return n + 1;
    } else if ((m > 0) && (n === 0)) {
        // RECURSIVE CASE
        return ackermann(m - 1, 1, indentation + 1);
    } else if ((m > 0) && (n > 0)) {
        // RECURSIVE CASE
        return ackermann(m - 1, ackermann(m, n - 1, indentation + 1), indentation + 1);
    }
}

document.write("<pre>");
document.write("Starting with m = 1, n = 1:<br />");
document.write(ackermann(1, 1) + "<br />");
document.write("Starting with m = 2, n = 3:<br />");
document.write(ackermann(2, 3) + "<br />");
document.write("</pre>");
</script>
```

When you run this code, the output's indentation (set by the `indentation` argument) tells you how deep on the call stack the given recursive function call is:

```
Starting with m = 1, n = 1:
ackermann(1, 1)
 ackermann(1, 0)
  ackermann(0, 1)
 ackermann(0, 2)
3
Starting with m = 2, n = 3:
ackermann(2, 3)
 ackermann(2, 2)
  ackermann(2, 1)
   ackermann(2, 0)
```

```
--snip--
    ackermann(0, 6)
   ackermann(0, 7)
  ackermann(0, 8)
9
```

You can also try `ackermann(3, 3)`, but anything with larger arguments will probably take far too long to calculate. To speed up the calculation, try commenting out all `print()` and `document.write()` calls except the ones that print the final return value of `ackermann()`.

Remember, even a recursive algorithm like the Ackermann function can be implemented as an iterative function. The iterative Ackermann algorithms are implemented in *ackermannIterative.py* and *ackermannIterative.html* in the downloadable resources at *https://nostarch.com/recursive-book-recursion*.

Summary

This chapter covered some classic recursive algorithms. For each, we asked the three important questions you should always ask when designing your own recursive functions: What is the base case? What arguments are passed to the recursive function call? How do these arguments become closer to the base case? If they don't, your function will continue to recurse until it causes a stack overflow.

The summation, string reversing, and palindrome detection recursive functions could have easily been implemented with a simple loop. The key giveaway is that they all make a single pass through the data given to them with no backtracking. As explained in Chapter 2, recursive algorithms are especially suited to problems that involve a tree-like structure and require backtracking.

The tree-like structures for solving the Tower of Hanoi puzzle suggest that it involves backtracking, as the program execution runs from top to bottom, left to right, in the tree. This makes it a prime candidate for recursion, especially since the solution requires two recursive calls of smaller towers.

The flood fill algorithm is directly applicable to graphics and drawing programs, as well as other algorithms to detect the shape of contiguous areas. If you've used the paint-bucket tool in a graphics program, you've likely used a version of the flood fill algorithm.

The Ackermann function is an excellent example of how quickly a recursive function can grow as its inputs increase. While it doesn't have many practical applications in day-to-day programming, no discussion about recursion would be complete without it. But as recursive as it is, like all recursive functions it can be implemented iteratively with a loop and a stack.

Further Reading

Wikipedia has more information on the Tower of Hanoi problem at *https://en.wikipedia.org/wiki/Tower_of_Hanoi*, and the Computerphile video

"Recursion 'Super Power' (in Python)" covers solving the Tower of Hanoi in Python at *https://youtu.be/8lhxIOAfDss*. The 3Blue1Brown two-part video series, "Binary, Hanoi, and Sierpiński," goes into even more detail by exploring the relationships among the Tower of Hanoi, binary numbers, and the Sierpiński Triangle fractal starting at *https://youtu.be/2SUvWfNJSsM*.

Wikipedia has an animation of the flood fill algorithm working on a small image at *https://en.wikipedia.org/wiki/Flood_fill*.

The Computerphile video "The Most Difficult Program to Compute?" discusses the Ackermann function at *https://youtu.be/i7sm9dzFtEI*. If you'd like to learn more about the Ackermann function's place in computability theory, the Hackers in Cambridge channel has a five-part video series on primitive recursive and partial recursive functions at *https://youtu.be/yaDQrOUK-KY*. The series requires a lot of mathematical thinking on the part of the viewer, but you don't need a lot of prior mathematical knowledge.

Practice Questions

Test your comprehension by answering the following questions:

1. What is the head of an array or string?
2. What is the tail of an array or string?
3. What are the three questions this chapter presents for each recursive algorithm?
4. What is the leap of faith in recursion?
5. What do you need to understand about the recursive function you are writing before you can take a leap of faith?
6. How does a linear data structure such as an array or string resemble a tree-like structure?
7. Does the recursive sum() function involve any backtracking over the data it works on?
8. In the flood fill program, try changing the im variable's strings to create a *C* shape that is not fully enclosed. What happens when you attempt to flood-fill the image from the middle of the *C*?
9. Answer the three questions about recursive solutions for each of the recursive algorithms presented in this chapter:

   a. What is the base case?

   b. What argument is passed to the recursive function call?

   c. How does this argument become closer to the base case?

   Then re-create the recursive algorithms from this chapter without looking at the original code.

Practice Projects

For practice, write a function for each of the following tasks:

1. Using the head-tail technique, create a recursive concat() function that is passed an array of strings and returns these strings concatenated together into a single string. For example, concat(['Hello', 'World']) should return HelloWorld.

2. Using the head-tail technique, create a recursive product() function that is passed an array of integers and returns the total multiplied product of them. This code will be almost identical to the sum() function in this chapter. However, note that the base case of an array with just one integer returns the integer, and the base case of an empty array returns 1.

3. Using the flood fill algorithm, count the number of "rooms," or enclosed spaces, in a 2D grid. You can do this by creating nested for loops that call the flood fill function on each character in the grid if it is a period, in order to change the periods into hash characters. For example, the following data would result in the program finding six places in the grid with periods, meaning there are five rooms (and the space outside all the rooms).

```
...##########....................................
...#........#....####.................##########
...#........#....#..#...###########...#........#
...##########....#..#...#..........#...##......#
.......#....#....####...#..........#....##.....#
.......#....#....#......###########.....##.....#
.......######....#.....................##....#
................####........####.........######
```

4

BACKTRACKING AND TREE TRAVERSAL ALGORITHMS

In previous chapters, you learned that recursion is especially suited for problems that involve a tree-like structure and backtracking, such as maze-solving algorithms. To see why, consider that a tree's trunk splits off into multiple branches. Those branches themselves split off into other branches. In other words, a tree has a recursive, self-similar shape.

A maze can be represented by a tree data structure, since mazes branch off into different paths, which in turn branch off into more paths. When you reach a dead end in a maze, you must backtrack to an earlier branching point.

The task of traversing tree graphs is tightly linked with many recursive algorithms, such as the maze-solving algorithm in this chapter and the maze-generation program in Chapter 11. We'll take a look at tree traversal algorithms and employ them to find certain names in a tree data structure. We'll also use tree traversal for an algorithm to obtain the deepest node in a tree. Finally, we'll see how mazes can be represented as a tree data structure, and employ tree traversal and backtracking to find a path from the start of the maze to the exit.

Using Tree Traversal

If you program in Python and JavaScript, you're used to working with list, array, and dictionary data structures. You'll encounter tree data structures only if you are dealing with low-level details of certain computer science algorithms such as abstract syntax trees, priority queues, Adelson-Velsky-Landis (AVL) trees, and other concepts beyond the scope of this book. However, trees themselves are simple enough concepts.

A *tree data structure* is a data structure composed of nodes that are connected to other nodes by edges. The *nodes* contain data, while the *edges* represent a relationship with another node. Nodes are also called *vertices*. The starting node of a tree is called the *root*, and the nodes at the end are called *leaves*. Trees always have exactly one root.

Parent nodes at the top have edges to zero or more *child nodes* beneath them. Therefore, leaves are the nodes that do not have children, parent nodes are the non-leaf nodes, and child nodes are all the non-root nodes. Nodes in a tree can have edges to multiple child nodes. The parent nodes that connect a child node to the root node are also called the child node's *ancestors*. The child nodes between a parent node and a leaf node are called the parent node's *descendants*. Parent nodes in a tree can have multiple child nodes. But every child node has exactly one parent, except for the root node, which has zero parents. In trees, only one path can exist between any two nodes.

Figure 4-1 shows an example of a tree and three examples of structures that are not trees.

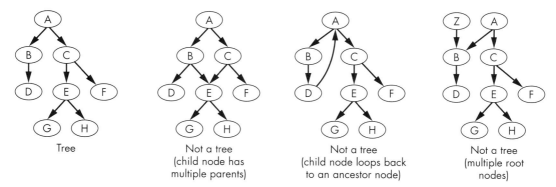

Figure 4-1: A tree (left) and three examples of non-trees

As you can see, child nodes must have one parent and not have an edge that creates a loop, or else the structure is no longer considered a tree. The recursive algorithms we cover in this chapter apply only to tree data structures.

A Tree Data Structure in Python and JavaScript

Tree data structures are often drawn growing downward, with the root at the top. Figure 4-2 shows a tree created with the following Python code (it's also valid JavaScript code):

```
root  = {'data': 'A', 'children': []}
node2 = {'data': 'B', 'children': []}
node3 = {'data': 'C', 'children': []}
node4 = {'data': 'D', 'children': []}
node5 = {'data': 'E', 'children': []}
node6 = {'data': 'F', 'children': []}
node7 = {'data': 'G', 'children': []}
node8 = {'data': 'H', 'children': []}
root['children'] = [node2, node3]
node2['children'] = [node4]
node3['children'] = [node5, node6]
node5['children'] = [node7, node8]
```

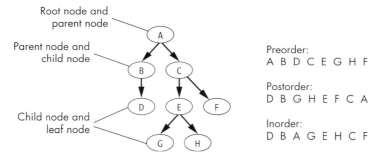

Preorder:
A B D C E G H F

Postorder:
D B G H E F C A

Inorder:
D B A G E H C F

Figure 4-2: A tree with root A and leaves D, G, H, and F, along with its traversal orders

Each node in the tree contains a piece of data (a string of a letter from A to H) and a list of its child nodes. The preorder, postorder, and inorder information in Figure 4-2 is explained in subsequent sections.

In the code for this tree, each node is represented by a Python dictionary (or JavaScript object) with a key data that stores the node's data, and a key children that has a list of other nodes. I use the root and node2 to node8 variables to store each node and make the code more readable, but they aren't required. The following Python/JavaScript code is equivalent to the previous code listing, though harder for humans to read:

```
root = {'data': 'A', 'children': [{'data': 'B', 'children':
[{'data': 'D', 'children': []}]}, {'data': 'C', 'children':
[{'data': 'E', 'children': [{'data': 'G', 'children': []},
{'data': 'H', 'children': []}]}, {'data': 'F', 'children': []}]}]}
```

The tree in Figure 4-2 is a specific kind of data structure called a *directed acyclic graph (DAG)*. In mathematics and computer science, a *graph* is a collection of nodes and edges, and a tree is a kind of graph. The graph is *directed* because its edges have one direction: from parent to child node. Edges in a DAG are not undirected—that is, bidirectional. (Trees in general do not have this restriction and can have edges in both directions, including from a child node back to its parent node.) The graph is *acyclic* because there are no loops, or *cycles*, from child nodes to their own ancestor nodes; the "branches" of the tree must keep growing in the same direction.

You can think of lists, arrays, and strings as linear trees; the root is the first element, and the nodes have only one child node. This linear tree terminates at its one leaf node. These linear trees are called *linked lists*, as each node has only one "next" node until the end of the list. Figure 4-3 shows a linked list that stores the characters in the word *HELLO*.

Figure 4-3: A linked list data structure storing HELLO. Linked lists can be considered a kind of tree data structure.

We'll use the code for the tree in Figure 4-2 for this chapter's examples. A tree traversal algorithm will visit each of the nodes in a tree by following the edges, starting from a root node.

Traversing the Tree

We can write code to access data in any node by starting from the root node in root. For example, after entering the tree code into the Python or JavaScript interactive shell, run the following:

```
>>> root['children'][1]['data']
'C'
>>> root['children'][1]['children'][0]['data']
'E'
```

Our tree traversal code can be written as a recursive function because tree data structures have a self-similar structure: a parent node has child nodes, and each child node is the parent node of its own children. Tree traversal algorithms ensure that your programs can access or modify the data in every node in the tree no matter its shape or size.

Let's ask the three questions about recursive algorithms for our tree traversal code:

What is the base case?   A leaf node, which has no more children and requires no more recursive calls, causing the algorithm to backtrack to a previous parent node.

What argument is passed to the recursive function call?   The node to traverse to, whose child nodes will be the next nodes to traverse.

How does this argument become closer to the base case?   There are no cycles in a DAG, so following the descendant nodes will always eventually reach a leaf node.

Keep in mind that tree data structures that are especially deep will cause a stack overflow as the algorithm traverses the deeper nodes. This happens because each level deeper into the tree requires yet another function call, and too many function calls without returning cause stack overflows. However, it's unlikely for broad, well-balanced trees to be that deep. If every node in a 1,000 level deep tree has two children, the tree would have about 2^{1000} nodes. That's more atoms than there are in the universe, and it's unlikely your tree data structure is that big.

Trees have three kinds of tree traversal algorithms: preorder, postorder, and inorder. We'll discuss each of these in the next three sections.

Preorder Tree Traversal

Preorder tree traversal algorithms access a node's data before traversing its child nodes. Use a preorder traversal if your algorithm needs to access the data in parent nodes before the data in their child nodes. For example, preorder traversals are used when you are creating a copy of the tree data structure, as you need to create the parent nodes before child nodes in the duplicate tree.

The following *preorderTraversal.py* program has a preorderTraverse() function that traverses each child node first, before accessing the node's data to print it to the screen:

Python
```
root = {'data': 'A', 'children': [{'data': 'B', 'children':
[{'data': 'D', 'children': []}]}, {'data': 'C', 'children':
[{'data': 'E', 'children': [{'data': 'G', 'children': []},
{'data': 'H', 'children': []}]}, {'data': 'F', 'children': []}]}]}

def preorderTraverse(node):
    print(node['data'], end=' ') # Access this node's data.
  ❶ if len(node['children']) > 0:
        # RECURSIVE CASE
        for child in node['children']:
            preorderTraverse(child) # Traverse child nodes.
    # BASE CASE
  ❷ return

preorderTraverse(root)
```

The equivalent JavaScript program is in *preorderTraversal.html*:

JavaScript
```
<script type="text/javascript">
root = {"data": "A", "children": [{"data": "B", "children":
[{"data": "D", "children": []}]}, {"data": "C", "children":
[{"data": "E", "children": [{"data": "G", "children": []},
{"data": "H", "children": []}]}, {"data": "F", "children": []}]}]};

function preorderTraverse(node) {
    document.write(node["data"] + " "); // Access this node's data.
  ❶ if (node["children"].length > 0) {
        // RECURSIVE CASE
        for (let i = 0; i < node["children"].length; i++) {
```

```
                preorderTraverse(node["children"][i]); // Traverse child nodes.
            }
        }
        // BASE CASE
    ❷ return;
}

preorderTraverse(root);
</script>
```

The output of these programs is the node data in preorder order:

```
A B D C E G H F
```

When you look at the tree in Figure 4-1, notice that preorder traversal order displays the data in left nodes before right nodes, and bottom nodes before top nodes.

All tree traversals begin by passing the root node to the recursive function. The function makes a recursive call and passes each of the root node's children as the argument. Since these child nodes have children of their own, the traversal continues until a leaf node with no children is reached. At this point, the function call simply returns.

The recursive case occurs if the node has any child nodes ❶, in which case a recursive call is made with each of the children as the node argument. Whether or not the node has children, the base case always happens at the end of the function when it returns ❷.

Postorder Tree Traversal

Postorder tree traversal traverses a node's child nodes before accessing the node's data. For example, this traversal is used when deleting a tree and ensuring that no child nodes are "orphaned" by deleting their parent nodes first, leaving the child node inaccessible to the root node. The code in the following *postorderTraversal.py* program is similar to the preorder traversal code in the previous section, except the recursive function call comes before the print() call:

Python
```
root = {'data': 'A', 'children': [{'data': 'B', 'children':
[{'data': 'D', 'children': []}]}, {'data': 'C', 'children':
[{'data': 'E', 'children': [{'data': 'G', 'children': []},
{'data': 'H', 'children': []}]}, {'data': 'F', 'children': []}]}]}

def postorderTraverse(node):
    for child in node['children']:
        # RECURSIVE CASE
        postorderTraverse(child) # Traverse child nodes.
    print(node['data'], end=' ') # Access this node's data.
    # BASE CASE
    return

postorderTraverse(root)
```

The *postorderTraversal.html* program has the equivalent JavaScript code:

JavaScript
```
<script type="text/javascript">
root = {"data": "A", "children": [{"data": "B", "children":
[{"data": "D", "children": []}]}, {"data": "C", "children":
[{"data": "E", "children": [{"data": "G", "children": []},
{"data": "H", "children": []}]}, {"data": "F", "children": []}]}]};

function postorderTraverse(node) {
    for (let i = 0; i < node["children"].length; i++) {
        // RECURSIVE CASE
        postorderTraverse(node["children"][i]); // Traverse child nodes.
    }
    document.write(node["data"] + " "); // Access this node's data.
    // BASE CASE
    return;
}

postorderTraverse(root);
</script>
```

The output of these programs is the node data in postorder order:

```
D B G H E F C A
```

The postorder traversal order of the nodes displays the data in left nodes before right nodes, and in bottom nodes before top nodes. When we compare the postorderTraverse() and preorderTraverse() functions, we find that the names are a bit of a misnomer: *pre* and *post* don't refer to the order in which nodes are visited. The nodes are always traversed in the same order; we go down the child nodes first (called a *depth-first search*) as opposed to visiting the nodes in each level before going deeper (called a *breadth-first search*). The *pre* and *post* refer to *when* the node's data is accessed: either before or after traversing the node's children.

Inorder Tree Traversal

Binary trees are tree data structures with at most two child nodes, often called the *left child* and *right child*. An *inorder tree traversal* traverses the left child node, then accesses the node's data, and then traverses the right child node. This traversal is used in algorithms that deal with binary search trees (which are beyond the scope of this book). The *inorderTraversal.py* program contains Python code that performs this kind of traversal:

Python
```
root = {'data': 'A', 'children': [{'data': 'B', 'children':
[{'data': 'D', 'children': []}]}, {'data': 'C', 'children':
[{'data': 'E', 'children': [{'data': 'G', 'children': []},
{'data': 'H', 'children': []}]}, {'data': 'F', 'children': []}]}]}

def inorderTraverse(node):
    if len(node['children']) >= 1:
        # RECURSIVE CASE
```

```
        inorderTraverse(node['children'][0]) # Traverse the left child.
    print(node['data'], end=' ') # Access this node's data.
    if len(node['children']) >= 2:
        # RECURSIVE CASE
        inorderTraverse(node['children'][1]) # Traverse the right child.
    # BASE CASE
    return

inorderTraverse(root)
```

The *inorderTraversal.html* program contains the equivalent JavaScript code:

```
<script type="text/javascript">
root = {"data": "A", "children": [{"data": "B", "children":
[{"data": "D", "children": []}]}, {"data": "C", "children":
[{"data": "E", "children": [{"data": "G", "children": []},
{"data": "H", "children": []}]}, {"data": "F", "children": []}]}]};

function inorderTraverse(node) {
    if (node["children"].length >= 1) {
        // RECURSIVE CASE
        inorderTraverse(node["children"][0]); // Traverse the left child.
    }
    document.write(node["data"] + " "); // Access this node's data.
    if (node["children"].length >= 2) {
        // RECURSIVE CASE
        inorderTraverse(node["children"][1]); // Traverse the right child.
    }
    // BASE CASE
    return;
}

inorderTraverse(root);
</script>
```

The output of these programs looks like this:

```
D B A G E H C F
```

Inorder traversal typically refers to the traversal of binary trees, although processing a node's data after traversing the first node and before traversing the last node would count as inorder traversal for trees of any size.

Finding Eight-Letter Names in a Tree

Instead of printing out the data in each node as we traverse them, we can use a *depth-first search* to find specific data in a tree data structure. We'll write an algorithm that searches the tree in Figure 4-4 for names that are exactly eight letters long. This is a rather contrived example, but it shows how an algorithm can use tree traversal to retrieve data out of a tree data structure.

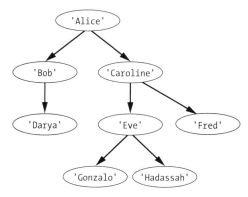

Figure 4-4: The tree that stores names in our depthFirstSearch.py and depthFirstSearch.html programs

Let's ask the three questions about recursive algorithms for our tree traversal code. Their answers are similar to the answers for the tree traversal algorithms:

What is the base case?   Either a leaf node causing the algorithm to backtrack, or a node containing an eight-letter name.

What argument is passed to the recursive function call?   The node to traverse to, whose child nodes will be the next nodes to traverse.

How does this argument become closer to the base case?   There are no cycles in a DAG, so following the descendant nodes will always eventually reach a leaf node.

The *depthFirstSearch.py* program contains Python code that performs a depth-first search with a preorder traversal:

```
root = {'name': 'Alice', 'children': [{'name': 'Bob', 'children':
[{'name': 'Darya', 'children': []}]}, {'name': 'Caroline',
'children': [{'name': 'Eve', 'children': [{'name': 'Gonzalo',
'children': []}, {'name': 'Hadassah', 'children': []}]}, {'name': 'Fred',
'children': []}]}]}

def find8LetterName(node):
    print(' Visiting node ' + node['name'] + '...')

    # Preorder depth-first search:
    print('Checking if ' + node['name'] + ' is 8 letters...')
  ❶ if len(node['name']) == 8: return node['name'] # BASE CASE

    if len(node['children']) > 0:
        # RECURSIVE CASE
        for child in node['children']:
            returnValue = find8LetterName(child)
            if returnValue != None:
                return returnValue
```

Python

```
          # Postorder depth-first search:
          #print('Checking if ' + node['name'] + ' is 8 letters...')
  ❷ #if len(node['name']) == 8: return node['name'] # BASE CASE

          # Value was not found or there are no children.
          return None # BASE CASE

  print('Found an 8-letter name: ' + str(find8LetterName(root)))
```

The *depthFirstSearch.html* program contains the equivalent JavaScript program:

JavaScript
```
<script type="text/javascript">
root = {'name': 'Alice', 'children': [{'name': 'Bob', 'children':
[{'name': 'Darya', 'children': []}]}, {'name': 'Caroline',
'children': [{'name': 'Eve', 'children': [{'name': 'Gonzalo',
'children': []}, {'name': 'Hadassah', 'children': []}]}, {'name': 'Fred',
'children': []}]}]};

function find8LetterName(node, value) {
    document.write("Visiting node " + node.name + "...<br />");

    // Preorder depth-first search:
    document.write("Checking if " + node.name + " is 8 letters...<br />");
  ❶ if (node.name.length === 8) return node.name; // BASE CASE

    if (node.children.length > 0) {
        // RECURSIVE CASE
        for (let child of node.children) {
            let returnValue = find8LetterName(child);
            if (returnValue != null) {
                return returnValue;
            }
        }
    }

    // Postorder depth-first search:
    document.write("Checking if " + node.name + " is 8 letters...<br />");
  ❷ //if (node.name.length === 8) return node.name; // BASE CASE

    // Value was not found or there are no children.
    return null; // BASE CASE
}

document.write("Found an 8-letter name: " + find8LetterName(root));
</script>
```

The output of these programs looks like this:

```
Visiting node Alice...
Checking if Alice is 8 letters...
Visiting node Bob...
Checking if Bob is 8 letters...
Visiting node Darya...
```

```
Checking if Darya is 8 letters...
Visiting node Caroline...
Checking if Caroline is 8 letters...
Found an 8-letter name: Caroline
```

The find8LetterName() function operates in the same way as our previous tree traversal functions, except instead of printing the node's data, the function checks the name stored in the node and returns the first eight-letter name it finds. You can change the preorder traversal to a postorder traversal by commenting out the earlier name length comparison and the Checking if line ❶ and uncommenting the later name length comparison and the Checking if line ❷. When you make this change, the first eight-letter name the function finds is Hadassah:

```
Visiting node Alice...
Visiting node Bob...
Visiting node Darya...
Checking if Darya is 8 letters...
Checking if Bob is 8 letters...
Visiting node Caroline...
Visiting node Eve...
Visiting node Gonzalo...
Checking if Gonzalo is 8 letters...
Visiting node Hadassah...
Checking if Hadassah is 8 letters...
Found an 8-letter name: Hadassah
```

While both traversal orders correctly find an eight-letter name, changing the order of a tree traversal can alter the behavior of your program.

Getting the Maximum Tree Depth

An algorithm can determine the deepest branch in a tree by recursively asking its child nodes how deep they are. The *depth* of a node is the number of edges between it and the root node. The root node itself has a depth of 0, the immediate child of the root node has a depth of 1, and so on. You may need this information as part of a larger algorithm or to gather information about the general size of the tree data structure.

We can have a function named getDepth() take a node for an argument and return the depth of its deepest child node. A leaf node (the base case) simply returns 0.

For example, given the root node of the tree in Figure 4-1, we could call getDepth() and pass it the root node (the A node). This would return the depth of its children, the B and C nodes, plus one. The function must make a recursive call to getDepth() to find out this information. Eventually, the A node would call getDepth() on C, which would call it on E. When E calls getDepth() with its two children, G and H, they both return 0, so getDepth() called on E returns 1, making getDepth() called on C return 2, and making getDepth() called on A (the root node) return 3. Our tree's greatest depth is three levels.

Let's ask our three recursive algorithm questions for the getDepth() function:

What is the base case? A leaf node with no children, which by its nature has a depth of one level.

What argument is passed to the recursive function call? The node whose greatest depth we want to find.

How does this argument become closer to the base case? A DAG has no cycles, so following the descendant nodes will eventually reach a leaf node.

The following *getDepth.py* program contains a recursive getDepth() function that returns the number of levels contained in the deepest node in the tree:

Python
```python
root = {'data': 'A', 'children': [{'data': 'B', 'children':
[{'data': 'D', 'children': []}]}, {'data': 'C', 'children':
[{'data': 'E', 'children': [{'data': 'G', 'children': []},
{'data': 'H', 'children': []}]}, {'data': 'F', 'children': []}]}]}

def getDepth(node):
    if len(node['children']) == 0:
        # BASE CASE
        return 0
    else:
        # RECURSIVE CASE
        maxChildDepth = 0
        for child in node['children']:
            # Find the depth of each child node:
            childDepth = getDepth(child)
            if childDepth > maxChildDepth:
                # This child is deepest child node found so far:
                maxChildDepth = childDepth
        return maxChildDepth + 1

print('Depth of tree is ' + str(getDepth(root)))
```

The *getDepth.html* program contains the JavaScript equivalent:

JavaScript
```javascript
<script type="text/javascript">
root = {"data": "A", "children": [{"data": "B", "children":
[{"data": "D", "children": []}]}, {"data": "C", "children":
[{"data": "E", "children": [{"data": "G", "children": []},
{"data": "H", "children": []}]}, {"data": "F", "children": []}]}]};

function getDepth(node) {
    if (node.children.length === 0) {
        // BASE CASE
        return 0;
    } else {
        // RECURSIVE CASE
        let maxChildDepth = 0;
        for (let child of node.children) {
            // Find the depth of each child node:
```

```
                let childDepth = getDepth(child);
                if (childDepth > maxChildDepth) {
                    // This child is deepest child node found so far:
                    maxChildDepth = childDepth;
                }
            }
        }
        return maxChildDepth + 1;
    }
}

document.write("Depth of tree is " + getDepth(root) + "<br />");
</script>
```

The output of these programs is as follows:

```
Depth of tree is 3
```

This matches what we see in Figure 4-2: the number of levels from the root node A down to the lowest nodes G and H is three levels.

Solving Mazes

While mazes come in all shapes and sizes, *simply connected mazes*, also called *perfect mazes*, contain no loops. A perfect maze has exactly one path between any two points, such as the start and exit. These mazes can be represented by a DAG.

For example, Figure 4-5 shows the maze that our maze program solves, and Figure 4-6 shows the DAG form of it. The capital *S* marks the start of the maze, and the capital *E* marks the exit. A few of the intersections that have been marked with lowercase letters in the maze correspond to nodes in the DAG.

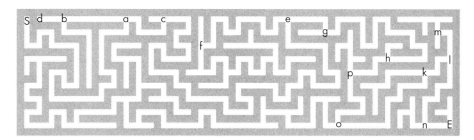

Figure 4-5: The maze solved by our maze program in this chapter. Some intersections have lowercase letters that correspond to nodes in Figure 4-6.

Figure 4-6: In this DAG representation of the maze, nodes represent intersections, and edges represent the north, south, east, or west path from the intersection. Some nodes have lowercase letters to correspond to intersections in Figure 4-5.

Because of this similarity in structure, we can use a tree traversal algorithm to solve the maze. The nodes in this tree graph represent intersections where the maze solver could choose one of the north, south, east, or west paths to follow to the next intersection. The root node is the start of the maze, and the leaf nodes represent dead ends.

The recursive case occurs when the tree traversal algorithm moves from one node to the next. If the tree traversal reaches a leaf node (a dead end in the maze), the algorithm has reached a base case and must backtrack to an earlier node and follow a different path. Once the algorithm reaches the exit node, the path it took from the root node represents the maze solution. Let's ask our three recursive algorithm questions about the maze-solving algorithm:

What is the base case?   Reaching a dead end or the exit of the maze.

What argument is passed to the recursive function call?   The x, y coordinates, along with the maze data and list of already visited x, y coordinates.

How does this argument become closer to the base case?   Like the flood fill algorithm, the x, y coordinates keep moving to neighboring coordinates until they eventually reach dead ends or the final exit.

This *mazeSolver.py* program contains the Python code for solving the maze stored in the MAZE variable:

Python
```
# Create the maze data structure:
# You can copy-paste this from inventwithpython.com/examplemaze.txt
MAZE = """
#######################################################################
#S#                   #         # #    #      #      #       #       #
# ##### ######### # ### ### # # # # ### # # ##### # ### # # ##### # ###
# # #   #     #       #     # # #   # #    # #       # # # #     # #  #
# # # ##### # ########### ### # ##### ##### ######### # # ##### ### # #
#   #   # # #       #   #   #   #         #     #   #   #   #   # # # #
######### # # ##### # ### # ########### ####### # # ##### ##### ### #
#       # # # #       # #     # # #   #     # # #       #         # #
# # ##### # # ### # # ####### # # # # # # ##### ### ### ######### # #
# # #   # # #   # # #   #     #   #   #   #   #   #       #       # #
### # # # # ### # # ##### ####### ########### # ### # ##### ##### ### #
#   # ## ## ## ##    #   #   #       #   #   # #     #     #   # #
# ### ####### ##### ### ### ####### ##### # ######### ### ### ##### ###
#   #   #       #   #     #   # #   # #     #   # #   # #   # #   # #
### ########### # ####### ####### ### # ##### # # ##### # # ### # ### #
# # #   #     # #     #   # #   #     # #   #     # #     # #   # #   #
# ### # # ####### # ### ##### # ####### ### ### # # ####### # # # ### #
#   #       #     #     #           #       #   #       # #       E#
#######################################################################
""".split('\n')

# Constants used in this program:
EMPTY = ' '
START = 'S'
EXIT = 'E'
```

```
PATH = '.'

# Get the height and width of the maze:
HEIGHT = len(MAZE)
WIDTH = 0
for row in MAZE: # Set WIDTH to the widest row's width.
    if len(row) > WIDTH:
        WIDTH = len(row)
# Make each row in the maze a list as wide as the WIDTH:
for i in range(len(MAZE)):
    MAZE[i] = list(MAZE[i])
    if len(MAZE[i]) != WIDTH:
        MAZE[i] = [EMPTY] * WIDTH # Make this a blank row.

def printMaze(maze):
    for y in range(HEIGHT):
        # Print each row.
        for x in range(WIDTH):
            # Print each column in this row.
            print(maze[y][x], end='')
        print() # Print a newline at the end of the row.
    print()

def findStart(maze):
    for x in range(WIDTH):
        for y in range(HEIGHT):
            if maze[y][x] == START:
                return (x, y) # Return the starting coordinates.

def solveMaze(maze, x=None, y=None, visited=None):
    if x == None or y == None:
        x, y = findStart(maze)
        maze[y][x] = EMPTY # Get rid of the 'S' from the maze.
    if visited == None:
      ❶ visited = [] # Create a new list of visited points.

    if maze[y][x] == EXIT:
        return True # Found the exit, return True.

    maze[y][x] = PATH # Mark the path in the maze.
  ❷ visited.append(str(x) + ',' + str(y))
  ❸ #printMaze(maze) # Uncomment to view each forward step.

    # Explore the north neighboring point:
    if y + 1 < HEIGHT and maze[y + 1][x] in (EMPTY, EXIT) and \
    str(x) + ',' + str(y + 1) not in visited:
        # RECURSIVE CASE
        if solveMaze(maze, x, y + 1, visited):
            return True # BASE CASE
    # Explore the south neighboring point:
    if y - 1 >= 0 and maze[y - 1][x] in (EMPTY, EXIT) and \
    str(x) + ',' + str(y - 1) not in visited:
        # RECURSIVE CASE
        if solveMaze(maze, x, y - 1, visited):
            return True # BASE CASE
```

```
        # Explore the east neighboring point:
        if x + 1 < WIDTH and maze[y][x + 1] in (EMPTY, EXIT) and \
        str(x + 1) + ',' + str(y) not in visited:
            # RECURSIVE CASE
            if solveMaze(maze, x + 1, y, visited):
                return True # BASE CASE
        # Explore the west neighboring point:
        if x - 1 >= 0 and maze[y][x - 1] in (EMPTY, EXIT) and \
        str(x - 1) + ',' + str(y) not in visited:
            # RECURSIVE CASE
            if solveMaze(maze, x - 1, y, visited):
                return True # BASE CASE

    maze[y][x] = EMPTY # Reset the empty space.
❹ #printMaze(maze) # Uncomment to view each backtrack step.

    return False # BASE CASE

printMaze(MAZE)
solveMaze(MAZE)
printMaze(MAZE)
```

The *mazeSolver.html* program contains the JavaScript equivalent:

JavaScript
```
<script type="text/javascript">
// Create the maze data structure:
// You can copy-paste this from inventwithpython.com/examplemaze.txt
let MAZE = `
#########################################################################
#S#                 #      # #   #       #      #   #             #
# ##### ######### # ### ### # # # # ### # # ##### # ### # # ##### # ###
# #   #     #     #     #     # # #   # #   # #     # # #     # #   #
# # # ##### # ########### ### # ##### ##### ######### # # ##### ### # #
#   #     # # #     #   #   #   #       #     #   #   #   #     #   # #
######### # # # ##### # ### # ########### ####### # # ##### ##### ### #
#     #   # # #     # #     # #   #   #   #   #       #   #         #   #
# # ##### # # ### # # ####### # # # # # # ##### ### ### ######### # #
# # #   # # #   # # #     #   #   #   #   #   #       #           # #
### # # # ### # # ##### ####### ########### # ### # ##### ##### ### #
#   # ##   # #   # #     #   #       #   #   # #     # #     #   # #
# ### ####### ##### ### ### ####### ##### # ######### ### ### ##### ###
#   #         #     #       #   # # # #     #   # # # #   # # # #   #
### ########### # ####### ####### ### # ##### # # ##### # # ### # ### #
#   #   #       # #     #   #   #       # # #     # # # # #   #
# ### # # ####### # ### ##### # ####### ### ### # # ####### # # # ### #
#     #         #   #     #         #   #       #   # #         E#
#########################################################################
`.split("\n");

// Constants used in this program:
const EMPTY = " ";
const START = "S";
const EXIT = "E";
const PATH = ".";
```

```
// Get the height and width of the maze:
const HEIGHT = MAZE.length;
let maxWidthSoFar = MAZE[0].length;
for (let row of MAZE) { // Set WIDTH to the widest row's width.
    if (row.length > maxWidthSoFar) {
        maxWidthSoFar = row.length;
    }
}
const WIDTH = maxWidthSoFar;
// Make each row in the maze a list as wide as the WIDTH:
for (let i = 0; i < MAZE.length; i++) {
    MAZE[i] = MAZE[i].split("");
    if (MAZE[i].length !== WIDTH) {
        MAZE[i] = EMPTY.repeat(WIDTH).split(""); // Make this a blank row.
    }
}

function printMaze(maze) {
    document.write("<pre>");
    for (let y = 0; y < HEIGHT; y++) {
        // Print each row.
        for (let x = 0; x < WIDTH; x++) {
            // Print each column in this row.
            document.write(maze[y][x]);
        }
        document.write("\n"); // Print a newline at the end of the row.
    }
    document.write("\n</ pre>");
}

function findStart(maze) {
    for (let x = 0; x < WIDTH; x++) {
        for (let y = 0; y < HEIGHT; y++) {
            if (maze[y][x] === START) {
                return [x, y]; // Return the starting coordinates.
            }
        }
    }
}

function solveMaze(maze, x, y, visited) {
    if (x === undefined || y === undefined) {
        [x, y] = findStart(maze);
        maze[y][x] = EMPTY; // Get rid of the 'S' from the maze.
    }
    if (visited === undefined) {
      ❶ visited = []; // Create a new list of visited points.
    }

    if (maze[y][x] == EXIT) {
        return true; // Found the exit, return true.
    }

    maze[y][x] = PATH; // Mark the path in the maze.
  ❷ visited.push(String(x) + "," + String(y));
```

```
❸ //printMaze(maze) // Uncomment to view each forward step.

   // Explore the north neighboring point:
   if ((y + 1 < HEIGHT) && ((maze[y + 1][x] == EMPTY) ||
   (maze[y + 1][x] == EXIT)) &&
   (visited.indexOf(String(x) + "," + String(y + 1)) === -1)) {
       // RECURSIVE CASE
       if (solveMaze(maze, x, y + 1, visited)) {
           return true; // BASE CASE
       }
   }
   // Explore the south neighboring point:
   if ((y - 1 >= 0) && ((maze[y - 1][x] == EMPTY) ||
   (maze[y - 1][x] == EXIT)) &&
   (visited.indexOf(String(x) + "," + String(y - 1)) === -1)) {
       // RECURSIVE CASE
       if (solveMaze(maze, x, y - 1, visited)) {
           return true; // BASE CASE
       }
   }
   // Explore the east neighboring point:
   if ((x + 1 < WIDTH) && ((maze[y][x + 1] == EMPTY) ||
   (maze[y][x + 1] == EXIT)) &&
   (visited.indexOf(String(x + 1) + "," + String(y)) === -1)) {
       // RECURSIVE CASE
       if (solveMaze(maze, x + 1, y, visited)) {
           return true; // BASE CASE
       }
   }
   // Explore the west neighboring point:
   if ((x - 1 >= 0) && ((maze[y][x - 1] == EMPTY) ||
   (maze[y][x - 1] == EXIT)) &&
   (visited.indexOf(String(x - 1) + "," + String(y)) === -1)) {
       // RECURSIVE CASE
       if (solveMaze(maze, x - 1, y, visited)) {
           return true; // BASE CASE
       }
   }

   maze[y][x] = EMPTY; // Reset the empty space.
❹ //printMaze(maze); // Uncomment to view each backtrack step.
   return false; // BASE CASE
}

printMaze(MAZE);
solveMaze(MAZE);
printMaze(MAZE);
</script>
```

A lot of this code is not directly related to the recursive maze-solving algorithm. The MAZE variable stores the maze data as a multiline string with hashtags to represent walls, an S for the starting point, and an E for the exit. This string is converted into a list that contains lists of strings, with each string representing a single character in the maze. This allows us to access MAZE[y][x] (note that y comes first) to get the character at the x, y coordinate in the original MAZE string. The printMaze() function can accept this list-of-list data structure and display the maze on the screen. The findStart() function accepts this data structure and returns the x, y coordinates of the S starting point. Feel free to edit the maze string yourself—although remember that, in order for the solving algorithm to work, the maze cannot have any loops.

The recursive algorithm is in the solveMaze() function. The arguments to this function are the maze data structure, the current x- and y-coordinates, and a visited list (which is created if none was supplied) ❶. The visited list contains all the coordinates that have previously been visited so that when the algorithm backtracks from a dead end to an earlier intersection, it knows which paths it has tried before and can try a different one. The path from the start to the exit is marked by replacing the spaces (matching the EMPTY constant) in the maze data structure with periods (from the PATH constant).

The maze-solving algorithm is similar to our flood fill program in Chapter 3 in that it "spreads" to neighboring coordinates, though when it reaches a dead end, it backtracks to an earlier intersection. The solveMaze() function receives the x, y coordinates indicating the algorithm's current location in the maze. If this is the exit, the function returns True, causing all the recursive calls to also return True. The maze data structure remains marked with the solution path.

Otherwise, the algorithm marks the current x, y coordinates in the maze data structure with a period and adds the coordinates to the visited list ❷. Then it looks to the x, y coordinates north of the current coordinates to see if that point is not off the edge of the map, is either the empty or exit space, and has not been visited before. If these conditions are met, the algorithm makes a recursive call to solveMaze() with the northern coordinates. If these conditions aren't met or the recursive call to solveMaze() returns False, the algorithm continues on to check the south, east, and west coordinates. Like the flood fill algorithm, recursive calls are made with the neighboring coordinates.

MODIFYING A LIST OR ARRAY IN PLACE

Python doesn't pass a copy of lists, and JavaScript doesn't pass a copy of arrays, to function calls. Rather, they pass a reference to the list. Therefore, any changes made to a list or array (such as the ones in maze and visited) remain even after the function returns. This is called modifying the list *in place*. For recursive functions, you can think of the maze data structure and collection of visited coordinates as a single copy shared among all the recursive function calls, unlike the x and y arguments. This is why the data structure in MAZE is still modified after the first call to solveMaze() returns.

To get a better idea of how this algorithm works, uncomment the two printMaze(MAZE) calls ❸ ❹ inside the solveMaze() function. These will display the maze data structure as it attempts new paths, reaches dead ends, backtracks, and tries different paths.

Summary

This chapter explored several algorithms that make use of tree data structures and backtracking, which are features of a problem that is suitable for solving with recursive algorithms. We covered tree data structures, which are composed of nodes that contain data and edges that relate nodes together in parent–child relationships. In particular, we examined a specific kind of tree called a directed acyclic graph (DAG) that is often used in recursive algorithms. A recursive function call is analogous to traversing to a child node in a tree, while returning from a recursive function call is analogous to backtracking to a previous parent node.

While recursion is overused for simple programming problems, it is well matched for problems that involve tree-like structures and backtracking. Using these ideas of tree-like structures, we wrote several algorithms for traversing, searching, and determining the depth of tree structures. We also showed that a simply connected maze has a tree-like structure, and employed recursion and backtracking to solve a maze.

Further Reading

There is far more to trees and tree traversal than the brief description of DAGs presented in this chapter. The Wikipedia articles at *https://en.wikipedia.org/wiki/Tree_(data_structure)* and *https://en.wikipedia.org/wiki/Tree_traversal* provide additional context for these concepts, which are often used in computer science.

The Computerphile YouTube channel also has a video titled "Maze Solving" at *https://youtu.be/rop0W4QDOUI* that discusses these concepts. V. Anton Spraul, author of *Think Like a Programmer* (No Starch Press, 2012), also has a video on maze solving titled "Backtracking" at *https://youtu.be/gBC_Fd8EE8A*. The freeCodeCamp organization (*https://freeCodeCamp.org*) has a video series on backtracking algorithms at *https://youtu.be/A80YzvNwqXA*.

In addition to maze solving, the recursive backtracker algorithm uses recursion to generate mazes. You can find out more about this and other maze-generating algorithms at *https://en.wikipedia.org/wiki/Maze_generation_algorithm#Recursive_backtracker*.

Practice Questions

Test your comprehension by answering the following questions:

1. What are nodes and edges?
2. What are root and leaf nodes?
3. What are the three tree traversal orders?
4. What does *DAG* stand for?
5. What is a cycle, and do DAGs have cycles?
6. What is a binary tree?
7. What are the child nodes in a binary tree called?
8. If a parent node has an edge to a child node, and the child node has an edge back to the parent node, is this graph considered a DAG?
9. What is backtracking in a tree traversal algorithm?

For the following tree traversal problems, you can use the Python/JavaScript code in "A Tree Data Structure in Python and JavaScript" in Chapter 4 for your tree and the multiline MAZE string from the *mazeSolver.py* and *mazeSolver.html* programs for the maze data.

10. Answer the three questions about recursive solutions for each of the recursive algorithms presented in this chapter:

    a. What is the base case?

    b. What argument is passed to the recursive function call?

    c. How does this argument become closer to the base case?

    Then re-create the recursive algorithms from this chapter without looking at the original code.

Practice Projects

For practice, write a function for each of the following tasks:

1. Create a reverse-inorder search, one that performs an inorder traversal but traverses the right child node before the left child node.
2. Create a function that, given a root node as an argument, proceeds to make the tree one level deeper by adding one child node to each leaf node in the original tree. This function will need to perform a tree traversal, detect when it has reached a leaf node, and then add one and only one child node to the leaf node. Be sure not to go on and add a child node to this new leaf node, as that will eventually cause a stack overflow.

5

DIVIDE-AND-CONQUER ALGORITHMS

Divide-and-conquer algorithms are those that split large problems into smaller subproblems, then divide those subproblems into ones that are smaller yet, until they become trivial to conquer. This approach makes recursion an ideal technique to use: the recursive case divides the problem into self-similar subproblems, and the base case occurs when the subproblem has been reduced to a trivial size. One benefit of this approach is that these problems can be worked on in parallel, allowing multiple central processing unit (CPU) cores or computers to work on them.

In this chapter, we'll look at some common algorithms that use recursion to divide and conquer, such as binary search, quicksort, and merge sort. We'll also reexamine summing an array of integers, this time with a divide-and-conquer approach. Finally, we'll take a look at the more esoteric

Karatsuba multiplication algorithm, developed in 1960, that laid the basis for computer hardware's fast integer multiplication.

Binary Search: Finding a Book in an Alphabetized Bookshelf

Let's say you have a bookshelf of 100 books. You can't remember which books you have or their exact locations on the shelf, but you do know that they are sorted alphabetically by title. To find your book *Zebras: The Complete Guide*, you wouldn't start at the beginning of the bookshelf, where *Aaron Burr Biography* is, but rather toward the end of the bookshelf. Your zebra book wouldn't be the very last book on the shelf if you also had books on zephyrs, zoos, and zygotes, but it would be close. Thus, you can use the facts that the books are in alphabetical order and that *Z* is the last letter of the alphabet as *heuristics*, or approximate clues, to look toward the end of the shelf rather than the beginning.

Binary search is a technique for locating a target item in a sorted list by repeatedly determining which half of the list the item is in. The most impartial way to search the bookshelf is to start with a book in the middle, and then ascertain if the target book you're looking for is in the left half or the right half.

You can then repeat this process, as shown in Figure 5-1: look at the book in the middle of your chosen half and then determine whether your target book is in the left-side quarter or the right-side quarter. You can do this until you either find the book, or find the place where the book should be but isn't and declare that the book doesn't exist on the shelf.

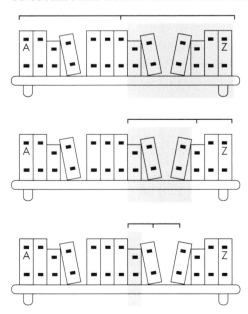

Figure 5-1: A binary search repeatedly determines which half of a range contains your target item in a sorted array of items.

This process scales efficiently; doubling the number of books to search adds only one step to the search process. A linear search of a shelf with 50 books takes 50 steps, and a linear search of a shelf with 100 books takes 100 steps. But a binary search of a shelf with 50 books takes only 6 steps, and a shelf with 100 books takes only 7 steps.

Let's ask the three recursion questions about our binary search implementation:

What is the base case?   Searching a range of items that is only one item in length.

What argument is passed to the recursive function call?   The indices of the left and right ends of the range in the list we are searching.

How does this argument become closer to the base case?   The range halves in size for each recursive call, so it eventually becomes one item long.

Examine the following binarySearch() function in our *binarySearch.py* program, which locates a value, needle, in a sorted list of values, haystack:

Python
```python
def binarySearch(needle, haystack, left=None, right=None):
    # By default, `left` and `right` are all of `haystack`:
    if left is None:
        left = 0 # `left` defaults to the 0 index.
    if right is None:
        right = len(haystack) - 1 # `right` defaults to the last index.

    print('Searching:', haystack[left:right + 1])

    if left > right: # BASE CASE
        return None # The `needle` is not in `haystack`.

    mid = (left + right) // 2
    if needle == haystack[mid]: # BASE CASE
        return mid # The `needle` has been found in `haystack`
    elif needle < haystack[mid]: # RECURSIVE CASE
        return binarySearch(needle, haystack, left, mid - 1)
    elif needle > haystack[mid]: # RECURSIVE CASE
        return binarySearch(needle, haystack, mid + 1, right)

print(binarySearch(13, [1, 4, 8, 11, 13, 16, 19, 19]))
```

The *binarySearch.html* program has this JavaScript equivalent:

JavaScript
```javascript
<script type="text/javascript">
function binarySearch(needle, haystack, left, right) {
    // By default, `left` and `right` are all of `haystack`:
    if (left === undefined) {
        left = 0; // `left` defaults to the 0 index.
    }
    if (right === undefined) {
        right = haystack.length - 1; // `right` defaults to the last index.
    }
```

```
    document.write("Searching: [" +
    haystack.slice(left, right + 1).join(", ") + "]<br />");

    if (left > right) { // BASE CASE
        return null; // The `needle` is not in `haystack`.
    }

    let mid = Math.floor((left + right) / 2);
    if (needle == haystack[mid]) { // BASE CASE
        return mid; // The `needle` has been found in `haystack`.
    } else if (needle < haystack[mid]) { // RECURSIVE CASE
        return binarySearch(needle, haystack, left, mid - 1);
    } else if (needle > haystack[mid]) { // RECURSIVE CASE
        return binarySearch(needle, haystack, mid + 1, right);
    }
}

document.write(binarySearch(13, [1, 4, 8, 11, 13, 16, 19, 19]));
</script>
```

When you run these programs, the list [1, 4, 8, 11, 13, 16, 19, 19] is searched for 13, and the output looks like this:

```
Searching: [1, 4, 8, 11, 13, 16, 19, 19]
Searching: [13, 16, 19, 19]
Searching: [13]
4
```

The target value 13 is indeed at index 4 in that list.

The code calculates the middle index (stored in mid) of the range defined by the left and right indices. At first, this range is the entire length of the items list. If the value at the mid index is the same as needle, then mid is returned. Otherwise, we need to figure out whether our target value is in the left half of the range (in which case, the new range to search is left to mid - 1) or in the right half (in which case, the new range to search is mid + 1 to end).

We already have a function that can search this new range: binarySearch() itself! A recursive call is made on the new range. If we ever get to the point where the right end of the search range comes before the left, we know that our search range has shrunk down to zero and our target value isn't to be found.

Notice that the code performs no actions after the recursive call returns; it immediately returns the return value of the recursive function call. This feature means that we could implement tail call optimization for this recursive algorithm, a practice we explain in Chapter 8. But also, it means that binary search can easily be implemented as an iterative algorithm that doesn't use recursive function calls. This book's downloadable resources at *https://nostarch.com/recursive-book-recursion* include the source code for an iterative binary search for you to compare with the recursive binary search.

Quicksort: Splitting an Unsorted Pile of Books into Sorted Piles

Remember that binarySearch()'s speed advantage comes from the fact that the values in items are sorted. If the values are out of order, the algorithm won't work. Enter *quicksort*, a recursive sorting algorithm developed by computer scientist Tony Hoare in 1959.

Quicksort uses a divide-and-conquer technique called *partitioning*. Think of partitioning this way: imagine you have a large pile of unalphabetized books. Grabbing one book and placing it in the right spot on the shelf means you'll spend a lot of time rearranging the bookshelf as it gets full. It would help if you first turned the pile of books into two piles: an *A* to *M* pile and an *N* to *Z* pile. (In this example, *M* would be our *pivot*.)

You haven't sorted the pile, but you have *partitioned* it. And partitioning is easy: the book doesn't have to go into the correct place in one of the two piles, it just has to go into the correct pile. Then you can further partition these two piles into four piles: *A* to *G*, *H* to *M*, *N* to *T*, and *U* to *Z*. This is shown in Figure 5-2. If you keep partitioning, you end up with piles that contain one book each (the base case), and the piles are now in sorted order. This means the books are now in sorted order as well. This repeated partitioning is how quicksort works.

For the first partitioning of *A* to *Z*, we select *M* as the pivot value because it's the middle letter between *A* and *Z*. However, if our collection of books consisted of one book about Aaron Burr and 99 books about zebras, zephyrs, zoos, zygotes, and other *Z* topics, our two partitioned piles would be heavily unbalanced. We would have the single Aaron Burr book in the *A* to *M* pile and every other book in the *M* to *Z* pile. The quicksort algorithm works fastest when the partitions are evenly balanced, so selecting a good pivot value at each partition step is important.

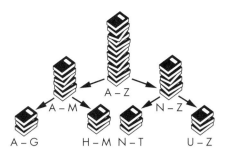

Figure 5-2: Quicksort works by repeatedly partitioning items into two sets.

However, if you don't know anything about the data you're sorting, it's impossible to select an ideal pivot. This is why the generic quicksort algorithm simply uses the last value in the range for the pivot value.

In our implementation, each call to quicksort() is given an array of items to sort. It is also given left and right arguments specifying the range of indices in that array to sort, similar to binarySearch()'s left and right arguments. The algorithm selects a pivot value to compare with the other values in the range, then places the values to either the left side of the range (if they're less than the pivot value) or the right side (if they're greater than the pivot value). This is the partition step. Next, the quicksort() function is recursively called on these two, smaller ranges until a range has been reduced to zero. The list becomes more and more sorted as the recursive calls are made, until finally the entire list is in the correct order.

Note that the algorithm modifies the array in place. See "Modifying a List or Array in Place" in Chapter 4 for details. Thus, the quicksort() function doesn't return a sorted array. The base case merely returns to stop producing more recursive calls.

Let's ask the three recursion questions about our binary search implementation:

What is the base case?   Being given a range to sort that contains zero or one item and that is already in sorted order.

What argument is passed to the recursive function call?   The indices of the left and right ends of the range in the list we are sorting.

How does this argument become closer to the base case?   The range halves in size for each recursive call, so it eventually becomes empty.

The following quicksort() function in the *quicksort.py* Python program sorts the values in the items list into ascending order:

```
def quicksort(items, left=None, right=None):
    # By default, `left` and `right` span the entire range of `items`:
    if left is None:
        left = 0 # `left` defaults to the 0 index.
    if right is None:
        right = len(items) - 1 # `right` defaults to the last index.
```

```
    print('\nquicksort() called on this range:', items[left:right + 1])
    print('...............The full list is:', items)

    if right <= left:  ❶
        # With only zero or one item, `items` is already sorted.
        return  # BASE CASE

    # START OF THE PARTITIONING
    i = left # i starts at the left end of the range.  ❷
    pivotValue = items[right] # Select the last value for the pivot.

    print('...................The pivot is:', pivotValue)

    # Iterate up to, but not including, the pivot:
    for j in range(left, right):
        # If a value is less than the pivot, swap it so that it's on the
        # left side of `items`:
        if items[j] <= pivotValue:
            # Swap these two values:
            items[i], items[j] = items[j], items[i]  ❸
            i += 1

    # Put the pivot on the left side of `items`:
    items[i], items[right] = items[right], items[i]
    # END OF THE PARTITIONING

    print('....After swapping, the range is:', items[left:right + 1])
    print('Recursively calling quicksort on:', items[left:i], 'and', items[i + 1:right + 1])

    # Call quicksort() on the two partitions:
    quicksort(items, left, i - 1)    # RECURSIVE CASE
    quicksort(items, i + 1, right)   # RECURSIVE CASE

myList = [0, 7, 6, 3, 1, 2, 5, 4]
quicksort(myList)
print(myList)
```

The *quicksort.html* program contains the JavaScript equivalent:

```
<script type="text/javascript">
function quicksort(items, left, right) {
    // By default, `left` and `right` span the entire range of `items`:
    if (left === undefined) {
        left = 0; // `left` defaults to the 0 index.
    }
    if (right === undefined) {
        right = items.length - 1; // `right` defaults to the last index.
    }

    document.write("<br /><pre>quicksort() called on this range: [" +
    items.slice(left, right + 1).join(", ") + "]</pre>");
    document.write("<pre>...............The full list is: [" + items.join(", ") + "]</pre>");

    if (right <= left) {  ❶
        // With only zero or one item, `items` is already sorted.
```

```
        return; // BASE CASE
    }

    // START OF THE PARTITIONING
    let i = left; ❷ // i starts at the left end of the range.
    let pivotValue = items[right]; // Select the last value for the pivot.

    document.write("<pre>...................The pivot is: " + pivotValue.toString() +
"</pre>");

    // Iterate up to, but not including, the pivot:
    for (let j = left; j < right; j++) {
        // If a value is less than the pivot, swap it so that it's on the
        // left side of `items`:
        if (items[j] <= pivotValue) {
            // Swap these two values:
            [items[i], items[j]] = [items[j], items[i]]; ❸
            i++;
        }
    }

    // Put the pivot on the left side of `items`:
    [items[i], items[right]] = [items[right], items[i]];
    // END OF THE PARTITIONING

    document.write("<pre>....After swapping, the range is: [" + items.slice(left, right +
1).join(", ") + "]</pre>");
    document.write("<pre>Recursively calling quicksort on: [" + items.slice(left, i).join(", ")
+ "] and [" + items.slice(i + 1, right + 1).join(", ") + "]</pre>");

    // Call quicksort() on the two partitions:
    quicksort(items, left, i - 1); // RECURSIVE CASE
    quicksort(items, i + 1, right); // RECURSIVE CASE
}

let myList = [0, 7, 6, 3, 1, 2, 5, 4];
quicksort(myList);
document.write("<pre>[" + myList.join(", ") + "]</pre>");
</script>
```

This code is similar to the code in the binary search algorithm. As defaults, we set the left and right ends of the range within the items array to the beginning and end of the entire array. If the algorithm reaches the base case of the right end at or before the left end (a range of one or zero items), the sorting is finished ❶.

In each call to quicksort(), we partition the items in the current range (defined by the indices in left and right), and then swap them around so that the items less than the pivot value end up on the left side of the range and the items greater than the pivot value end up on the right side of the range. For example, if 42 is the pivot value in the array [81, 48, 94, 87, 83, 14, 6, 42], a partitioned array would be [14, 6, 42, 81, 48, 94, 87, 83].

Note that a partitioned array is not the same thing as a sorted one: although the two items to the left of 42 are less than 42, and the five items to the right of 42 are greater than 42, the items are not in sorted order.

The bulk of the quicksort() function is the partitioning step. To get an idea of how partitioning works, imagine an index j that begins at the left end of the range and moves to the right end ❷. We compare the item at index j with the pivot value and then move right to compare the next item. The pivot value can be arbitrarily chosen from any value in the range, but we'll always use the value at the right end of the range.

Imagine a second index i that also begins at the left end. If the item at index j is less than or equal to the pivot, the items at indices i and j are swapped ❸ and i is increased to the next index. So while j always increases (that is, moves right) after each comparison with the pivot value, i increases only if the item at index j is less than or equal to the pivot.

The names i and j are commonly used for variables that hold array indices. Someone else's quicksort() implementation may instead use j and i, or even completely different variables. The important thing to remember is that two variables store indices and behave as shown here.

As an example, let's work through the first partitioning of the array [0, 7, 6, 3, 1, 2, 5, 4], and the range defined by left of 0 and right of 7 to cover the full size of the array. The pivot will be the value at the right end, 4. The i and j index begin at index 0, the left end of the range. At each step, index j always moves to the right. Index i moves only if the value at index j is less than or equal to the pivot value. The items array, the i index, and the j index begin as follows:

```
items:    [0, 7, 6, 3, 1, 2, 5, 4]
indices:   0  1  2  3  4  5  6  7
           ^
i = 0      i
j = 0      j
```

The value at index j (which is 0) is less than or equal to the pivot value (which is 4), so swap the values at i and j. This results in no actual change since i and j are the same index. Also, increase i so that it moves to the right. The j index increases for every comparison with the pivot value. The state of the variables now looks like this:

```
items:    [0, 7, 6, 3, 1, 2, 5, 4]
indices:   0  1  2  3  4  5  6  7
              ^
i = 1         i
j = 1         j
```

The value at index j (which is 7) is not less than or equal to the pivot value (which is 4), so don't swap the values. Remember, j always increases, but i increases only after a swap is performed—so i is always either at or to the left of j. The state of the variables now looks like this:

```
items:    [0, 7, 6, 3, 1, 2, 5, 4]
indices:   0  1  2  3  4  5  6  7
              ^
i = 1         i  ^
j = 2            j
```

The value at index j (which is 6) is not less than or equal to the pivot value (which is 4), so don't swap the values. The state of the variables now looks like this:

```
items:    [0, 7, 6, 3, 1, 2, 5, 4]
indices:   0  1  2  3  4  5  6  7
              ^
i = 1         i     ^
j = 3               j
```

The value at index j (which is 3) is less than or equal to the pivot value (which is 4), so swap the values at i and j. The 7 and 3 swap positions. Also, increase i so that it moves to the right. The state of the variables now looks like this:

```
items:    [0, 3, 6, 7, 1, 2, 5, 4]
indices:   0  1  2  3  4  5  6  7
                 ^
i = 2            i     ^
j = 4                  j
```

The value at index j (which is 1) is less than or equal to the pivot value (which is 4), so swap the values at i and j. The 6 and 1 swap positions. Also, increase i so that it moves to the right. The state of the variables now looks like this:

```
items:    [0, 3, 1, 7, 6, 2, 5, 4]
indices:   0  1  2  3  4  5  6  7
                    ^
i = 3               i     ^
j = 5                     j
```

The value at index j (which is 2) is less than or equal to the pivot value (which is 4), so swap the values at i and j. The 7 and 2 swap positions. Also, increase i so that it moves to the right. The state of the variables now looks like this:

```
items:   [0, 3, 1, 2, 6, 7, 5, 4]
indices:  0  1  2  3  4  5  6  7
                        ^
i = 4                   i     ^
j = 6                         j
```

The value at index j (which is 6) is not less than or equal to the pivot value (which is 4), so don't swap the values. The state of the variables now looks like this:

```
items:   [0, 3, 1, 2, 6, 7, 5, 4]
indices:  0  1  2  3  4  5  6  7
                        ^
i = 4                   i        ^
j = 7                            j
```

We've reached the end of the partitioning. The index j is at the pivot value (which is always the rightmost value in the range), so let's swap i and j one last time to make sure the pivot is not on the right half of the partition. The 6 and 4 swap positions. The state of the variables now looks like this:

```
items:   [0, 3, 1, 2, 4, 7, 5, 6]
indices:  0  1  2  3  4  5  6  7
                        ^
i = 4                   i        ^
j = 7                            j
```

Notice what is happening with the i index: this index will always receive the values smaller than the pivot value as a result of swapping; then the i index moves right to receive future smaller-than-the-pivot values. As a result, everything to the left of the i index is smaller than or equal to the pivot, and everything to the right of the i index is greater than the pivot.

The entire process repeats as we recursively call quicksort() on the left and right partitions. When we partition these two halves (and then partition the four halves of these two halves with more recursive quicksort() calls, and so on), the entire array ends up sorted.

When we run these programs, the output shows the process of sorting the [0, 7, 6, 3, 1, 2, 5, 4] list. The rows of periods are meant to help you line up the output when writing the code:

```
quicksort() called on this range: [0, 7, 6, 3, 1, 2, 5, 4]
...............The full list is: [0, 7, 6, 3, 1, 2, 5, 4]
...................The pivot is: 4
....After swapping, the range is: [0, 3, 1, 2, 4, 7, 5, 6]
Recursively calling quicksort on: [0, 3, 1, 2] and [7, 5, 6]

quicksort() called on this range: [0, 3, 1, 2]
...............The full list is: [0, 3, 1, 2, 4, 7, 5, 6]
...................The pivot is: 2
....After swapping, the range is: [0, 1, 2, 3]
Recursively calling quicksort on: [0, 1] and [3]
```

```
quicksort() called on this range: [0, 1]
...............The full list is: [0, 1, 2, 3, 4, 7, 5, 6]
...................The pivot is: 1
....After swapping, the range is: [0, 1]
Recursively calling quicksort on: [0] and []

quicksort() called on this range: [0]
...............The full list is: [0, 1, 2, 3, 4, 7, 5, 6]

quicksort() called on this range: []
...............The full list is: [0, 1, 2, 3, 4, 7, 5, 6]

quicksort() called on this range: [3]
...............The full list is: [0, 1, 2, 3, 4, 7, 5, 6]

quicksort() called on this range: [7, 5, 6]
...............The full list is: [0, 1, 2, 3, 4, 7, 5, 6]
...................The pivot is: 6
....After swapping, the range is: [5, 6, 7]
Recursively calling quicksort on: [5] and [7]

quicksort() called on this range: [5]
...............The full list is: [0, 1, 2, 3, 4, 5, 6, 7]

quicksort() called on this range: [7]
...............The full list is: [0, 1, 2, 3, 4, 5, 6, 7]

Sorted: [0, 1, 2, 3, 4, 5, 6, 7]
```

Quicksort is a commonly used sorting algorithm because it is straightforward to implement and, well, quick. The other commonly used sorting algorithm, merge sort, is also fast and uses recursion. We cover it next.

Merge Sort: Merging Small Piles of Playing Cards into Larger Sorted Piles

Computer scientist John von Neumann developed *merge sort* in 1945. It uses a divide-merge approach: each recursive call to mergeSort() divides the unsorted list into halves until they've been whittled down into lists of lengths of zero or one. Then, as the recursive calls return, these smaller lists are merged together into sorted order. When the last recursive call has returned, the entire list will have been sorted.

For example, the divide step takes a list, such as [2, 9, 8, 5, 3, 4, 7, 6], and splits it into two lists, like [2, 9, 8, 5] and [3, 4, 7, 6], to pass to two recursive function calls. At the base case, the lists have been divided into lists of zero or one item. A list with nothing or one item is naturally sorted. After the recursive calls return, the code merges these small, sorted lists together into larger sorted lists until finally the entire list is sorted. Figure 5-3 shows an example using merge sort on playing cards.

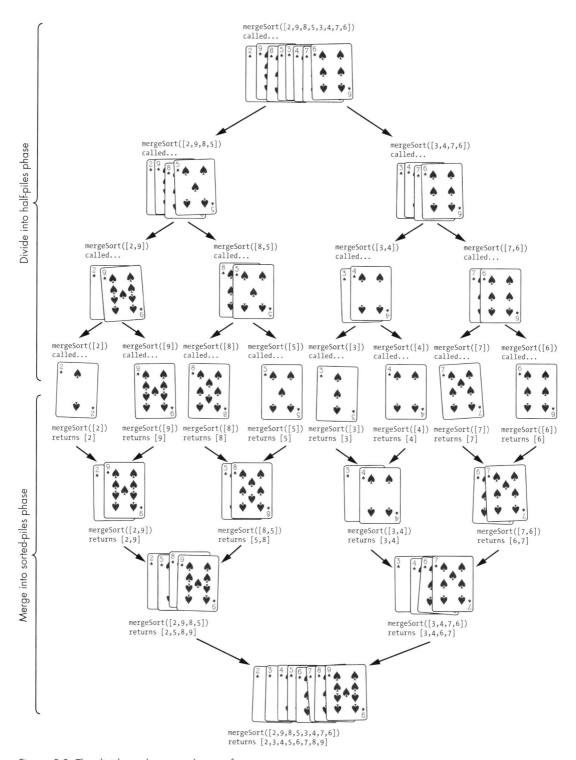

Figure 5-3: The divide and merge phases of merge sort

For example, at the end of the division phase, we have eight separate lists of single numbers: [2], [9], [8], [5], [3], [4], [7], [6]. A list of just one number is naturally in sorted order. Merging two sorted lists into a larger sorted list involves looking at the start of both smaller lists and appending the smaller value to the larger list. Figure 5-4 shows an example of merging [2, 9] and [5, 8]. This is repeatedly done in the merge phase until the end result is that the original mergeSort() call returns the full list in sorted order.

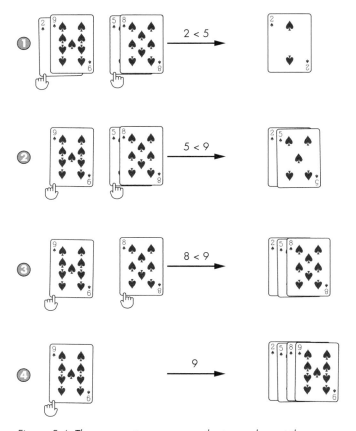

Figure 5-4: The merge step compares the two values at the start of the smaller sorted lists and moves them to the larger sorted list. Merging four cards requires only four steps.

Let's ask our three recursive algorithm questions about the merge sort algorithm:

What is the base case?   Being given a list to sort that has zero or one item in it, which is already in sorted order.

What argument is passed to the recursive function call?   Lists made from the left and right halves of the original list to sort.

How does this argument become closer to the base case?   The lists passed to the recursive call are half the size of the original list, so they eventually become a list of zero or one item.

The following mergeSort() function in the *mergeSort.py* Python program sorts the values in the items list into ascending order:

```
import math

def mergeSort(items):
    print('.....mergeSort() called on:', items)

    # BASE CASE - Zero or one item is naturally sorted:
    if len(items) == 0 or len(items) == 1:
        return items ❶

    # RECURSIVE CASE - Pass the left and right halves to mergeSort():
    # Round down if items doesn't divide in half evenly:
    iMiddle = math.floor(len(items) / 2) ❷

    print('...............Split into:', items[:iMiddle], 'and', items[iMiddle:])

    left = mergeSort(items[:iMiddle]) ❸
    right = mergeSort(items[iMiddle:])

    # BASE CASE - Returned merged, sorted data:
    # At this point, left should be sorted and right should be
    # sorted. We can merge them into a single sorted list.
    sortedResult = []
    iLeft = 0
    iRight = 0
    while (len(sortedResult) < len(items)):
        # Append the smaller value to sortedResult.
        if left[iLeft] < right[iRight]: ❹
            sortedResult.append(left[iLeft])
            iLeft += 1
        else:
            sortedResult.append(right[iRight])
            iRight += 1

        # If one of the pointers has reached the end of its list,
        # put the rest of the other list into sortedResult.
        if iLeft == len(left):
            sortedResult.extend(right[iRight:])
            break
        elif iRight == len(right):
            sortedResult.extend(left[iLeft:])
            break

    print('The two halves merged into:', sortedResult)

    return sortedResult # Returns a sorted version of items.

myList = [2, 9, 8, 5, 3, 4, 7, 6]
myList = mergeSort(myList)
print(myList)
```

```
<script type="text/javascript">
function mergeSort(items) {
    document.write("<pre>" + ".....mergeSort() called on: [" +
    items.join(", ") + "]</pre>");

    // BASE CASE - Zero or one item is naturally sorted:
    if (items.length === 0 || items.length === 1) { // BASE CASE
        return items; ❶
    }

    // RECURSIVE CASE - Pass the left and right halves to mergeSort():
    // Round down if items doesn't divide in half evenly:
    let iMiddle = Math.floor(items.length / 2); ❷

    document.write("<pre>...............Split into: [" + items.slice(0, iMiddle).join(", ") +
    "] and [" + items.slice(iMiddle).join(", ") + "]</pre>");

    let left = mergeSort(items.slice(0, iMiddle)); ❸
    let right = mergeSort(items.slice(iMiddle));

    // BASE CASE - Returned merged, sorted data:
    // At this point, left should be sorted and right should be
    // sorted. We can merge them into a single sorted list.
    let sortedResult = [];
    let iLeft = 0;
    let iRight = 0;
    while (sortedResult.length < items.length) {
        // Append the smaller value to sortedResult.
        if (left[iLeft] < right[iRight]) { ❹
            sortedResult.push(left[iLeft]);
            iLeft++;
        } else {
            sortedResult.push(right[iRight]);
            iRight++;
        }

        // If one of the pointers has reached the end of its list,
        // put the rest of the other list into sortedResult.
        if (iLeft == left.length) {
            Array.prototype.push.apply(sortedResult, right.slice(iRight));
            break;
        } else if (iRight == right.length) {
            Array.prototype.push.apply(sortedResult, left.slice(iLeft));
            break;
        }
    }

    document.write("<pre>The two halves merged into: [" + sortedResult.join(", ") +
    "]</pre>");

    return sortedResult; // Returns a sorted version of items.
}
```

```
let myList = [2, 9, 8, 5, 3, 4, 7, 6];
myList = mergeSort(myList);
document.write("<pre>[" + myList.join(", ") + "]</pre>");
</script>
```

The mergeSort() function (and all the recursive calls to the mergeSort() function) takes an unsorted list and returns a sorted list. The first step in this function is to check for the base case of a list containing only zero or one item ❶. This list is already sorted, so the function returns the list as is.

Otherwise, the function determines the middle index of the list ❷ so that we know where to split it into the left- and right-half lists to pass to two recursive function calls ❸. The recursive function calls return sorted lists, which we store in the left and right variables.

The next step is to merge these two sorted half lists into one sorted full list named sortedResult. We'll maintain two indices for the left and right lists named iLeft and iRight. Inside a loop, the smaller of the two values ❹ is appended to sortedResult, and its respective index variable (either iLeft or iRight) is incremented. If either iLeft or iRight reaches the end of its list, the remaining items in the other half's list are appended to sortedResult.

Let's follow an example of the merging step if the recursive calls have returned [2, 9] for left and [5, 8] for right. Since these lists were returned from mergeSort() calls, we can always assume they are sorted. We must merge them into a single sorted list in sortedResult for the current mergeSort() call to return to its caller.

The iLeft and iRight indices begin at 0. We compare the value at left [iLeft] (which is 2) and right[iRight] (which is 5) to find the smaller one:

```
sortedResult = []
        left: [2, 9]     right: [5, 8]
     indices:  0  1              0  1
  iLeft = 0    ^
 iRight = 0                      ^
```

Since left[iLeft]'s value, 2, is the smaller of the values, we append it to sortedResult and increase iLeft from 0 to 1. The state of the variables is now as follows:

```
sortedResult = [2]
        left: [2, 9]     right: [5, 8]
     indices:  0  1              0  1
  iLeft = 1       ^
 iRight = 0                      ^
```

Comparing left[iLeft] and right[iRight] again, we find that of 9 and 5, right[iRight]'s 5 is smaller. The code appends the 5 to sortedResult and increases iRight from 0 to 1. The state of the variables is now the following:

```
sortedResult = [2, 5]
        left: [2, 9]     right: [5, 8]
```

```
    indices:   0  1              0  1
  iLeft = 1           ^
iRight = 1                           ^
```

Comparing left[iLeft] and right[iRight] again, we find that, of 9 and 8, right[iRight]'s 8 is smaller. The code appends the 8 to sortedResult and increases iRight from 0 to 1. Here's the state of the variables now:

```
sortedResult = [2, 5, 8]
      left: [2, 9]    right: [5, 8]
   indices:   0  1           0  1
  iLeft = 1           ^
iRight = 2                          ^
```

Because iRight is now 2 and equal to the length of the right list, the remaining items in left from the iLeft index to the end are appended to sortedResult, as no more items remain in right to compare them to. This leaves sortedResult as [2, 5, 8, 9], the sorted list it needs to return. This merging step is performed for every call to mergeSort() to produce the final sorted list.

When we run the *mergeSort.py* and *mergeSort.html* programs, the output shows the process of sorting the [2, 9, 8, 5, 3, 4, 7, 6] list:

```
.....mergeSort() called on: [2, 9, 8, 5, 3, 4, 7, 6]
...............Split into: [2, 9, 8, 5] and [3, 4, 7, 6]
.....mergeSort() called on: [2, 9, 8, 5]
...............Split into: [2, 9] and [8, 5]
.....mergeSort() called on: [2, 9]
...............Split into: [2] and [9]
.....mergeSort() called on: [2]
.....mergeSort() called on: [9]
The two halves merged into: [2, 9]
.....mergeSort() called on: [8, 5]
...............Split into: [8] and [5]
.....mergeSort() called on: [8]
.....mergeSort() called on: [5]
The two halves merged into: [5, 8]
The two halves merged into: [2, 5, 8, 9]
.....mergeSort() called on: [3, 4, 7, 6]
...............Split into: [3, 4] and [7, 6]
.....mergeSort() called on: [3, 4]
...............Split into: [3] and [4]
.....mergeSort() called on: [3]
.....mergeSort() called on: [4]
The two halves merged into: [3, 4]
.....mergeSort() called on: [7, 6]
...............Split into: [7] and [6]
.....mergeSort() called on: [7]
.....mergeSort() called on: [6]
The two halves merged into: [6, 7]
The two halves merged into: [3, 4, 6, 7]
The two halves merged into: [2, 3, 4, 5, 6, 7, 8, 9]
[2, 3, 4, 5, 6, 7, 8, 9]
```

As you can see from the output, the function divides the [2, 9, 8, 5, 3, 4, 7, 6] list into [2, 9, 8, 5] and [3, 4, 7, 6] and passes these to recursive mergeSort() calls. The first list is further split into [2, 9] and [8, 5]. That [2, 9] list is split into [2] and [9]. These single-value lists cannot be divided anymore, so we have reached our base case. These lists are merged back into sorted order as [2, 9]. The function divides the [8, 5] list into [8] and [5], reaches the base case, and then merges back into [5, 8].

The [2, 9] and [5, 8] lists are individually in sorted order. Remember, mergeSort() doesn't simply *concatenate* the lists into [2, 9, 5, 8], which would not be in sorted order. Rather, the function *merges* them into the sorted list [2, 5, 8, 9]. By the time the original mergeSort() call returns, the full list it returns is completely sorted.

Summing an Array of Integers

We already covered summing an array of integers in Chapter 3 with the head-tail technique. In this chapter, we'll use a divide-and-conquer strategy. Since the associative property of addition means that adding 1 + 2 + 3 + 4 is the same as adding the sums of 1 + 2 and 3 + 4, we can divide a large array of numbers to sum into two smaller arrays of numbers to sum.

The benefit is that for larger sets of data to process, we could farm out the subproblems to different computers and have them all work together in parallel. There's no need to wait for the first half of the array to be summed before another computer can start summing the second half. This is a large advantage of the divide-and-conquer technique, as CPUs aren't getting much faster but we can have multiple CPUs work simultaneously.

Let's ask the three questions about recursive algorithms for our summation function:

What is the base case? Either an array containing zero numbers (where we return 0) or an array containing one number (where we return the number).

What argument is passed to the recursive function call? Either the left half or the right half of the array of numbers.

How does this argument become closer to the base case? The size of the array of numbers is halved each time, eventually becoming an array containing zero or one number.

The *sumDivConq.py* Python program implements the divide-and-conquer strategy for adding numbers in the sumDivConq() function:

Python
```
def sumDivConq(numbers):
    if len(numbers) == 0: # BASE CASE
      ❶ return 0
    elif len(numbers) == 1: # BASE CASE
      ❷ return numbers[0]
    else: # RECURSIVE CASE
      ❸ mid = len(numbers) // 2
        leftHalfSum = sumDivConq(numbers[0:mid])
```

```
            rightHalfSum = sumDivConq(numbers[mid:len(numbers) + 1])
        ❹ return leftHalfSum + rightHalfSum

nums = [1, 2, 3, 4, 5]
print('The sum of', nums, 'is', sumDivConq(nums))
nums = [5, 2, 4, 8]
print('The sum of', nums, 'is', sumDivConq(nums))
nums = [1, 10, 100, 1000]
print('The sum of', nums, 'is', sumDivConq(nums))
```

The *sumDivConq.html* program contains the JavaScript equivalent:

JavaScript
```
<script type="text/javascript">
function sumDivConq(numbers) {
    if (numbers.length === 0) { // BASE CASE
      ❶ return 0;
    } else if (numbers.length === 1) { // BASE CASE
      ❷ return numbers[0];
    } else { // RECURSIVE CASE
      ❸ let mid = Math.floor(numbers.length / 2);
        let leftHalfSum = sumDivConq(numbers.slice(0, mid));
        let rightHalfSum = sumDivConq(numbers.slice(mid, numbers.length + 1));
      ❹ return leftHalfSum + rightHalfSum;
    }
}

let nums = [1, 2, 3, 4, 5];
document.write('The sum of ' + nums + ' is ' + sumDivConq(nums) + "<br />");
nums = [5, 2, 4, 8];
document.write('The sum of ' + nums + ' is ' + sumDivConq(nums) + "<br />");
nums = [1, 10, 100, 1000];
document.write('The sum of ' + nums + ' is ' + sumDivConq(nums) + "<br />");
</script>
```

The output of this program is:

```
The sum of [1, 2, 3, 4, 5] is 15
The sum of [5, 2, 4, 8] is 19
The sum of [1, 10, 100, 1000] is 1111
```

The sumDivConq() function first checks the numbers array for having either zero or one number in it. These trivial base cases are easy to sum since they require no addition: return either 0 ❶ or the lone number in the array ❷. Everything else is a recursive case; the middle index of the array is calculated ❸ so that separate recursive calls with the left half and right half of the numbers array are made. The sum of these two return values becomes the return value for the current sumDivConq() call ❹.

Because of the associative nature of addition, there's no reason an array of numbers must be added sequentially by a single computer. Our program carries out all operations on the same computer, but for large arrays or calculations more complicated than addition, our program could send the halves to other computers to complete. The problem can be divided into similar subproblems, which is a huge hint that a recursive approach can be taken.

Karatsuba Multiplication

The * operator makes multiplication easy to do in high-level programming languages such as Python and JavaScript. But low-level hardware needs a way to perform multiplication using more primitive operations. We could multiply two integers using only addition with a loop, such as in the following Python code to multiply 5678 * 1234:

```
>>> x = 5678
>>> y = 1234
>>> product = 0
>>> for i in range(x):
...     product += y
...
>>> product
7006652
```

However, this code doesn't scale efficiently for large integers. *Karatsuba multiplication* is a fast, recursive algorithm discovered in 1960 by Anatoly Karatsuba that can multiply integers using addition, subtraction, and a precomputed multiplication table of all products from single-digit numbers. This multiplication table, shown in Figure 5-5, is called a *lookup table*.

Our algorithm won't need to multiply single-digit numbers because it can just look them up in the table. By using memory to store precomputed values, we increase memory usage to decrease CPU runtime.

	0	1	2	3	4	5	6	7	8	9
0	0	0	0	0	0	0	0	0	0	0
1	0	1	2	3	4	5	6	7	8	9
2	0	2	4	6	8	10	12	14	16	18
3	0	3	6	9	12	15	18	21	24	27
4	0	4	8	12	16	20	24	28	32	36
5	0	5	10	15	20	25	30	35	40	45
6	0	6	12	18	24	30	36	42	48	54
7	0	7	14	21	28	35	42	49	56	63
8	0	8	16	24	32	40	48	56	64	72
9	0	9	18	27	36	45	54	63	72	81

Figure 5-5: A lookup table, such as this table of products of all single-digit numbers, saves our program from repeat calculations as the computer stores the precomputed values in memory for later retrieval.

We'll implement Karatsuba multiplication in a high-level language like Python or JavaScript as though the * operator didn't already exist. Our karatsuba() function accepts two integer arguments, x and y, to multiply. The Karatsuba algorithm has five steps, and the first three involve making recursive calls to karatsuba() with arguments that are smaller, broken-down integers derived from x and y. The base case occurs when the x and y arguments are both single-digit numbers, in which case the product can be found in the precomputed lookup table.

We also define four more variables: a and b are each half of the digits of x, and c and d are each half of the digits of y, as shown in Figure 5-6. For example, if x and y are 5678 and 1234, respectively, then a is 56, b is 78, c is 12, and d is 34.

Figure 5-6: The integers to multiply, x and y, are divided into halves a, b, c, and d.

Here are the five steps of the Karatsuba algorithm:

1. Multiply a and c either from the multiplication lookup table or from a recursive call to karatsuba().
2. Multiply b and d either from the multiplication lookup table or from a recursive call to karatsuba().
3. Multiply a + c and b + d either from the multiplication lookup table or from a recursive call to karatsuba().
4. Calculate step 3 – step 2 – step 1.
5. Pad the step 1 and step 4 results with zeros; then add them to step 2.

The result of step 5 is the product of x and y. The specifics of how to pad the step 1 and step 4 results with zeros are explained later in this section.

Let's ask our three recursive algorithm questions about the karatsuba() function:

What is the base case? Multiplying single-digit numbers, which can be done with a precomputed lookup table.

What argument is passed to the recursive function call? The a, b, c, and d values derived from the x and y arguments.

How does this argument become closer to the base case? Since a, b, c, and d are each half of the digits of x and y and themselves are used for the next recursive call's x and y arguments, the recursive call's arguments become closer and closer to the single-digit numbers the base case requires.

Our Python implementation for Karatsuba multiplication is in the *karatsubaMultiplication.py* program:

```
import math

# Create a lookup table of all single-digit multiplication products:
MULT_TABLE = {} ❶
for i in range(10):
    for j in range(10):
```

```
            MULT_TABLE[(i, j)] = i * j

def padZeros(numberString, numZeros, insertSide):
    """Return a string padded with zeros on the left or right side."""
    if insertSide == 'left':
        return '0' * numZeros + numberString
    elif insertSide == 'right':
        return numberString + '0' * numZeros

def karatsuba(x, y):
    """Multiply two integers with the Karatsuba algorithm. Note that
    the * operator isn't used anywhere in this function."""
    assert isinstance(x, int), 'x must be an integer'
    assert isinstance(y, int), 'y must be an integer'
    x = str(x)
    y = str(y)

    # At single digits, look up the products in the multiplication table:
    if len(x) == 1 and len(y) == 1: # BASE CASE
        print('Lookup', x, '*', y, '=', MULT_TABLE[(int(x), int(y))])
        return MULT_TABLE[(int(x), int(y))]

    # RECURSIVE CASE
    print('Multiplying', x, '*', y)

    # Pad with prepended zeros so that x and y are the same length:
    if len(x) < len(y): ❷
        # If x is shorter than y, pad x with zeros:
        x = padZeros(x, len(y) - len(x), 'left')
    elif len(y) < len(x):
        # If y is shorter than x, pad y with zeros:
        y = padZeros(y, len(x) - len(y), 'left')
    # At this point, x and y have the same length.

    halfOfDigits = math.floor(len(x) / 2) ❸

    # Split x into halves a & b, split y into halves c & d:
    a = int(x[:halfOfDigits])
    b = int(x[halfOfDigits:])
    c = int(y[:halfOfDigits])
    d = int(y[halfOfDigits:])

    # Make the recursive calls with these halves:
    step1Result = karatsuba(a, c) ❹ # Step 1: Multiply a & c.
    step2Result = karatsuba(b, d) # Step 2: Multiply b & d.
    step3Result = karatsuba(a + b, c + d) # Step 3: Multiply a + b & c + d.

    # Step 4: Calculate Step 3 - Step 2 - Step 1:
    step4Result = step3Result - step2Result - step1Result ❺

    # Step 5: Pad these numbers, then add them for the return value:
    step1Padding = (len(x) - halfOfDigits) + (len(x) - halfOfDigits)
    step1PaddedNum = int(padZeros(str(step1Result), step1Padding, 'right'))

    step4Padding = (len(x) - halfOfDigits)
```

```
    step4PaddedNum = int(padZeros(str(step4Result), step4Padding, 'right'))

    print('Solved', x, 'x', y, '=', step1PaddedNum + step2Result + step4PaddedNum)

    return step1PaddedNum + step2Result + step4PaddedNum ❻

# Example: 1357 x 2468 = 3349076
print('1357 * 2468 =', karatsuba(1357, 2468))
```

The JavaScript equivalent is in *karatsubaMultiplication.html*:

```javascript
<script type="text/javascript">

// Create a lookup table of all single-digit multiplication products:
let MULT_TABLE = {}; ❶
for (let i = 0; i < 10; i++) {
    for (let j = 0; j < 10; j++) {
        MULT_TABLE[[i, j]] = i * j;
    }
}

function padZeros(numberString, numZeros, insertSide) {
    // Return a string padded with zeros on the left or right side.
    if (insertSide === "left") {
        return "0".repeat(numZeros) + numberString;
    } else if (insertSide === "right") {
        return numberString + "0".repeat(numZeros);
    }
}

function karatsuba(x, y) {
    // Multiply two integers with the Karatsuba algorithm. Note that
    // the * operator isn't used anywhere in this function.
    console.assert(Number.isInteger(x), "x must be an integer");
    console.assert(Number.isInteger(y), "y must be an integer");
    x = x.toString();
    y = y.toString();

    // At single digits, look up the products in the multiplication table:
    if ((x.length === 1) && (y.length === 1)) { // BASE CASE
        document.write("Lookup " + x.toString() + " * " + y.toString() + " = " +
        MULT_TABLE[[parseInt(x), parseInt(y)]] + "<br />");
        return MULT_TABLE[[parseInt(x), parseInt(y)]];
    }

    // RECURSIVE CASE
    document.write("Multiplying " + x.toString() + " * " + y.toString() +
    "<br />");

    // Pad with prepended zeros so that x and y are the same length:
    if (x.length < y.length) { ❷
        // If x is shorter than y, pad x with zeros:
        x = padZeros(x, y.length - x.length, "left");
    } else if (y.length < x.length) {
        // If y is shorter than x, pad y with zeros:
```

```
        y = padZeros(y, x.length - y.length, "left");
    }
    // At this point, x and y have the same length.

    let halfOfDigits = Math.floor(x.length / 2); ❸

    // Split x into halves a & b, split y into halves c & d:
    let a = parseInt(x.substring(0, halfOfDigits));
    let b = parseInt(x.substring(halfOfDigits));
    let c = parseInt(y.substring(0, halfOfDigits));
    let d = parseInt(y.substring(halfOfDigits));

    // Make the recursive calls with these halves:
    let step1Result = karatsuba(a, c); ❹ // Step 1: Multiply a & c.
    let step2Result = karatsuba(b, d); // Step 2: Multiply b & d.
    let step3Result = karatsuba(a + b, c + d); // Step 3: Multiply a + b & c + d.

    // Step 4: Calculate Step 3 - Step 2 - Step 1:
    let step4Result = step3Result - step2Result - step1Result; ❺

    // Step 5: Pad these numbers, then add them for the return value:
    let step1Padding = (x.length - halfOfDigits) + (x.length - halfOfDigits);
    let step1PaddedNum = parseInt(padZeros(step1Result.toString(), step1Padding, "right"));

    let step4Padding = (x.length - halfOfDigits);
    let step4PaddedNum = parseInt(padZeros((step4Result).toString(), step4Padding, "right"));

    document.write("Solved " + x + " x " + y + " = " +
    (step1PaddedNum + step2Result + step4PaddedNum).toString() + "<br />");

    return step1PaddedNum + step2Result + step4PaddedNum; ❻
}

// Example: 1357 x 2468 = 3349076
document.write("1357 * 2468 = " + karatsuba(1357, 2468).toString() + "<br />");
</script>
```

When you run this code, the output looks like this:

```
Multiplying 1357 * 2468
Multiplying 13 * 24
Lookup 1 * 2 = 2
Lookup 3 * 4 = 12
Lookup 4 * 6 = 24
Solved 13 * 24 = 312
Multiplying 57 * 68
Lookup 5 * 6 = 30
Lookup 7 * 8 = 56
Multiplying 12 * 14
Lookup 1 * 1 = 1
Lookup 2 * 4 = 8
Lookup 3 * 5 = 15
Solved 12 * 14 = 168
Solved 57 * 68 = 3876
Multiplying 70 * 92
```

```
Lookup 7 * 9 = 63
Lookup 0 * 2 = 0
Multiplying 7 * 11
Lookup 0 * 1 = 0
Lookup 7 * 1 = 7
Lookup 7 * 2 = 14
Solved 07 * 11 = 77
Solved 70 * 92 = 6440
Solved 1357 * 2468 = 3349076
1357 * 2468 = 3349076
```

The first part of this program happens before karatsuba() is called. Our program needs to create the multiplication lookup table in the MULT_TABLE variable ❶. Normally, lookup tables are hardcoded directly in the source code, from MULT_TABLE[[0, 0]] = 0 to MULT_TABLE[[9, 9]] = 81. But to reduce the amount of typing, we'll use nested for loops to generate each product. Accessing MULT_TABLE[[m, n]] gives us the product of integers m and n.

Our karatsuba() function also relies on a helper function named pad Zeros(), which pads a string of digits with additional zeros on the left or right side of the string. This padding is done in the fifth step of the Karatsuba algorithm. For example, padZeros("42", 3, "left") returns the string 00042, while padZeros("99", 1, "right") returns the string 990.

The karatsuba() function itself first checks for the base case, where x and y are single-digit numbers. These can be multiplied using the lookup table, and their product is immediately returned. Everything else is a recursive case.

We need to convert the x and y integers into strings and adjust them so that they contain the same number of digits. If one of these numbers is shorter than the other, zeros are padded to the left side. For example, if x is 13 and y is 2468, our function calls padZeros() so that x can be replaced with 0013. This is required because we then create the a, b, c, and d variables to each contain one-half of the digits of x and y ❷. The a and c variables must have the same number of digits for the Karatsuba algorithm to work, as do the b and d variables.

Note that we use division and rounding down to calculate how much is half of the digits of x ❸. These mathematical operations are as complicated as multiplication and might not be available to the low-level hardware we are programming the Karatsuba algorithm for. In a real implementation, we could use another lookup table for these values: HALF_TABLE = [0, 0, 1, 1, 2, 2, 3, 3...], and so on. Looking up HALF_TABLE[n] would evaluate to half of n, rounded down. An array of a mere 100 items would be sufficient for all but the most astronomical numbers and save our program from division and rounding. But our programs are for demonstration, so we'll just use the / operator and built-in rounding functions.

Once these variables are set up correctly, we can begin making the recursive function calls ❹. The first three steps involve recursive calls with arguments a and b, c and d, and finally a + b and c + d. The fourth step subtracts the results of the first three steps from each other ❺. The fifth step pads the results of the first and fourth steps with zeros on the right side, then adds them to the results of the second step ❻.

The Algebra Behind the Karatsuba Algorithm

These steps may seem like magic, so let's dive into the algebra that shows why they work. Let's use 1,357 for x and 2,468 for y as the integers we want to multiply. Let's also consider a new variable, n, for the number of digits in x or y. Since a is 13 and b is 57, we can calculate the original x as $10^{n/2} \times a + b$, which is $10^2 \times 13 + 57$ or $1,300 + 57$, or $1,357$. Similarly, y is the same as $10^{n/2} \times c + d$.

This means that the product of $x \times y = (10^{n/2} \times a + b) \times (10^{n/2} \times c + d)$. Doing a bit of algebra, we can rewrite this equation as $x \times y = 10^n \times ac + 10^{n/2} \times (ad + bc) + bd$. With our example numbers, this means $1,357 \times 2,468 = 10,000 \times (13 \times 24) + 100 \times (13 \times 68 + 57 \times 24) + (57 \times 68)$. Both sides of this equation evaluate to 3,349,076.

We've broken the multiplication of xy into the multiplications of ac, ad, bc, and bd. This forms the basis of our recursive function: we've defined the multiplication of x and y by using multiplication of smaller numbers (remember, a, b, c, and d are half the digits of x or y) that approach the base case of multiplying single-digit numbers. And we can perform single-digit multiplication with a lookup table rather than multiplying.

So we need to recursively compute ac (the first step of the Karatsuba algorithm) and bd (the second step). We also need to calculate $(a + b)(c + d)$ for the third step, which we can rewrite as $ac + ad + bc + bd$. We already have ac and bd from the first two steps, so subtracting those gives us $ad + bc$. This means we need only one multiplication (and one recursive call) to calculate $(a + b)(c + d)$ instead of two to calculate $ad + bc$. And $ad + bc$ is needed for the $10^{n/2} \times (ad + bc)$ part of our original equation.

Multiplying by the 10^n and $10^{n/2}$ powers of 10 can be done by padding zero digits: for example, $10,000 \times 123$ is $1,230,000$. So, there's no need to make recursive calls for those multiplications. In the end, multiplying $x \times y$ can be broken into multiplying three smaller products with three recursive calls: `karatsuba(a, c)`, `karatsuba(b, d)`, and `karatsuba((a + b), (c + d))`.

With some careful study of this section, you can understand the algebra behind the Karatsuba algorithm. What I can't understand is how Anatoly Karatsuba was clever enough to devise this algorithm in less than a week as a 23-year-old student in the first place.

Summary

Dividing problems into smaller, self-similar problems is at the heart of recursion, making these divide-and-conquer algorithms especially suited for recursive techniques. In this chapter, we created a divide-and-conquer version of Chapter 3's program for summing numbers in an array. One benefit of this version is that upon dividing a problem into multiple subproblems, the subproblems can be farmed out to other computers to work on in parallel.

A binary search algorithm searches a sorted array by repeatedly narrowing the range to search in half. While a linear search starts searching at the beginning and searches the entire array, a binary search takes advantage of the array's sorted order to home in on the item it is looking for. The performance improvement is so great that it may be worthwhile to sort an unsorted array in order to enable a binary search on its items.

We covered two popular sorting algorithms in this chapter: quicksort and merge sort. Quicksort divides an array into two partitions based on a pivot value. The algorithm then recursively partitions these two partitions, repeating the process until the partitions are the size of a single item. At this point, the partitions, and the items in them, are in sorted order. Merge sort takes an opposite approach. The algorithm splits the array into smaller arrays first, and then merges the smaller arrays into sorted order afterward.

Finally, we covered Karatsuba multiplication, a recursive algorithm for performing integer multiplication when the * multiplication operator isn't available. This comes up in low-level hardware programming that doesn't offer a built-in multiplication instruction. The Karatsuba algorithm breaks down multiplying two integers into three multiplications of smaller integers. To multiply single-digit numbers for the base case, the algorithm stores every product from 0×0 to 9×9 in a lookup table.

The algorithms in this chapter are part of many data structure and algorithm courses that freshman computer science students take. In the next chapter, we'll continue to look at other algorithms at the heart of computing with algorithms that calculate permutations and combinations.

Further Reading

The Computerphile channel on YouTube has videos on quicksort at *https:// youtu.be/XE4VP_8Y0BU* and merge sort at *https://youtu.be/kgBjXUE_Nwc*. If you want a more comprehensive tutorial, the free "Algorithmic Toolbox" online course covers many of the same topics that a freshman data structures and algorithms course would cover, including binary search, quicksort, and merge sort. You can sign up for this Coursera course at *https:// www.coursera.org/learn/algorithmic-toolbox*.

Sorting algorithms are often compared to each other in lessons on big O algorithm analysis, which you can read about in Chapter 13 of my book *Beyond the Basic Stuff with Python* (No Starch Press, 2020). You can read this chapter online at *https://inventwithpython.com/beyond*. Python developer Ned Batchelder describes big O and "how code slows as your data grows" in his 2018 PyCon talk of the same name at *https://youtu.be/duvZ-2UK0fc*.

Divide-and-conquer algorithms are useful because they often can be run on multiple computers in parallel. Guy Steele Jr. gives a Google TechTalk titled "Four Solutions to a Trivial Problem" on this topic at *https://youtu.be/ftcIcn8AmSY*.

Professor Tim Roughgarden produced a video lecture for Stanford University on Karatsuba multiplication at *https://youtu.be/JCbZayFr9RE*.

To help your understanding of quicksort and merge sort, obtain a pack of playing cards or simply write numbers on index cards and practice sorting them by hand according to the rules of these two algorithms. This offline approach can help you remember the pivot-and-partition of quicksort and the divide-merge of merge sort.

Practice Questions

Test your comprehension by answering the following questions:

1. What is a benefit of the divide-and-conquer summing algorithm in this chapter compared to the head-tail summing algorithm in Chapter 3?

2. If a binary search of 50 books on a shelf takes six steps, how many steps would it take to search twice as many books?

3. Can a binary search algorithm search an unsorted array?

4. Is partitioning the same thing as sorting?

5. What happens in quicksort's partition step?

6. What is the pivot value in quicksort?

7. What is the base case of quicksort?

8. How many recursive calls does the `quicksort()` function have?

9. How is the array [0, 3, 1, 2, 5, 4, 7, 6] not properly partitioned with a pivot value of 4?

10. What is the base case of merge sort?

11. How many recursive calls does the `mergeSort()` function have?

12. What is the resultant array when the merge sort algorithm sorts the arrays [12, 37, 38, 41, 99] and [2, 4, 14, 42]?

13. What is a lookup table?

14. In the Karatsuba algorithm that multiplies integers x and y, what do the a, b, c, and d variables store?

15. Answer the three questions about recursive solutions for each of the recursive algorithms presented in this chapter:

    a. What is the base case?

    b. What argument is passed to the recursive function call?

    c. How does this argument become closer to the base case?

    Then re-create the recursive algorithms from this chapter without looking at the original code.

Practice Projects

For practice, write a function for each of the following tasks:

1. Create a version of the `karatsuba()` function that has a multiplication lookup table of products from 0×0 to 999×999 rather than 0×0 to 9×9. Get a rough estimate of how long it takes to calculate `karatsuba(12345678, 87654321)` 10,000 times in a loop with this larger lookup table compared to the original lookup table. If this still runs too quickly to measure, increase the number of iterations to 100,000 or 1,000,000 or more. (Hint: you should delete or comment out the `print()` and `document.write()` calls inside the `karatsuba()` function for this timing test.)

2. Create a function that performs a linear search on a large array of integers 10,000 times. Get a rough estimate of how long this takes, increasing the number of iterations to 100,000 or 1,000,000 if the program executes too quickly. Compare this with how long a second function takes to sort the array once before performing the same number of binary searches.

6

PERMUTATIONS AND COMBINATIONS

Problems involving permutations and combinations are especially suited to recursion. These are common in *set theory*, a branch of mathematical logic that deals with the selection, arrangement, and manipulation of collections of objects.

Dealing with small sets in our short-term memory is simple. We can easily come up with every possible order (that is, *permutation*) or combination of a set of three or four objects. Ordering and combining items in a larger set requires the same process but quickly turns into an impossible task for our human brains. At that point, it becomes practical to bring in computers to handle the combinatorial explosion that occurs as we add more objects to a set.

At its heart, calculating permutations and combinations of large groups involves calculating permutations and combinations of smaller groups. This makes these calculations suitable for recursion. In this chapter, we'll look at recursive algorithms for generating all possible permutations and combinations of characters in a string. We'll expand on this to generate all possible combinations of balanced parentheses (orderings of open parentheses correctly matched to closing parentheses). And finally, we will calculate the power set of a set—that is, the set of all possible subsets of a set.

Many of the recursive functions in this chapter have an argument named indent. This isn't used by the actual recursive algorithms; rather, it is used by their debugging output so that you can see which level of recursion produced the output. The indentation is increased by one space for each recursive call and rendered in the debugging output as periods so that it's easy to count the level of indentation.

The Terminology of Set Theory

This chapter doesn't cover set theory as completely as a math or computer science textbook would. But it covers enough to justify starting with an explanation of the discipline's basic terminology, as doing so will make the rest of this chapter easier to understand. A *set* is a collection of unique objects, called *elements*, or *members*. For example, the letters A, B, and C form a set of three letters. In mathematics (and in Python code syntax), sets are written inside curly braces, with the objects separated by commas: {A, B, C}.

Order doesn't matter for a set; the set {A, B, C} is the same set as {C, B, A}. Sets have distinct elements, meaning there are no duplicates: {A, C, A, B} has repeat As and so is not a set.

A set is a *subset* of another set if it has only members of the other set. For example, {A, C} and {B, C} are both subsets of {A, B, C}, but {A, C, D} is not a subset of it. Conversely, {A, B, C} is a *superset* to {A, C} and also to {B, C} because it contains all their elements. The *empty set* { } is a set that contains no members at all. Empty sets are considered subsets of every possible set.

A subset can also include all the elements of the other set. For example, {A, B, C} is a subset of {A, B, C}. But a *proper subset*, or *strict subset*, is a subset that does not have all the set's elements. No set is a proper subset of itself: so {A, B, C} is a subset but not a proper subset of {A, B, C}. All other subsets are proper subsets. Figure 6-1 shows a graphical representation of the set {A, B, C} and some of its subsets.

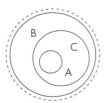

Figure 6-1: The set {A, B, C} within the dashed lines and some of its subsets {A, B, C}, {A, C}, and { } within the solid lines. The circles represent sets, and the letters represent elements.

A *permutation* of a set is a specific ordering of all elements in the set. For example, the set {A, B, C} has six permutations: ABC, ACB, BAC, BCA, CAB, and CBA. We call these *permutations without repetition*, or *permutations without replacement*, because each element doesn't appear in the permutation more than once.

A *combination* is a selection of elements of a set. More formally, a *k-combination* is a subset of *k* elements from a set. Unlike permutations, combinations don't have an ordering. For example, the 2-combinations of the set {A, B, C} are {A, B}, {A, C}, and {B, C}. The 3-combination of the set {A, B, C} is {A, B, C}.

The term *n choose k* refers to the number of possible combinations (without repetition) of *k* elements that can be selected from a set of *n* elements. (Some mathematicians use the term *n choose r*.) This concept has nothing to do with the elements themselves, just the number of them. For example, 4 choose 2 is 6, because there are six ways to choose two elements from a set of four elements like {A, B, C, D}: {A, B}, {A, C}, {A, D}, {B, C}, {B, D}, and {C, D}. Meanwhile, 3 choose 3 is 1, because there's only one 3-combination from a set of three elements like {A, B, C}; that is, {A, B, C} itself. The formula for calculating *n* choose *k* is $(n!) / (k! \times (n - k)!)$. Recall that *n*! is the notation for factorials: 5! is $5 \times 4 \times 3 \times 2 \times 1$.

The term *n multichoose k* refers to the number of possible combinations *with repetition* of *k* elements that can be selected from a set of *n* elements. Because *k*-combinations are sets and sets do not have duplicate elements, a *k*-combination does not have repetition. When we use *k*-combinations with duplicate elements, we specifically call them *k-combinations with repetition*.

Keep in mind that, both with and without repetition, you can think of permutation as a certain arrangement of all elements in a set, while a combination is an orderless selection of certain elements from a set. Permutations have an ordering and use all the elements from a set, while combinations don't have an ordering and use any number of elements from a set. To get a better idea of these terms, Table 6-1 shows the difference between permutations and combinations, with and without repetition, of the set {A, B, C}.

Table 6-1: All Possible Permutations and Combinations, with and without Repetition, of the Set {A, B, C}

	Permutations	Combinations
Without repetition	ABC, ACB, BAC, BCA, CAB	(None), A, B, C, AB, AC, BC, ABC
With repetition	AAA, AAB, AAC, ABA, ABB, ABC, ACA, ACB, ACC, BAA, BAB, BAC, BBA, BBB, BBC, BCA, BCB, BCC, CAA, CAB, CAC, CBA, CBB, CBC, CCA, CCB, CCC	(None), A, B, C, AA, AB, AC, BB, BC, CC, AAA, AAB, AAC, ABB, ABC, ACC, BBB, BBC, BCC, CCC

It's surprising how quickly the number of permutations and combinations grows as we add elements to a set. This *combinatorial explosion* is captured by the formulas in Table 6-2. For example, a set of 10 elements has 10!, or 3,628,800, possible permutations, but a set of twice as many elements has 20!, or 2,432,902,008,176,640,000, permutations.

Table 6-2: Calculating the Number of Possible Permutations and Combinations, with and without Repetition, of a Set of *n* Elements

	Permutations	Combinations
Without repetition	$n!$	2^n
With repetition	n^n	$2n$ choose n, or $(2n)! / (n!)^2$

Note that permutations without repetition are always the same size as the set. For example, the permutations of {A, B, C} are always three letters long: ABC, ACB, BAC, and so forth. However, permutations with repetition can be of any length. Table 6-1 shows the three-letter permutations of {A, B, C} ranging from AAA to CCC, but you could also, for example, have five-letter permutations with repetition ranging from AAAAA to CCCCC. The number of permutations with repetition of *n* elements that are *k* elements long is n^k. Table 6-2 lists it as n^n for permutations with repetition that are also *n* elements long.

Ordering matters for permutations, but not for combinations. While AAB, ABA, and BAA are considered the same combination with repetition, they are considered three separate permutations with repetition.

Finding All Permutations Without Repetition: A Wedding Seating Chart

Imagine you must arrange the seating chart for a wedding reception with delicate social requirements. Some of the guests hate each other, while others demand to sit near an influential guest. The seats at the rectangular table form one long, straight row, rather than a circle. It'd be helpful for your planning to see every possible ordering of guests—that is, every permutation without repetition of the set of guests. No repetition occurs, because each guest appears in the seating chart only once.

Let's use a simple example of Alice, Bob, and Carol, or {A, B, C}. Figure 6-2 shows all six possible permutations of these three wedding guests.

One way we can determine the number of permutations without repetition is with a head-tail recursive strategy. We select one element from the set as the head. We then get every permutation of the rest of the elements (which constitute the tail), and for each permutation we place the head in every possible location in the permutation.

In our ABC example, we'll start with Alice (A) as the head and Bob and Carol (BC) as the tail. The permutations of {B, C} are BC and CB. (How we got BC and CB is explained in the next paragraph, so just put that question aside for now.) We'll put A in every possible location in BC. That is, we put Alice before Bob (ABC), in between Bob and Carol (BAC), and after Carol (BCA). This creates the permutations ABC, BAC, and BCA. We also put A in every possible position in CB, creating ACB, CAB, and CBA. This creates all six permutations of Alice, Bob, and Carol sitting at the reception table. Now we can pick the arrangement that results in the fewest fights (or the most fights, if you want a memorable wedding reception).

Figure 6-2: All six possible permutations of three wedding guests at a table

Of course, to get every permutation of {B, C}, we'd recursively repeat the process with B as the head and C as the tail. The permutation of a single character is the character itself; this is our base case. By putting the head B in every possible location in C, we get the BC and CB permutations we used in the previous paragraph. Remember that, while order doesn't matter with sets (as {B, C} is the same as {C, B}), it does matter with permutations (BC is not a duplicate of CB).

Our recursive permutation function accepts as an argument a string of characters and returns an array of strings of every possible permutation of those characters. Let's ask the three questions about our recursive algorithms for this function:

What is the base case?   An argument of a single character string or empty string, which returns an array of just that string.

What argument is passed to the recursive function call?   The string argument missing one character. A separate recursive call is made for each character missing.

How does this argument become closer to the base case?   The size of the string shrinks and eventually becomes a single-character string.

The recursive permutations algorithm is implemented in *permutations.py*:

```
def getPerms(chars, indent=0):
    print('.' * indent + 'Start of getPerms("' + chars + '")')
    if len(chars) == 1: ❶
        # BASE CASE
        print('.' * indent + 'When chars = "' + chars + '" base case returns', chars)
        return [chars]

    # RECURSIVE CASE
    permutations = []
    head = chars[0] ❷
    tail = chars[1:]
```

```python
        tailPermutations = getPerms(tail, indent + 1)
        for tailPerm in tailPermutations: ❸
            print('.' * indent + 'When chars =', chars, 'putting head', head, 'in all places in',
tailPerm)
            for i in range(len(tailPerm) + 1): ❹
                newPerm = tailPerm[0:i] + head + tailPerm[i:]
                print('.' * indent + 'New permutation:', newPerm)
                permutations.append(newPerm)
        print('.' * indent + 'When chars =', chars, 'results are', permutations)
        return permutations

print('Permutations of "ABCD":')
print('Results:', ','.join(getPerms('ABCD')))
```

The equivalent JavaScript program is in *permutations.html*:

```javascript
<script type="text/javascript">
function getPerms(chars, indent) {
    if (indent === undefined) {
        indent = 0;
    }
    document.write('.'.repeat(indent) + 'Start of getPerms("' + chars + '")<br />');
    if (chars.length === 1) { ❶
        // BASE CASE
        document.write('.'.repeat(indent) + "When chars = \"" + chars +
        "\" base case returns " + chars + "<br />");
        return [chars];
    }
    // RECURSIVE CASE
    let permutations = [];
    let head = chars[0]; ❷
    let tail = chars.substring(1);
    let tailPermutations = getPerms(tail, indent + 1);
    for (tailPerm of tailPermutations) { ❸
        document.write('.'.repeat(indent) + "When chars = " + chars +
        " putting head " + head + " in all places in " + tailPerm + "<br />");
        for (let i = 0; i < tailPerm.length + 1; i++) { ❹
            let newPerm = tailPerm.slice(0, i) + head + tailPerm.slice(i);
            document.write('.'.repeat(indent) + "New permutation: " + newPerm + "<br />");
            permutations.push(newPerm);
        }
    }
    document.write('.'.repeat(indent) + "When chars = " + chars +
    " results are " + permutations + "<br />");
    return permutations;
}

document.write("<pre>Permutations of \"ABCD\":<br />");
document.write("Results: " + getPerms("ABCD") + "</pre>");
</script>
```

The output of these programs is the following:

```
Permutations of "ABCD":
Start of getPerms("ABCD")
.Start of getPerms("BCD")
..Start of getPerms("CD")
...Start of getPerms("D")
...When chars = "D" base case returns D
..When chars = CD putting head C in all places in D
..New permutation: CD
..New permutation: DC
..When chars = CD results are ['CD', 'DC']
.When chars = BCD putting head B in all places in CD
.New permutation: BCD
.New permutation: CBD
.New permutation: CDB
.When chars = BCD putting head B in all places in DC
.New permutation: BDC
.New permutation: DBC
.New permutation: DCB
.When chars = BCD results are ['BCD', 'CBD', 'CDB', 'BDC', 'DBC', 'DCB']
--snip--
When chars = ABCD putting head A in all places in DCB
New permutation: ADCB
New permutation: DACB
New permutation: DCAB
New permutation: DCBA
When chars = ABCD results are ['ABCD', 'BACD', 'BCAD', 'BCDA', 'ACBD', 'CABD',
'CBAD', 'CBDA', 'ACDB','CADB', 'CDAB', 'CDBA', 'ABDC', 'BADC', 'BDAC', 'BDCA',
'ADBC', 'DABC', 'DBAC', 'DBCA', 'ADCB', 'DACB', 'DCAB', 'DCBA']
Results: ABCD,BACD,BCAD,BCDA,ACBD,CABD,CBAD,CBDA,ACDB,CADB,CDAB,CDBA,ABDC,
BADC,BDAC,BDCA,ADBC,DABC,DBAC,DBCA,ADCB,DACB,DCAB,DCBA
```

When getPerms() is called, it first checks for the base case ❶. If the chars string is only one character long, it can have only one permutation: the chars string itself. The function returns this string in an array.

Otherwise, in the recursive case, the function splits the chars argument's first character into the head variable and the rest into the tail variable ❷. The function makes a recursive call to getPerms() to get all the permutations of the string in tail. A first for loop ❸ iterates over each of these permutations, and a second for loop ❹ creates a new permutation by placing the head character in every possible place in the string.

For example, if getPerms() is called with ABCD for the chars argument, head is A and tail is BCD. The getPerms('BCD') call returns an array of the tail permutations, ['BCD', 'CBD', 'CDB', 'BDC', 'DBC', 'DCB']. The first for loop starts with the BCD permutation, and the second for loop places the A string in head in each possible place, producing ABCD, BACD, BCAD, BCDA. This is repeated with the remaining tail permutations, and the entire list is then returned by the getPerms() function.

Getting Permutations with Nested Loops:
A Less-Than-Ideal Approach

Let's say we have a simple bicycle lock, as in Figure 6-3, with a four-digit combination. The combination has 10,000 possible permutations of digits (0000 to 9999), but only one will unlock it. (They are called *combination locks*; however, in this context it'd be more accurate to call them *permutations with repetition locks*, since the order matters.)

Now let's say we have a much simpler lock with only the five letters A to E. We can calculate the number of possible combinations as 5^4, or $5 \times 5 \times 5 \times 5$, or 625. A combination lock of k characters, each character selected from a set of n possibilities, is n^k. But getting a list of the combinations themselves is a bit more involved.

Figure 6-3: A four-digit combination bicycle lock has 10^4, or 10,000, possible permutations with repetition (photo courtesy of Shaun Fisher, CC BY 2.0 license).

One way to get permutations with repetition is with *nested loops*—that is, a loop within another loop. The inner loop goes through every element in a set, whereas the outer loop does the same while repeating the inner loop. Creating all possible k-character permutations, each character selected from a set of n possibilities, requires k nested loops.

For example, *nestedLoopPermutations.py* contains code that generates all 3-combinations of {A, B, C, D, E}:

Python
```
for a in ['A', 'B', 'C', 'D', 'E']:
    for b in ['A', 'B', 'C', 'D', 'E']:
        for c in ['A', 'B', 'C', 'D', 'E']:
            for d in ['A', 'B', 'C', 'D', 'E']:
                print(a, b, c, d)
```

And *nestedLoopPermutations.html* contains the equivalent JavaScript program:

```
<script>
for (a of ['A', 'B', 'C', 'D', 'E']) {
    for (b of ['A', 'B', 'C', 'D', 'E']) {
        for (c of ['A', 'B', 'C', 'D', 'E']) {
            for (d of ['A', 'B', 'C', 'D', 'E']) {
                document.write(a + b + c + d + "<br />")
            }
        }
    }
}
</script>
```

The output of these programs looks like this:

```
A A A A
A A A B
A A A C
A A A D
A A A E
A A B A
A A B B
--snip--
E E E C
E E E D
E E E E
```

The problem with generating permutations with four nested loops is that it works only for permutations that are exactly four characters. Nested loops cannot generate permutations for arbitrary lengths. Instead, we can use a recursive function, as described in the next section.

You can remember the difference between permutations with and without repetition with the examples in this chapter. Permutations *without* repetition go through all possible orderings of the elements in a set, like our wedding guest seating chart example. Permutations *with* repetition go through all the possible combinations of a combination lock; the order matters, and the same element can appear more than once.

Permutations with Repetition: A Password Cracker

Imagine you have received a sensitive encrypted file from a recently deceased journalist. In their final message, the journalist told you the file contains records of tax evasion by a nefarious trillionaire. They didn't have the password to decrypt the file, but they did know that it is exactly four characters long; also, the possible characters are the numbers 2, 4, and 8 and the letters J, P, and B. These characters can appear more than once. For example, possible passwords are JPB2, JJJJ, and 2442.

To generate a list of all possible four-character passwords based on this information, you want to obtain all possible four-element permutations with repetition of the set {J, P, B, 2, 4, 8}. Each of the four characters in the password can be one of the six possible characters, making $6 \times 6 \times 6 \times 6$, or 6^4, or 1,296 possible permutations. We want to generate the permutations of {J, P, B, 2, 4, 8}, and not the combinations, because the ordering matters; JPB2 is a different password from B2JP.

Let's ask the three recursive algorithm questions about our permutations function. Instead of k, we'll use the more descriptive name permLength:

What is the base case? A permLength argument of 0, meaning a permutation zero characters long, signals that the prefix argument now contains the complete permutation and so prefix should be returned in an array.

What argument is passed to the recursive function call? The chars string of the characters to get permutations of, a permLength argument that begins as the length of chars, and a prefix argument that begins as the blank string. Recursive calls decrement the permLength argument while appending a character from chars to the prefix argument.

How does this argument become closer to the base case? Eventually, the permLength argument decrements to 0.

The algorithm for recursive permutations with repetition is implemented in *permutationsWithRepetition.py*:

```
def getPermsWithRep(chars, permLength=None, prefix=''):
    indent = '.' * len(prefix)
    print(indent + 'Start, args=("' + chars + '", ' + str(permLength) + ', "' + prefix + '")')
    if permLength is None:
        permLength = len(chars)

    # BASE CASE
    if (permLength == 0): ❶
        print(indent + 'Base case reached, returning', [prefix])
        return [prefix]

    # RECURSIVE CASE
    # Create a new prefix by adding each character to the current prefix.
    results = []
    print(indent + 'Adding each char to prefix "' + prefix + '".')
    for char in chars:
        newPrefix = prefix + char ❷

        # Decrease permLength by one because we added one character to the prefix.
        results.extend(getPermsWithRep (chars, permLength - 1, newPrefix)) ❸
    print(indent + 'Returning', results)
    return results


print('All permutations with repetition of JPB123:')
print(getPermsWithRep('JPB123', 4))
```

```
<script type="text/javascript">
function getPermsWithRep(chars, permLength, prefix) {
    if (permLength === undefined) {
        permLength = chars.length;
    }
    if (prefix === undefined) {
        prefix = "";
    }
    let indent = ".".repeat(prefix.length);
    document.write(indent + "Start, args=(\"" + chars + "\", " + permLength +
", \"" + prefix + "\")<br />");

    // BASE CASE
    if (permLength === 0) { ❶
        document.write(indent + "Base case reached, returning " + [prefix] + "<br />");
        return [prefix];
    }

    // RECURSIVE CASE
    // Create a new prefix by adding each character to the current prefix.
    let results = [];
    document.write(indent + "Adding each char to prefix \"" + prefix + "\".<br />");
    for (char of chars) {
        let newPrefix = prefix + char; ❷

        // Decrease permLength by one because we added one character to the prefix.
        results = results.concat(getPermsWithRep(chars, permLength - 1, newPrefix)); ❸
    }
    document.write(indent + "Returning " + results + "<br />");
    return results;
}

document.write("<pre>All permutations with repetition of JPB123:<br />");
document.write(getPermsWithRep('JPB123', 4) + "</pre>");
</script>
```

The output of these programs is shown here:

```
All permutations with repetition of JPB123:
Start, args=("JPB123", 4, "")
Adding each char to prefix "".
.Start, args=("JPB123", 3, "J")
.Adding each char to prefix "J".
..Start, args=("JPB123", 2, "JJ")
..Adding each char to prefix "JJ".
...Start, args=("JPB123", 1, "JJJ")
...Adding each char to prefix "JJJ".
....Start, args=("JPB123", 0, "JJJJ")
....Base case reached, returning ['JJJJ']
....Start, args=("JPB123", 0, "JJJP")
....Base case reached, returning ['JJJP']
```

```
--snip--
Returning ['JJJJ', 'JJJP', 'JJJB', 'JJJ1', 'JJJ2', 'JJJ3',
'JJPJ', 'JJPP', 'JJPB', 'JJP1', 'JJP2', 'JJP3', 'JJBJ', 'JJBP',
'JJBB', 'JJB1', 'JJB2', 'JJB3', 'JJ1J', 'JJ1P', 'JJ1B', 'JJ11',
'JJ12', 'JJ13', 'JJ2J', 'JJ2P', 'JJ2B', 'JJ21', 'JJ22', 'JJ23',
'JJ3J', 'JJ3P', 'JJ3B', 'JJ31', 'JJ32', 'JJ33', 'JPJJ',
--snip--
```

The getPermsWithRep() function has a prefix string argument that begins
as a blank string by default. When the function is called, it first checks for
the base case ❶. If permLength, the length of the permutations, is 0, an array
with prefix is returned.

Otherwise, in the recursive case, for each character in the chars argument the function creates a new prefix ❷ to pass to the recursive getPerms
WithRep() call. This recursive call passes permLength - 1 for the permLength
argument.

The permLength argument starts at the length of the permutations and
decreases by one for each recursive call ❸. And the prefix argument starts
as the blank string and increases by one character for each recursive call.
So by the time the base case of k == 0 is reached, the prefix string is the full
permutation length of k.

For example, let's consider the case of calling getPermsWithRep('ABC', 2).
The prefix argument defaults to the blank string. The function makes a
recursive call with each character of ABC concatenated to the blank prefix
string as the new prefix. Calling getPermsWithRep('ABC', 2) makes these three
recursive calls:

- getPermsWithRep('ABC', 1, 'A')
- getPermsWithRep('ABC', 1, 'B')
- getPermsWithRep('ABC', 1, 'C')

Each of these three calls will make its own three recursive calls, but will
pass 0 for permLength instead of 1. The base case occurs when permLength == 0,
so these return their prefixes. This is how all nine of the permutations are
generated. The getPermsWithRep() function generates permutations of larger
sets the same way.

Getting K-Combinations with Recursion

Recall that order is not significant for combinations in the way it is for permutations. Yet generating all *k*-combinations of a set is a bit tricky because
you don't want your algorithm to generate duplicates: if you create the
AB 2-combination from the set {A, B, C}, you don't want to also create BA,
because it's the same 2-combination as AB.

To figure out how we can write recursive code to solve this problem,
let's see how a tree can visually describe generating all the *k*-combinations
of a set. Figure 6-4 shows a tree with all the combinations from the set
{A, B, C, D}.

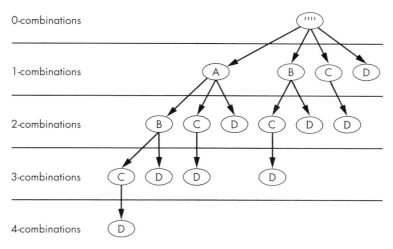

0-combinations

1-combinations

2-combinations

3-combinations

4-combinations

Figure 6-4: Tree showing every possible k-combination (from 0 to 4) from the set {A, B, C, D}

To gather, for example, 3-combinations from this tree, start at the root node at the top and do a depth-first tree traversal to the 3-combinations level, while memorizing each node's letter on the way to the bottom. (Depth-first searches are discussed in Chapter 4.) Our first 3-combination would be going from the root to A in the 1-combination level, then down to B in the 2-combination level, then to C in the 3-combination level, where we stop with our complete 3-combination: ABC. For the next combination, we traverse from the root to A to B to D, giving us the combination ABD. We continue doing this for ACD and BCD. Our tree has four nodes in the 3-combination level, and four 3-combinations from {A, B, C, D}: ABC, ABD, ACD, and BCD.

Notice that we create the tree in Figure 6-4 by starting with a blank string for the root node. This is the 0-combination level, and it applies to all combinations of zero selections from the set; it's simply an empty string. The child nodes of the root are all elements from the set. In our case, that is all four elements from {A, B, C, D}. While sets don't have an order, we need to be consistent in using the ABCD order of the set while generating this tree. This is because every node's children consist of the letters after it in the ABCD string: all A nodes have children B, C, and D; all B nodes have children C and D; all C nodes have one D child; and all D nodes have no child nodes.

While it's not directly related to the recursive combination function, also notice the pattern in the number of *k*-combinations at each level:

- The 0-combination and 4-combination levels both have one combination: the empty string and ABCD, respectively.

- The 1-combination and 3-combination levels both have four combinations: A, B, C, D and ABC, ABD, ACD, BCD, respectively.

- The 2-combination level in the middle has the most combinations at six: AB, AC, AD, BC, BD, and CD.

The reason the number of combinations increases, peaks in the middle, and then decreases is that the *k*-combinations are mirrors of each other. For example, the 1-combinations are made from the elements not selected for the 3-combinations:

- The 1-combination A is the mirror of the 3-combination BCD.
- The 1-combination B is the mirror of the 3-combination ACD.
- The 1-combination C is the mirror of the 3-combination ABD.
- The 1-combination D is the mirror of the 3-combination ABC.

We'll create a function called getCombos() that takes two arguments: a chars string with the letters to get combinations from, and the size of the combinations k. The return value is an array of strings of combinations from the string chars, each of length k.

We'll use a head-tail technique with the chars argument. For example, say we call getCombos('ABC', 2) to get all the 2-combinations from {A, B, C}. The function will set A as the head and BC as the tail. Figure 6-5 shows the tree for selecting 2-combinations from {A, B, C}.

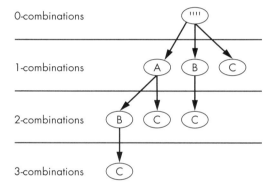

Figure 6-5: Tree showing every possible 2-combination from the set {A, B, C}

Let's ask our three recursive algorithm questions:

What is the base case?   The first base case is a k argument of 0, meaning that a 0-combination is requested, which is always an array of the blank string no matter what chars is. The second case occurs if chars is the blank string, which is an empty array since no possible combinations can be made from a blank string.

What argument is passed to the recursive function call?   For the first recursive call, the tail of chars and k - 1 are passed. For the second recursive call, the tail of chars and k are passed.

How does this argument become closer to the base case?   Since the recursive calls decrement k and remove the heads from the chars arguments, eventually the k argument decrements to 0 or the chars argument becomes the blank string.

The Python code for generating combinations is in *combinations.py*:

Python

```
def getCombos(chars, k, indent=0):
    debugMsg = '.' * indent + "In getCombos('" + chars + "', " + str(k) + ")"
    print(debugMsg + ', start.')
    if k == 0:
        # BASE CASE
        print(debugMsg + " base case returns ['']")
        # If k asks for 0-combinations, return '' as the selection of
        # zero letters from chars.
        return ['']
    elif chars == '':
        # BASE CASE
        print(debugMsg + ' base case returns []')
        return [] # A blank chars has no combinations, no matter what k is.

    # RECURSIVE CASE
    combinations = []
❶  # First part, get the combos that include the head:
    head = chars[:1]
    tail = chars[1:]
    print(debugMsg + " part 1, get combos with head '" + head + "'")
❷  tailCombos = getCombos(tail, k - 1, indent + 1)
    print('.' * indent + "Adding head '" + head + "' to tail combos:")
    for tailCombo in tailCombos:
        print('.' * indent + 'New combination', head + tailCombo)
        combinations.append(head + tailCombo)

❸  # Second part, get the combos that don't include the head:
    print(debugMsg + " part 2, get combos without head '" + head + "')")
❹  combinations.extend(getCombos(tail, k, indent + 1))

    print(debugMsg + ' results are', combinations)
    return combinations

print('2-combinations of "ABC":')
print('Results:', getCombos('ABC', 2))
```

The equivalent JavaScript program is in *combinations.html*:

```
<script type="text/javascript">
function getCombos(chars, k, indent) {
    if (indent === undefined) {
        indent = 0;
    }
    let debugMsg = ".".repeat(indent) + "In getCombos('" + chars + "', " + k + ")";
    document.write(debugMsg + ", start.<br />");
    if (k == 0) {
        // BASE CASE
        document.write(debugMsg + " base case returns ['']<br />");
        // If k asks for 0-combinations, return '' as the selection of zero letters from chars.
        return [""];
    } else if (chars == "") {
        // BASE CASE
        document.write(debugMsg + " base case returns []<br />");
```

```
        return []; // A blank chars has no combinations, no matter what k is.
    }

    // RECURSIVE CASE
    let combinations = [];
    // First part, get the combos that include the head: ❶
    let head = chars.slice(0, 1);
    let tail = chars.slice(1, chars.length);
    document.write(debugMsg + " part 1, get combos with head '" + head + "'<br />");
    let tailCombos = getCombos(tail, k - 1, indent + 1); ❷
    document.write(".".repeat(indent) + "Adding head '" + head + "' to tail combos:<br />");
    for (tailCombo of tailCombos) {
        document.write(".".repeat(indent) + "New combination " + head + tailCombo + "<br />");
        combinations.push(head + tailCombo);
    }
    // Second part, get the combos that don't include the head: ❸
    document.write(debugMsg + " part 2, get combos without head '" + head + "')<br />");
    combinations = combinations.concat(getCombos(tail, k, indent + 1)); ❹

    document.write(debugMsg + " results are " + combinations + "<br />");
    return combinations;
}

document.write('<pre>2-combinations of "ABC":<br />');
document.write("Results: " + getCombos("ABC", 2) + "<br /></pre>");
</script>
```

The output of these programs is the following:

```
2-combinations of "ABC":
In getCombos('ABC', 2), start.
In getCombos('ABC', 2) part 1, get combos with head 'A'
.In getCombos('BC', 1), start.
.In getCombos('BC', 1) part 1, get combos with head 'B'
..In getCombos('C', 0), start.
..In getCombos('C', 0) base case returns ['']
.Adding head 'B' to tail combos:
.New combination B
.In getCombos('BC', 1) part 2, get combos without head 'B')
..In getCombos('C', 1), start.
..In getCombos('C', 1) part 1, get combos with head 'C'
...In getCombos('', 0), start.
...In getCombos('', 0) base case returns ['']
..Adding head 'C' to tail combos:
..New combination C
..In getCombos('C', 1) part 2, get combos without head 'C')
...In getCombos('', 1), start.
...In getCombos('', 1) base case returns []
..In getCombos('C', 1) results are ['C']
.In getCombos('BC', 1) results are ['B', 'C']
Adding head 'A' to tail combos:
New combination AB
New combination AC
In getCombos('ABC', 2) part 2, get combos without head 'A')
.In getCombos('BC', 2), start.
```

```
.In getCombos('BC', 2) part 1, get combos with head 'B'
..In getCombos('C', 1), start.
..In getCombos('C', 1) part 1, get combos with head 'C'
...In getCombos('', 0), start.
...In getCombos('', 0) base case returns ['']
..Adding head 'C' to tail combos:
..New combination C
..In getCombos('C', 1) part 2, get combos without head 'C')
...In getCombos('', 1), start.
...In getCombos('', 1) base case returns []
..In getCombos('C', 1) results are ['C']
.Adding head 'B' to tail combos:
.New combination BC
.In getCombos('BC', 2) part 2, get combos without head 'B')
..In getCombos('C', 2), start.
..In getCombos('C', 2) part 1, get combos with head 'C'
...In getCombos('', 1), start.
...In getCombos('', 1) base case returns []
..Adding head 'C' to tail combos:
..In getCombos('C', 2) part 2, get combos without head 'C')
...In getCombos('', 2), start.
...In getCombos('', 2) base case returns []
..In getCombos('C', 2) results are []
.In getCombos('BC', 2) results are ['BC']
In getCombos('ABC', 2) results are ['AB', 'AC', 'BC']
Results: ['AB', 'AC', 'BC']
```

Every getCombos() function call has two recursive calls for the two parts of the algorithm. For our getCombos('ABC', 2) example, the first part ❶ is to get all the combinations that include the head A. In the tree, this generates all the combinations *under* the A node in the 1-combination level.

We can do this by passing the tail and k - 1 to the first recursive function call: getCombos('BC', 1) ❷. We add A to each combination that this recursive function call returns. Let's use the leap-of-faith principle and just assume our getCombos() correctly returns a list of *k*-combinations, ['B', 'C'], even though we haven't finished writing it yet. We now have all the *k*-combinations that include the head A in an array to hold our results: ['AB', 'AC'].

The second part ❸ gets all the combinations that don't include the head A. In the tree, this generates all the combinations *to the right* of the A node in the 1-combination level. We can do this by passing the tail and k to the second recursive function call: getCombos('BC', 2). This returns ['BC'], since BC is the only 2-combination of BC.

The results from getCombos('ABC', 2)'s two recursive calls, ['AB', 'AC'] and ['BC'], are concatenated together and returned: ['AB', 'AC', 'BC'] ❹. The getCombos() function generates combinations of larger sets the same way.

Get All Combinations of Balanced Parentheses

A string has *balanced parentheses* if every opening parenthesis is followed by exactly one closing parenthesis. For example, '()()' and '(())' are strings of two balanced parentheses pairs, but ')(()' and '((()' are not balanced. These strings are also called *Dyck words*, after mathematician Walther von Dyck.

A common coding interview question is to write a recursive function that, given the number of pairs of parentheses, produces all possible combinations of balanced parentheses. For example, a getBalancedParens(3) call should return ['((()))', '(()())', '(())()', '()(())', '()()()']. Note that calling getBalancedParens(*n*) returns strings that are $2n$ characters in length, since each string consists of *n* pairs of parentheses.

We could try to solve this problem by finding all permutations of the pairs of parenthesis characters, but that would result in both balanced and unbalanced parentheses strings. Even if we filtered out the invalid strings later, 2*n*! permutations exist for *n* pairs of parentheses. That algorithm is far too slow to be practical.

Instead, we can implement a recursive function to generate all strings of balanced parentheses. Our getBalancedParens() function takes an integer of the number of pairs of parentheses and returns a list of balanced parentheses strings. The function builds these strings by adding either an opening or closing parenthesis. An opening parenthesis can be added only if opening parentheses remain to be used. A closing parenthesis can be added only if more opening parentheses have been added than closing parentheses so far.

We'll track the number of opening and closing parentheses remaining to be used with function parameters named openRem and closeRem. The string currently being built is another function parameter named current, which serves a similar purpose as the prefix parameter in the *permutationsWithRepetition* program. The first base case occurs when openRem and closeRem are both 0 and no more parentheses remain to be added to the current string. The second base case happens after the two recursive cases have received the lists of balanced parentheses strings after adding an opening and/or closing parenthesis (if possible).

Let's ask the three recursive algorithm questions about the getBalanced Parens() function:

What is the base case?   When the number of opening and closing parentheses remaining to be added to the string being built has reached 0. A second base case always occurs after the recursive cases have finished.

What argument is passed to the recursive function call?   The total number of pairs of parentheses (pairs), the remaining number of opening and closing parentheses to add (openRem and closeRem), and the string currently being built (current).

How does this argument become closer to the base case?   As we add more opening and closing parentheses to current, we decrement the openRem and closeRem arguments until they become 0.

The *balancedParentheses.py* file contains the Python code for our balanced parentheses recursive function:

```python
def getBalancedParens(pairs, openRem=None, closeRem=None, current='', indent=0):
    if openRem is None: ❶
        openRem = pairs
    if closeRem is None:
        closeRem = pairs

    print('.' * indent, end='')
    print('Start of pairs=' + str(pairs) + ', openRem=' +
    str(openRem) + ', closeRem=' + str(closeRem) + ', current="' + current + '"')
    if openRem == 0 and closeRem == 0: ❷
        # BASE CASE
        print('.' * indent, end='')
        print('1st base case. Returning ' + str([current]))
        return [current] ❸

    # RECURSIVE CASE
    results = []
    if openRem > 0: ❹
        print('.' * indent, end='')
        print('Adding open parenthesis.')
        results.extend(getBalancedParens(pairs, openRem - 1, closeRem,
        current + '(', indent + 1))
    if closeRem > openRem: ❺
        print('.' * indent, end='')
        print('Adding close parenthesis.')
        results.extend(getBalancedParens(pairs, openRem, closeRem - 1,
        current + ')', indent + 1))

    # BASE CASE
    print('.' * indent, end='')
    print('2nd base case. Returning ' + str(results))
    return results ❻

print('All combinations of 2 balanced parentheses:')
print('Results:', getBalancedParens(2))
```

The *balancedParentheses.html* file contains the JavaScript equivalent of this program:

```html
<script type="text/javascript">
function getBalancedParens(pairs, openRem, closeRem, current, indent) {
    if (openRem === undefined) { ❶
        openRem = pairs;
    }
    if (closeRem === undefined) {
        closeRem = pairs;
    }
    if (current === undefined) {
        current = "";
    }
```

```
        if (indent === undefined) {
            indent = 0;
        }

        document.write(".".repeat(indent) + "Start of pairs=" +
        pairs + ", openRem=" + openRem + ", closeRem=" +
        closeRem + ", current=\"" + current + "\"<br />");
        if (openRem === 0 && closeRem === 0) { ❷
            // BASE CASE
            document.write(".".repeat(indent) +
            "1st base case. Returning " + [current] + "<br />");
            return [current]; ❸
        }

        // RECURSIVE CASE
        let results = [];
        if (openRem > 0) { ❹
            document.write(".".repeat(indent) + "Adding open parenthesis.<br />");
            Array.prototype.push.apply(results, getBalancedParens(
            pairs, openRem - 1, closeRem, current + '(', indent + 1));
        }
        if (closeRem > openRem) { ❺
            document.write(".".repeat(indent) + "Adding close parenthesis.<br />");
            results = results.concat(getBalancedParens(
            pairs, openRem, closeRem - 1, current + ')', indent + 1));
        }

        // BASE CASE
        document.write(".".repeat(indent) + "2nd base case. Returning " + results + "<br />");
        return results; ❻
    }

document.write(<pre>"All combinations of 2 balanced parentheses:<br />");
document.write("Results: ", getBalancedParens(2), "</pre>");
</script>
```

The output of these programs looks like this:

```
All combinations of 2 balanced parentheses:
Start of pairs=2, openRem=2, closeRem=2, current=""
Adding open parenthesis.
.Start of pairs=2, openRem=1, closeRem=2, current="("
.Adding open parenthesis.
..Start of pairs=2, openRem=0, closeRem=2, current="(("
..Adding close parenthesis.
...Start of pairs=2, openRem=0, closeRem=1, current="(()"
...Adding close parenthesis.
....Start of pairs=2, openRem=0, closeRem=0, current="(())"
....1st base case. Returning ['(())']
...2nd base case. Returning ['(())']
..2nd base case. Returning ['(())']
.Adding close parenthesis.
..Start of pairs=2, openRem=1, closeRem=1, current="()"
..Adding open parenthesis.
...Start of pairs=2, openRem=0, closeRem=1, current="()("
```

```
...Adding close parenthesis.
....Start of pairs=2, openRem=0, closeRem=0, current="()()"
....1st base case. Returning ['()()']
...2nd base case. Returning ['()()']
..2nd base case. Returning ['()()']
.2nd base case. Returning ['(())', '()()']
2nd base case. Returning ['(())', '()()']
Results: ['(())', '()()']
```

The getBalancedParens() function ❶ requires one argument, the number of pairs of parentheses, when called by the user. However, it needs to pass additional information in the arguments to its recursive calls. These include the number of opening parentheses that remain to be added (openRem), the number of closing parentheses that remain to be added (closeRem), and the current balanced parentheses string being built (current). Both openRem and closeRem start as the same value as the pairs argument, and current starts as the blank string. An indent argument is used only for the debugging output to show the program's level of recursive function call.

The function first checks the number of opening and closing parentheses remaining to be added ❷. If both are 0, we've reached the first base case, and the string in current is finished. Since the getBalancedParens() function returns a list of strings, we put current in a list and return it ❸.

Otherwise, the function continues on to the recursive case. If possible opening parentheses remain ❹, the function calls getBalancedParens() with an opening parenthesis added to the current argument. If more closing parentheses are remaining than opening parentheses ❺, the function calls getBalancedParens() with a closing parenthesis added to the current argument. This check ensures that an unmatched closing parenthesis won't be added, as this would make the string unbalanced, such as the second closing parenthesis in ()).

After these recursive cases is an unconditional base case that returns all the strings returned from the two recursive function calls (and, of course, the recursive function calls made by these recursive function calls, and so on) ❻.

Power Set: Finding All Subsets of a Set

The *power set* of a set is the set of every possible subset of that set. For example, the power set of {A, B, C} is {{ }, {A}, {B}, {C}, {A, B}, {A, C}, {B, C}, {A, B, C}}. This is equivalent to the set of every possible *k*-combination of a set. After all, the power set of {A, B, C} contains all its 0-combinations, 1-combinations, 2-combinations, and 3-combinations.

If you're looking for a real-world example in which you would need to generate the power set of a set, imagine a job interviewer asked you to generate the power set of a set. It is astronomically unlikely you'll need to generate the power set of a set for any other reason, including the job you are interviewing for.

To find every power set of a set, we could reuse our existing getCombos() function, calling it repeatedly with each possible *k* argument. This approach is taken by the *powerSetCombinations.py* and *powerSetCombinations.html* programs in the downloadable resources file from *https://nostarch.com/recursive-book-recursion*.

However, we can use a more efficient way to generate power sets. Let's consider the power set of {A, B}, which is {{A, B}, {A}, {B}, { }}. Now say we add one more element, C, to the set and want to generate the power set of {A, B, C}. We have the four sets in the power set of {A, B} we already generated; in addition, we have these same four sets but with the element C added to them: {{A, B, C}, {A, C}, {B, C}, {C}}. Table 6-3 shows the pattern of how adding more elements to a set adds more sets to its power set.

Table 6-3: How Power Sets Grow as New Elements (in Bold) Are Added to the Set

Set with new element	New sets to the power set	Complete power set
{ }	{ }	{{ }}
{A}	{A}	{{ }, **{A}**}
{A, B}	{B}, {A, B}	{{ }, {A}, **{B}**, **{A, B}**}
{A, B, C}	{C}, {A, C}, {B, C}, {A, B, C}	{{ }, {A}, {B}, **{C}**, {A, B}, **{A, C}**, **{B, C}**, **{A, B, C}**}
{A, B, C, D}	{D}, {A, D}, {B, D}, {C, D}, {A, B, D}, {A, C, D}, {B, C, D}, {A, B, C, D}	{{ }, {A}, {B}, {C}, **{D}**, {A, B}, {A, C}, **{A, D}**, {B, C}, **{B, D}**, **{C, D}**, {A, B, C}, {A, B, D}, {A, C, D}, **{B, C, D}**, **{A, B, C, D}**}

The power sets of larger sets are similar to the power sets of smaller sets, hinting that we can create a recursive function to generate them. The base case is an empty set, and its power set is a set of just the empty set. We can use a head-tail technique for this recursive function. For each new element we add, we want to get the power set of the tail to add to our full power set. We also add the head element to each set in the tail power set. Together, these form the full power set for the chars argument.

Let's ask the three recursive algorithm questions about our power set algorithm:

What is the base case?   If chars is the blank string (the empty set), the function returns an array with just a blank string, since the empty set is the only subset of the empty set.

What argument is passed to the recursive function call?   The tail of chars is passed.

How does this argument become closer to the base case?   Since the recursive calls remove the heads from the chars arguments, eventually the chars argument becomes the blank string.

The getPowerSet() recursive function is implemented in *powerSet.py*:

```python
def getPowerSet(chars, indent=0):
    debugMsg = '.' * indent + 'In getPowerSet("' + chars + '")'
    print(debugMsg + ', start.')

❶   if chars == '':
        # BASE CASE
        print(debugMsg + " base case returns ['']")
        return ['']

    # RECURSIVE CASE
    powerSet = []
    head = chars[0]
    tail = chars[1:]

    # First part, get the sets that don't include the head:
    print(debugMsg, "part 1, get sets without head '" + head + "'")
❷   tailPowerSet = getPowerSet(tail, indent + 1)

    # Second part, get the sets that include the head:
    print(debugMsg, "part 2, get sets with head '" + head + "'")
    for tailSet in tailPowerSet:
        print(debugMsg, 'New set', head + tailSet)
❸       powerSet.append(head + tailSet)

    powerSet = powerSet + tailPowerSet
    print(debugMsg, 'returning', powerSet)
❹   return powerSet

print('The power set of ABC:')
print(getPowerSet('ABC'))
```

The equivalent JavaScript code is in *powerSet.html*:

```javascript
<script type="text/javascript">
function getPowerSet(chars, indent) {
    if (indent === undefined) {
        indent = 0;
    }
    let debugMsg = ".".repeat(indent) + 'In getPowerSet("' + chars + '")';
    document.write(debugMsg + ", start.<br />");

    if (chars == "") { ❶
        // BASE CASE
        document.write(debugMsg + " base case returns ['']<br />");
        return [''];
    }

    // RECURSIVE CASE
    let powerSet = [];
    let head = chars[0];
    let tail = chars.slice(1, chars.length);
```

```
    // First part, get the sets that don't include the head:
    document.write(debugMsg +
    " part 1, get sets without head '" + head + "'<br />");
    let tailPowerSet = getPowerSet(tail, indent + 1); ❷

    // Second part, get the sets that include the head:
    document.write(debugMsg +
    " part 2, get sets with head '" + head + "'<br />");
    for (tailSet of tailPowerSet) {
        document.write(debugMsg + " New set " + head + tailSet + "<br />");
        powerSet.push(head + tailSet); ❸
    }

    powerSet = powerSet.concat(tailPowerSet);
    document.write(debugMsg + " returning " + powerSet + "<br />");
    return powerSet; ❹
}

document.write("<pre>The power set of ABC:<br />")
document.write(getPowerSet("ABC") + "<br /></pre>");
</script>
```

The programs output the following:

```
The power set of ABC:
In getPowerSet("ABC"), start.
In getPowerSet("ABC") part 1, get sets without head 'A'
.In getPowerSet("BC"), start.
.In getPowerSet("BC") part 1, get sets without head 'B'
..In getPowerSet("C"), start.
..In getPowerSet("C") part 1, get sets without head 'C'
...In getPowerSet(""), start.
...In getPowerSet("") base case returns ['']
..In getPowerSet("C") part 2, get sets with head 'C'
..In getPowerSet("C") New set C
..In getPowerSet("C") returning ['C', '']
.In getPowerSet("BC") part 2, get sets with head 'B'
.In getPowerSet("BC") New set BC
.In getPowerSet("BC") New set B
.In getPowerSet("BC") returning ['BC', 'B', 'C', '']
In getPowerSet("ABC") part 2, get sets with head 'A'
In getPowerSet("ABC") New set ABC
In getPowerSet("ABC") New set AB
In getPowerSet("ABC") New set AC
In getPowerSet("ABC") New set A
In getPowerSet("ABC") returning ['ABC', 'AB', 'AC', 'A', 'BC', 'B', 'C', '']
['ABC', 'AB', 'AC', 'A', 'BC', 'B', 'C', '']
```

The `getPowerSet()` function accepts a single argument: the string `chars`, which contains the characters of the original set. The base case occurs when `chars` is the blank string ❶, representing an empty set. Recall that the power set is the set of all subsets of the original set. Thus, the power set of the empty set is simply a set containing the empty set, since the empty set is the only subset of the empty set. This is why the base case returns `['']`.

The recursive case is split into two parts. The first part is acquiring the power set of the tail of `chars`. We'll use the leap-of-faith principle and just assume the call to `getPowerSet()` returns the power set of the tail correctly ❷, even though at this point we'd still be in the process of writing the code for `getPowerSet()`.

To form the complete power set of `chars`, the second part of the recursive case forms new sets by adding the head to each of the tail power sets ❸. Together with the sets from the first part, this forms the power set of `chars` to return at the end of the function ❹.

Summary

Permutations and combinations are two problem domains that many programmers don't know how to even begin to approach. While recursion is often an overly complicated solution for common programming problems, it's well suited for the complexity of the tasks in this chapter.

The chapter began with a brief introduction to set theory. This lays the basis for the data structures that our recursive algorithms operate on. A set is a collection of distinct elements. A subset consists of none, some, or all the elements of a set. While sets have no ordering for their elements, a permutation is a specific ordering of the elements in a set. And a combination, which has no ordering, is a specific selection of none, some, or all the elements in a set. A k-combination of a set is a subset of k elements selected from the set.

Permutations and combinations can include an element once or can repeat elements. We call these permutations or combinations without repetition and with repetition, respectively. These are implemented by different algorithms.

This chapter also tackled the balanced parentheses problem that is commonly used in coding interviews. Our algorithm builds the strings of balanced parentheses by starting with a blank string and adding opening and closing parentheses. This approach involves backtracking to earlier strings, making recursion an ideal technique.

Finally, this chapter featured a recursive function for generating power sets—that is, sets of all possible k-combinations of the elements of a set. The recursive function we create to do this is much more efficient than repeatedly calling our combinations function for each possible size of subset.

Further Reading

Generating permutations and combinations only scratches the surface of what you can do with permutations and combinations, as well as the field of mathematical logic known as *set theory*. The following Wikipedia articles provide plenty of further details on these topics, as do the Wikipedia articles that each links to:

- *https://en.wikipedia.org/wiki/Set_theory*
- *https://en.wikipedia.org/wiki/Combination*
- *https://en.wikipedia.org/wiki/Permutation*

The Python standard library comes with implementations of permutation, combination, and other algorithms in its `itertools` module. This module is documented at *https://docs.python.org/3/library/itertools.html*.

Permutations and combinations are also covered in statistics and probability math courses. Khan Academy's unit on counting, permutations, and combinations can be found online at *https://www.khanacademy.org/math/statistics-probability/counting-permutations-and-combinations*.

Practice Questions

Test your comprehension by answering the following questions:

1. Do sets have a specific order for their elements? Do permutations? Do combinations?

2. How many permutations (without repetition) are there of a set of *n* elements?

3. How many combinations (without repetition) are there of a set of *n* elements?

4. Is {A, B, C} a subset of {A, B, C}?

5. What is the formula for calculating *n choose k*, the number of possible combinations of *k* elements selected from a set of *n* elements?

6. Identify which of the following are permutations or combinations, with or without repetition:

    a. AAA, AAB, AAC, ABA, ABB, ABC, ACA, ACB, ACC, BAA, BAB, BAC, BBA, BBB, BBC, BCA, BCB, BCC, CAA, CAB, CAC, CBA, CBB, CBC, CCA, CCB, CCC

    b. ABC, ACB, BAC, BCA, CAB

    c. (None), A, B, C, AB, AC, BC, ABC

    d. (None), A, B, C, AA, AB, AC, BB, BC, CC, AAA, AAB, AAC, ABB, ABC, ACC, BBB, BBC, BCC, CCC

7. Draw a tree graph that can be used to generate all possible combinations of the set {A, B, C, D}.

8. Answer the three questions about recursive solutions for each of the recursive algorithms presented in this chapter:

   a. What is the base case?

   b. What argument is passed to the recursive function call?

   c. How does this argument become closer to the base case?

   Then re-create the recursive algorithms from this chapter without looking at the original code.

Practice Projects

For practice, write a function for the following task:

1. The permutation function in this chapter operates on characters in a string value. Modify it so that the sets are represented by lists (in Python) or arrays (in JavaScript) and the elements can be values of any data type. For example, your new function should be able to generate permutations of integer values, rather than strings.

2. The combination function in this chapter operates on characters in a string value. Modify it so that the sets are represented by lists (in Python) or arrays (in JavaScript) and the elements can be values of any data type. For example, your new function should be able to generate combinations of integer values, rather than strings.

7

MEMOIZATION AND DYNAMIC PROGRAMMING

In this chapter, we'll explore memoization, a technique for making recursive algorithms run faster. We'll discuss what memoization is, how it should be applied, and its usefulness in the areas of functional programming and dynamic programming. We'll use the Fibonacci algorithm from Chapter 2 to demonstrate memoizing code we write and the memoization features we can find in the Python standard library. We'll also learn why memoization can't be applied to every recursive function.

Memoization

Memoization is the technique of remembering the return values from a function for the specific arguments supplied to it. For example, if someone asked me to find the square root of 720, which is the number that when multiplied by itself results in 720, I'd have to sit down with pencil and paper for a few minutes (or call `Math.sqrt(720)` in JavaScript or `math.sqrt(720)` in Python) to figure it out: 26.832815729997478. If they asked me again a few seconds later, I wouldn't have to repeat my calculation because I'd already have the answer at hand. By caching previously calculated results, memoization makes a trade-off to save on execution time by increasing memory usage.

Confusing *memoization* with *memorization* is a modern mistake made by many. (Feel free to make a memo to remind yourself of the difference.)

Top-Down Dynamic Programming

Memoization is a common strategy in *dynamic programming*, a computer programming technique that involves breaking a large problem into overlapping subproblems. This might sound a lot like the ordinary recursion we've already seen. The key difference is that dynamic programming uses recursion with repeated recursive cases; these are the *overlapping* subproblems.

For example, let's consider the recursive Fibonacci algorithm from Chapter 2. Making a recursive `fibonacci(6)` function call will in turn call `fibonacci(5)` and `fibonacci(4)`. Next, `fibonacci(5)` will call `fibonacci(4)` and `fibonacci(3)`. The subproblems of the Fibonacci algorithm overlap, because the `fibonacci(4)` call, and many others, are repeated. This makes generating Fibonacci numbers a dynamic programming problem.

An inefficiency exists here: performing those same calculations multiple times is unnecessary, because `fibonacci(4)` will always return the same thing, the integer 3. Instead, our program could just remember that if the argument to our recursive function is 4, the function should immediately return 3.

Figure 7-1 shows a tree diagram of all the recursive calls, including the redundant function calls that memoization can optimize. Meanwhile, quicksort and merge sort are recursive divide-and-conquer algorithms, but their subproblems do not overlap; they are unique. Dynamic programming techniques aren't applied to these sorting algorithms.

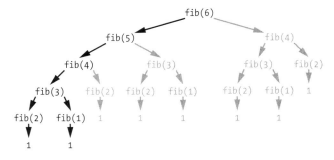

Figure 7-1: A tree diagram of the recursive function calls made starting with `fibonacci(6)`. The redundant function calls are in gray.

One approach in dynamic programming is to memoize the recursive function so that previous calculations are remembered for future function calls. Overlapping subproblems become trivial if we can reuse previous return values.

Using recursion with memoization is called *top-down dynamic programming*. This process takes a large problem and divides it into smaller overlapping subproblems. A contrasting technique, *bottom-up dynamic programming*, starts with the smaller subproblems (often related to the base case) and "builds up" to the solution of the original, large problem. The iterative Fibonacci algorithm, which begins with the base cases of the first and second Fibonacci numbers, is an example of bottom-up dynamic programming. Bottom-up approaches don't use recursive functions.

Note that there is no such thing as top-down recursion or bottom-up recursion. These are commonly used but incorrect terms. All recursion is already top-down, so *top-down recursion* is redundant. And no bottom-up approach uses recursion, so there's no such thing as *bottom-up recursion*.

Memoization in Functional Programming

Not all functions can be memoized. To see why, we must discuss *functional programming*, a programming paradigm that emphasizes writing functions that don't modify global variables or any *external state* (such as files on the hard drive, internet connections, or database contents). Some programming languages, such as Erlang, Lisp, and Haskell, are heavily designed around functional programming concepts. But you can apply functional programming features to almost any programming language, including Python and JavaScript.

Functional programming includes the concepts of deterministic and nondeterministic functions, side effects, and pure functions. The sqrt() function mentioned in the introduction is a *deterministic* function because it always returns the same value when passed the same argument. However, Python's random.randint() function, which returns a random integer, is *nondeterministic* because even when passed the same arguments, it can return different values. The time.time() function, which returns the current time, is also nondeterministic because time is constantly moving forward.

Side effects are any changes a function makes to anything outside of its own code and local variables. To illustrate this, let's create a subtract() function that implements Python's subtraction operator (-):

Python
```
>>> def subtract(number1, number2):
...     return number1 - number2
...
>>> subtract(123, 987)
-864
```

This subtract() function has no side effects; calling this function doesn't affect anything in the program outside of its code. There's no way to tell from the program's or the computer's state whether the subtract() function has been called once, twice, or a million times before. A function might modify local variables inside the function, but these changes are local to the function and remain isolated from the rest of the program.

Now consider an addToTotal() function, which adds the numeric argument to a global variable named TOTAL:

```
>>> TOTAL = 0
>>> def addToTotal(amount):
...     global TOTAL
...     TOTAL += amount
...     return TOTAL
...
>>> addToTotal(10)
10
>>> addToTotal(10)
20
>>> TOTAL
20
```

The addToTotal() function does have a side effect, because it modifies an element that exists outside of the function: the TOTAL global variable.

Side effects can be more than mere changes to global variables. They include updating or deleting files, printing text onscreen, opening a database connection, authenticating to a server, or any other manipulation of data outside of the function. Any trace that a function call leaves behind after returning is a side effect.

If a function is deterministic and has no side effects, it's known as a *pure function*. Only pure functions should be memoized. You'll see why in the next sections when we memoize the recursive Fibonacci function and the impure functions of the doNotMemoize program.

Memoizing the Recursive Fibonacci Algorithm

Let's memoize our recursive Fibonacci function from Chapter 2. Remember that this function is extraordinarily inefficient: on my computer, the recursive fibonacci(40) call takes 57.8 seconds to compute. Meanwhile, an iterative version of fibonacci(40) is literally too fast for my code profiler to measure: 0.000 seconds.

Memoization can greatly speed up the recursive version of the function. For example, Figure 7-2 shows the number of function calls the original and memoized fibonacci() functions make for the first 20 Fibonacci numbers. The original, non-memoized function is doing an extraordinary amount of unnecessary computation.

The number of function calls sharply increases for the original fibonacci() function (top) but only slowly grows for the memoized fibonacci() function (bottom).

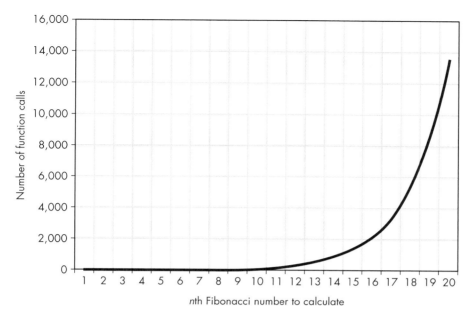

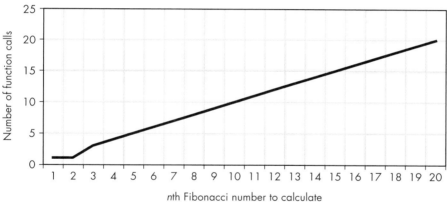

Figure 7-2: The number of function calls sharply increases for the original `fibonacci()` function (top) but grows only slowly for the memoized `fibonacci()` function (bottom).

The Python version of the memoized Fibonacci algorithm is in *fibonacci ByRecursionMemoized.py*. The additions to the original *fibonacciByRecursion .html* program from Chapter 2 have been marked in bold:

```python
fibonacciCache = {} ❶ # Create the global cache.

def fibonacci(nthNumber, indent=0):
    global fibonacciCache
    indentation = '.' * indent
    print(indentation + 'fibonacci(%s) called.' % (nthNumber))
```

```python
    if nthNumber in fibonacciCache:
        # If the value was already cached, return it.
        print(indentation + 'Returning memoized result: %s' % (fibonacciCache[nthNumber]))
        return fibonacciCache[nthNumber] ❷

    if nthNumber == 1 or nthNumber == 2:
        # BASE CASE
        print(indentation + 'Base case fibonacci(%s) returning 1.' % (nthNumber))
        fibonacciCache[nthNumber] = 1 ❸ # Update the cache.
        return 1
    else:
        # RECURSIVE CASE
        print(indentation + 'Calling fibonacci(%s) (nthNumber - 1).' % (nthNumber - 1))
        result = fibonacci(nthNumber - 1, indent + 1)

        print(indentation + 'Calling fibonacci(%s) (nthNumber - 2).' % (nthNumber - 2))
        result = result + fibonacci(nthNumber - 2, indent + 1)

        print('Call to fibonacci(%s) returning %s.' % (nthNumber, result))
        fibonacciCache[nthNumber] = result ❹ # Update the cache.
        return result

print(fibonacci(10))
print(fibonacci(10)) ❺
```

The JavaScript version of the memoized Fibonacci algorithm is in *fibonacci ByRecursionMemoized.html*. The additions to the original *fibonacciByRecursion .html* program from Chapter 2 have been marked in bold:

JavaScript

```javascript
<script type="text/javascript">

❶ let fibonacciCache = {}; // Create the global cache.

function fibonacci(nthNumber, indent) {
    if (indent === undefined) {
        indent = 0;
    }
    let indentation = '.'.repeat(indent);
    document.write(indentation + "fibonacci(" + nthNumber + ") called.
<br />");

    if (nthNumber in fibonacciCache) {
        // If the value was already cached, return it.
        document.write(indentation +
        "Returning memoized result: " + fibonacciCache[nthNumber] + "<br />");
      ❷ return fibonacciCache[nthNumber];
    }

    if (nthNumber === 1 || nthNumber === 2) {
        // BASE CASE
        document.write(indentation +
        "Base case fibonacci(" + nthNumber + ") returning 1.<br />");
      ❸ fibonacciCache[nthNumber] = 1; // Update the cache.
        return 1;
```

```
            } else {
                // RECURSIVE CASE
                document.write(indentation +
                "Calling fibonacci(" + (nthNumber - 1) + ") (nthNumber - 1).<br />");
                let result = fibonacci(nthNumber - 1, indent + 1);

                document.write(indentation +
                "Calling fibonacci(" + (nthNumber - 2) + ") (nthNumber - 2).<br />");
                result = result + fibonacci(nthNumber - 2, indent + 1);

                document.write(indentation + "Returning " + result + ".<br />");
            ❹ fibonacciCache[nthNumber] = result; // Update the cache.
                return result;
            }
        }

    document.write("<pre>");
    document.write(fibonacci(10) + "<br />");
 ❺ document.write(fibonacci(10) + "<br />");
    document.write("</pre>");
    </script>
```

If you compare the output of this program to the original recursive Fibonacci program in Chapter 2, you'll find it's much shorter. This reflects the massive reduction of computation needed to achieve the same results:

```
fibonacci(10) called.
Calling fibonacci(9) (nthNumber - 1).
.fibonacci(9) called.
.Calling fibonacci(8) (nthNumber - 1).
..fibonacci(8) called.
..Calling fibonacci(7) (nthNumber - 1).
--snip--
.......Calling fibonacci(2) (nthNumber - 1).
........fibonacci(2) called.
........Base case fibonacci(2) returning 1.
.......Calling fibonacci(1) (nthNumber - 2).
........fibonacci(1) called.
........Base case fibonacci(1) returning 1.
Call to fibonacci(3) returning 2.
......Calling fibonacci(2) (nthNumber - 2).
.......fibonacci(2) called.
.......Returning memoized result: 1
--snip--
Calling fibonacci(8) (nthNumber - 2).
.fibonacci(8) called.
.Returning memoized result: 21
Call to fibonacci(10) returning 55.
55
fibonacci(10) called.
Returning memoized result: 55
55
```

To memoize this function, we'll create a dictionary (in Python) or object (in JavaScript) in a global variable named `fibonacciCache` ❶. Its keys are the arguments passed for the `nthNumber` parameter, and its values are the integers returned by the `fibonacci()` function given that argument. Every function call first checks if its `nthNumber` argument is already in the cache. If so, the cached return value is returned ❷. Otherwise, the function runs as normal (though it also adds the result to the cache just before the function returns ❸ ❹).

The memoized function is effectively expanding the number of base cases in the Fibonacci algorithm. The original base cases are only for the first and second Fibonacci numbers: they immediately return 1. But every time a recursive case returns an integer, it becomes a base case for all future `fibonacci()` calls with that argument. The result is already in `fibonacciCache` and can be immediately returned. If you've already called `fibonacci(99)` once before, it becomes a base case just like `fibonacci(1)` and `fibonacci(2)`. In other words, memoization improves the performance of recursive functions with overlapping subproblems by increasing the number of base cases. Notice that the second time our program tries to find the 10th Fibonacci number ❺, it immediately returns the memoized result: 55.

Keep in mind that while memoization can reduce the number of redundant function calls a recursive algorithm makes, it doesn't necessarily reduce the growth of frame objects on the call stack. Memoization won't prevent stack overflow errors. Once again, you may be better off forgoing a recursive algorithm for a more straightforward iterative one.

Python's functools Module

Implementing a cache by adding a global variable and code to manage it for every function you'd like to memoize can be quite a chore. Python's standard library has a `functools` module with a function decorator named `@lru_cache()` that automatically memoizes the function it decorates. In Python syntax, this means adding `@lru_cache()` to the line preceding the function's `def` statement.

The cache can have a memory size limit set. The *lru* in the decorator name stands for the *least recently used* cache replacement policy, meaning that the least recently used entry is replaced with new entries when the cache limit is reached. The LRU algorithm is simple and fast, though other cache replacement policies are available for different software requirements.

The *fibonacciFunctools.py* program demonstrates the use of the `@lru_cache()` decorator. The additions to the original *fibonacciByRecursion.py* program from Chapter 2 have been marked in bold:

Python
```
import functools

@functools.lru_cache()
def fibonacci(nthNumber):
    print('fibonacci(%s) called.' % (nthNumber))
```

```
    if nthNumber == 1 or nthNumber == 2:
        # BASE CASE
        print('Call to fibonacci(%s) returning 1.' % (nthNumber))
        return 1
    else:
        # RECURSIVE CASE
        print('Calling fibonacci(%s) (nthNumber - 1).' % (nthNumber - 1))
        result = fibonacci(nthNumber - 1)

        print('Calling fibonacci(%s) (nthNumber - 2).' % (nthNumber - 2))
        result = result + fibonacci(nthNumber - 2)

        print('Call to fibonacci(%s) returning %s.' % (nthNumber, result))
        return result

print(fibonacci(99))
```

Compared to the additions required to implement our own cache in *fibonacciByRecursionMemoized.py*, using Python's @lru_cache() decorator is much simpler. Normally, calculating fibonacci(99) with the recursive algorithm would take a few centuries. With memoization, our program displays the 218922995834555169026 result in a few milliseconds.

Memoization is a useful technique for recursive functions with overlapping subproblems, but it can be applied to any pure function to speed up runtime at the expense of computer memory.

What Happens When You Memoize Impure Functions?

You should not add the @lru_cache to functions that are not pure, meaning they are nondeterministic or have side effects. Memoization saves time by skipping the code in the function and returning the previously cached return value. This is fine for pure functions but can cause various bugs for impure functions.

In nondeterministic functions, such as a function that returns the current time, memoization causes the function to return incorrect results. For functions with side effects, such as printing text to the screen, memoization causes the function to skip the intended side effect. The *doNotMemoize.py* program demonstrates what happens when the @lru_cache function decorator (described in the previous section) memoizes these impure functions:

Python
```
import functools, time, datetime

@functools.lru_cache()
def getCurrentTime():
    # This nondeterministic function returns different values each time
    # it's called.
    return datetime.datetime.now()

@functools.lru_cache()
def printMessage():
    # This function displays a message on the screen as a side effect.
```

```
    print('Hello, world!')

print('Getting the current time twice:')
print(getCurrentTime())
print('Waiting two seconds...')
time.sleep(2)
print(getCurrentTime())

print()

print('Displaying a message twice:')
printMessage()
printMessage()
```

When you run this program, the output looks like this:

```
Getting the current time twice:
2022-07-30 16:25:52.136999
Waiting two seconds...
2022-07-30 16:25:52.136999

Displaying a message twice:
Hello, world!
```

Notice that the second call to getCurrentTime() returns the same result as the first call despite being called two seconds later. And of the two calls to printMessage(), only the first call results in displaying the Hello, world! message on the screen.

These bugs are subtle because they don't cause an obvious crash, but rather cause the functions to behave incorrectly. No matter how you memoize your functions, be sure to thoroughly test them.

Summary

Memoization (not memorization) is an optimization technique that can speed up recursive algorithms that have overlapping subproblems by remembering the previous results of identical calculations. Memoization is a common technique in the field of dynamic programming. By trading computer memory usage for improved runtime, memoization makes some otherwise intractable recursive functions possible.

However, memoization won't prevent stack overflow errors. Keep in mind that memoization is not a replacement for using a simple iterative solution. Code that uses recursion for the sake of recursion is not automatically more elegant than non-recursive code.

Memoized functions must be pure—that is, they must be deterministic (returning the same values given the same arguments each time) and not have side effects (affecting anything about the computer or program outside of the function). Pure functions are often used in functional programming, which is a programming paradigm that makes heavy use of recursion.

Memoization is implemented by creating a data structure called a *cache* for each function to memoize. You can write this code yourself, but Python has a built-in `@functools.lru_cache()` decorator that can automatically memoize the function it decorates.

Further Reading

There's more to dynamic programming algorithms than simply memoizing functions. These algorithms are often used in both coding interviews and programming competitions. Coursera offers a free "Dynamic Programming, Greedy Algorithms" course at *https://www.coursera.org/learn/dynamic-programming-greedy-algorithms*. The freeCodeCamp organization also has a series on dynamic programming at *https://www.freecodecamp.org/news/learn-dynamic-programing-to-solve-coding-challenges*.

If you'd like to learn more about the LRU cache and other cache-related functions, the official Python documentation for the `functools` module is at *https://docs.python.org/3/library/functools.html*. More information about other kinds of cache replacement algorithms is mentioned on Wikipedia at *https://en.wikipedia.org/wiki/Cache_replacement_policies*.

Practice Questions

Test your comprehension by answering the following questions:

1. What is memoization?
2. How do dynamic programming problems differ from regular recursion problems?
3. What does functional programming emphasize?
4. What two characteristics must a function have in order to be a pure function?
5. Is a function that returns the current date and time a deterministic function?
6. How does memoization improve the performance of recursive functions with overlapping subproblems?
7. Would adding the `@lru_cache()` function decorator to a merge sort function improve its performance? Why or why not?
8. Is changing the value in a function's local variable an example of a side effect?
9. Does memoization prevent stack overflows?

8

TAIL CALL OPTIMIZATION

In the previous chapter, we covered using memoization to optimize recursive functions. This chapter explores a technique called *tail call optimization*, which is a feature provided by a compiler or interpreter to avoid stack overflows. Tail call optimization is also called *tail call elimination*, or *tail recursion elimination*.

This chapter is meant to explain tail call optimization, not to endorse it. I would go so far as to recommend *never* using tail call optimization. As you'll see, rearranging your function's code to use tail call optimization often makes it far less understandable. You should consider tail call optimization to be more of a hack or workaround to make recursion work when you shouldn't be using a recursive algorithm in the first place. Remember, a complex recursive solution is not automatically an elegant solution; simple coding problems should be solved with simple non-recursive methods.

Many implementations of popular programming languages don't even offer tail call optimization as a feature. These include interpreters and compilers for Python, JavaScript, and Java. However, tail call optimization is a technique you should become familiar with in case you come across it in the code projects you work on.

How Tail Recursion and Tail Call Optimization Work

To make use of tail call optimization, a function must use *tail recursion*. In tail recursion, the recursive function call is the last action of a recursive function. In code, this looks like a return statement returning the results of a recursive call.

To see this in action, recall the *factorialByRecursion.py* and *factorialByRecursion.html* programs in Chapter 2. These programs calculated the factorial of an integer; for instance, 5! is equivalent to $5 \times 4 \times 3 \times 2 \times 1$, or 120. These calculations can be performed recursively because factorial(n) is equivalent to n * factorial(n - 1), with the base case of n == 1 returning 1.

Let's rewrite these programs to use tail recursion. The following *factorialTailCall.py* program has a factorial() function that uses tail recursion:

Python
```
def factorial(number, accum=1):
    if number == 1:
        # BASE CASE
        return accum
    else:
        # RECURSIVE CASE
        return factorial(number - 1, accum * number)

print(factorial(5))
```

The *factorialTailCall.html* program has the equivalent JavaScript code:

JavaScript
```
<script type="text/javascript">
function factorial(number, accum=1) {
    if (number === 1) {
        // BASE CASE
        return accum;
    } else {
        // RECURSIVE CASE
        return factorial(number - 1, accum * number);
    }
}

document.write(factorial(5));
</script>
```

Notice that the factorial() function's recursive case ends with a return statement returning the results of a recursive call to factorial(). To allow the interpreter or compiler to implement tail call optimization, the last action a recursive function makes must be to return the results of the recursive call. No instructions can occur between making the recursive call and the return statement. The base case returns the accum parameter. This is the accumulator, explained in the next section.

To understand how tail call optimization works, remember from Chapter 1 what happens when a function is called. First, a frame object is created and stored on the call stack. If the function call calls another function, another frame object is created and placed on top of the first frame object on the call stack. When a function returns, your program automatically deletes the frame object from the top of the stack.

A stack overflow happens when too many function calls are made without returning, causing the number of frame objects to exceed the capacity of the call stack. This capacity is 1,000 function calls for Python and about 10,000 for JavaScript programs. While these amounts are more than enough for typical programs, recursive algorithms could exceed this limit and cause a stack overflow that crashes your program.

Recall from Chapter 2 that a frame object stores the local variables in the function call as well as the return address of the instruction to return to when the function finishes. However, if the last action in the recursive case of a function is to return the results of a recursive function call, there's no need to retain the local variables. The function does nothing involving the local variables after the recursive call, so the current frame object can be deleted immediately. The next frame object's return address information can be the same as the old deleted frame object's return address.

Since the current frame object is deleted instead of retained on the call stack, the call stack never grows in size and can never cause a stack overflow!

Recall from Chapter 1 that all recursive algorithms can be implemented with a stack and a loop. Since tail call optimization removes the need for a call stack, we are effectively using recursion to simulate a loop's iterative code. However, earlier in this book I stated that the problems suitable for recursive solutions involve a tree-like data structure and backtracking. Without a call stack, no tail recursive function could possibly do any backtracking work. In my view, every algorithm that can be implemented with tail recursion would be easier and more readable to implement with a loop instead. There's nothing automatically more elegant about using recursion for recursion's sake.

Accumulators in Tail Recursion

The disadvantage of tail recursion is that it requires rearranging your recursive function so that the last action is returning the recursive call's return value. This can make our recursive code even more unreadable. Indeed, the factorial() function in this chapter's *factorialTailCall.py* and *factorialTailCall.html* programs is a bit harder to comprehend than the version in Chapter 2's *factorialByRecursion.py* and *factorialByRecursion.html* programs.

In the case of our tail call factorial() function, a new parameter named accum follows the calculated product as recursive function calls are made. This is known as an *accumulator* parameter, and it keeps track of a partial result of a calculation that would otherwise have been stored in a local variable. Not all tail recursive functions use accumulators, but they act as a workaround for tail recursion's inability to use local variables after the final recursive call. Notice that in *factorialByRecursion.py*'s factorial() function, the recursive case was return number * factorial(number - 1). The multiplication happens after the factorial(number - 1) recursive call. The accum accumulator takes the place of the number local variable.

Also notice that the base case for factorial() no longer returns 1; rather, it returns the accum accumulator. By the time factorial() is called with number == 1 and the base case is reached, accum stores the final result to return. Adjusting your code to use tail call optimization often involves changing the base case to return the accumulator's value.

You can think of the factorial(5) function call as transforming into the following return, as shown in Figure 8-1.

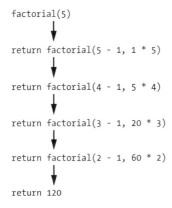

```
factorial(5)

return factorial(5 - 1, 1 * 5)

return factorial(4 - 1, 5 * 4)

return factorial(3 - 1, 20 * 3)

return factorial(2 - 1, 60 * 2)

return 120
```

Figure 8-1: The process of trans-formations that factorial(5) makes to the integer 120

Rearranging your recursive calls as the last action in the function and adding accumulators can make your code even harder to understand than typical recursive code. But that's not the only downside of tail recursion, as we'll see in the next section.

Limitations of Tail Recursion

Tail recursive functions require rearranging their code to make them suitable for the tail call optimization feature of the compiler or interpreter. However, not all compilers and interpreters offer tail call optimization as a feature. Notably, CPython (the Python interpreter downloaded from *https://python.org*) does not implement tail call optimization. Even if you write your recursive functions with the recursive call as the last action, it will still cause stack overflows after enough function calls are made.

Not only that, but CPython will likely never have tail call optimization as a feature. Guido van Rossum, the creator of the Python programming language, has explained that tail call optimization can make programs harder to debug. Tail call optimization removes frame objects from the call stack, which in turn removes the debugging information that frame objects can provide. He also points out that once tail call optimization is implemented, Python programmers will begin to write code that depends on the feature, and their code won't run on non-CPython interpreters that don't implement tail call optimization.

Finally, and I concur, van Rossum disagrees with the idea that recursion is a fundamentally important part of day-to-day programming. Computer scientists and mathematicians tend to place recursion on a pedestal. But tail call optimization is simply a workaround hack to make some recursive algorithms actually workable, rather than simply crashing with a stack overflow.

While CPython doesn't feature tail call optimization, this doesn't mean another compiler or interpreter that implements the Python language couldn't have tail call optimization. Unless tail call optimization is explicitly a part of a programming language specification, it is not a feature of a programming language, but rather of individual compilers or interpreters of a programming language.

The lack of tail call optimization is not unique to Python. The Java compiler since version 8 also doesn't support tail call optimization. Tail call optimization is a part of the ECMAScript 6 version of JavaScript; however, as of 2022, only the Safari web browser's implementation of JavaScript actually supports it. One way to determine whether your programming language's compiler or interpreter implements this feature is to write a tail recursive factorial function and try to calculate the factorial of 100,000. If the program crashes, tail call optimization is not implemented.

Personally, I take the stance that the tail recursion technique should never be used. As stated in Chapter 2, any recursive algorithm can be implemented with a loop and a stack. Tail call optimization prevents stack overflows by effectively removing the use of the call stack. Therefore, all tail recursive algorithms can be implemented with a loop alone. Since the code for loops is much simpler than a recursive function, a loop should be used wherever tail call optimization could be employed.

Additionally, potential problems exist even if tail call optimization is implemented. Since tail recursion is possible only when the last action of a function is returning the recursive call's return value, it's impossible to do tail recursion for algorithms that require two or more recursive calls. For example, take the Fibonacci sequence algorithm calls `fibonacci(n - 1)` and `fibonacci(n - 2)`. While tail call optimization can be performed for the latter recursive call, the first recursive call will cause a stack overflow for large-enough arguments.

Tail Recursion Case Studies

Let's examine some of the recursive functions demonstrated earlier in this book to see if they are good candidates for tail recursion. Keep in mind that because Python and JavaScript do not actually implement tail call optimization, these tail recursive functions will still result in a stack overflow error. These case studies are for demonstration purposes only.

Tail Recursive Reverse String

The first example is the program to reverse a string that we made in Chapter 3. The Python code for this tail recursive function is in *reverse StringTailCall.py*:

Python
```
❶ def rev(theString, accum=''):
       if len(theString) == 0:
           # BASE CASE
       ❷ return accum
       else:
           # RECURSIVE CASE
           head = theString[0]
           tail = theString[1:]
       ❸ return rev(tail, head + accum)

text = 'abcdef'
print('The reverse of ' + text + ' is ' + rev(text))
```

The JavaScript equivalent is in *reverseStringTailCall.html*:

JavaScript
```
   <script type="text/javascript">
❶ function rev(theString, accum='') {
       if (theString.length === 0) {
           // BASE CASE
       ❷ return accum;
       } else {
           // RECURSIVE CASE
           let head = theString[0];
           let tail = theString.substring(1, theString.length);
       ❸ return rev(tail, head + accum);
       }
   }

   let text = "abcdef";
   document.write("The reverse of " + text + " is " + rev(text) + "<br />");
   </script>
```

The conversion of the original recursive functions in *reverseString.py* and *reverseString.html* involves adding an accumulator parameter. The accumulator, named accum, is set to the blank string by default if no argument is passed for it ❶. We also change the base case from return '' to return accum ❷, and the recursive case from return rev(tail) + head (which performs a string concatenation after the recursive call returns) to return rev(tail, head + accum) ❸. You can think of the rev('abcdef') function call as transforming into the following return, as shown in Figure 8-2.

By effectively using the accumulator as a local variable shared across function calls, we can make the rev() function tail recursive.

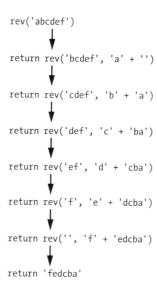

```
rev('abcdef')
      ↓
return rev('bcdef', 'a' + '')
      ↓
return rev('cdef', 'b' + 'a')
      ↓
return rev('def', 'c' + 'ba')
      ↓
return rev('ef', 'd' + 'cba')
      ↓
return rev('f', 'e' + 'dcba')
      ↓
return rev('', 'f' + 'edcba')
      ↓
return 'fedcba'
```

Figure 8-2: The process of trans-
formations that rev('abcdef')
makes to the string fedcba

Tail Recursive Find Substring

Some recursive functions naturally end up using the tail recursion pattern.
If you look at the findSubstringRecursive() function in the *findSubstring.py* and
findSubstring.html programs in Chapter 2, you'll notice that the last action
for the recursive case is to return the value of the recursive function call.
No adjustments are needed to make this function tail recursive.

Tail Recursive Exponents

The *exponentByRecursion.py* and *exponentByRecursion.html* programs, also
from Chapter 2, are not good candidates for tail recursion. These programs have two recursive cases for when the n parameter is even or odd.
This is fine: as long as all the recursive cases return the return value of the
recursive function call as their last action, the function can use tail call
optimization.

However, notice the Python code for the n is even recursive case:

Python
```
--snip--
    elif n % 2 == 0:
        # RECURSIVE CASE (when n is even)
        result = exponentByRecursion(a, n / 2)
        return result * result
--snip--
```

And notice the equivalent JavaScript recursive case:

JavaScript
```
--snip--
    } else if (n % 2 === 0) {
        // RECURSIVE CASE (when n is even)
        result = exponentByRecursion(a, n / 2);
        return result * result;
--snip--
```

This recursive case does not have the recursive call as its last action. We could get rid of the result local variable, and instead call the recursive function twice. This would reduce the recursive case to the following:

```
--snip--
return exponentByRecursion(a, n / 2) * exponentByRecursion(a, n / 2)
--snip--
```

However, now we have two recursive calls to exponentByRecursion(). Not only does this needlessly double the amount of computation the algorithm performs, but the last action performed by the function is to multiply the two return values. This is the same problem the recursive Fibonacci algorithm has: if the recursive function has multiple recursive calls, at least one of those recursive calls can't be the last action of the function.

Tail Recursive Odd-Even

To determine whether an integer is odd or even, you can use the % modulus operator. The expression number % 2 == 0 will be True if number is even, and False if number is odd. However, if you'd prefer to overengineer a more "elegant" recursive algorithm, you can implement the following isOdd() function in *isOdd.py* (the rest of *isOdd.py* is presented later in this section):

Python
```
def isOdd(number):
    if number == 0:
        # BASE CASE
        return False
    else:
        # RECURSIVE CASE
        return not isOdd(number - 1)
print(isOdd(42))
print(isOdd(99))
--snip--
```

The JavaScript equivalent is in *isOdd.html*:

JavaScript
```
<script type="text/javascript">

function isOdd(number) {
    if (number === 0) {
        // BASE CASE
        return false;
```

```
        } else {
            // RECURSIVE CASE
            return !isOdd(number - 1);
        }
    }
    document.write(isOdd(42) + "<br />");
    document.write(isOdd(99) + "<br />");
    --snip--
```

We have two base cases for isOdd(). When the number argument is 0, the function returns False to indicate *even*. For simplicity, our implementation of isOdd() works for only positive integers. The recursive case returns the opposite of isOdd(number - 1).

You can see why this works with an example: when isOdd(42) is called, the function can't determine if 42 is even or odd but does know that the answer is the opposite of whether 41 is odd or even. The function will return not isOdd(41). This function call, in turn, returns the opposite Boolean value of isOdd(40), and so on, until isOdd(0) returns False. The number of recursive function calls determines the number of not operators that act on return values before the final return value is returned.

However, this recursive function results in stack overflows for large-number arguments. Calling isOdd(100000) results in 100,001 function calls without returning—which far exceeds the capacity of any call stack. We can rearrange the code in the function so that the last action of the recursive case is returning the results of the recursive function call, making the function tail recursive. We do this in isOddTailCall() in *isOdd.py*. Here is the rest of the *isOdd.py* program:

Python
```
--snip--
def isOddTailCall(number, inversionAccum=False):
    if number == 0:
        # BASE CASE
        return inversionAccum
    else:
        # RECURSIVE CASE
        return isOddTailCall(number - 1, not inversionAccum)

print(isOddTailCall(42))
print(isOddTailCall(99))
```

The JavaScript equivalent is in the rest of *isOdd.html*:

JavaScript
```
--snip--
function isOddTailCall(number, inversionAccum) {
    if (inversionAccum === undefined) {
        inversionAccum = false;
    }

    if (number === 0) {
        // BASE CASE
        return inversionAccum;
    } else {
```

```
        // RECURSIVE CASE
        return isOddTailCall(number - 1, !inversionAccum);
    }
}

document.write(isOdd(42) + "<br />");
document.write(isOdd(99) + "<br />");
</script>
```

If this Python and JavaScript code is run by an interpreter that supports tail call optimization, calling isOddTailCall(100000) won't result in a stack overflow. However, tail call optimization is still much slower than simply using the % modulus operator to determine oddness or evenness.

If you think recursion, with or without tail recursion, is an incredibly inefficient way to determine whether a positive integer is odd, you are absolutely correct. Unlike iterative solutions, recursion can fail from stack overflows. Adding tail call optimization to prevent stack overflows doesn't fix the efficiency flaws of using recursion inappropriately. As a technique, recursion is not automatically better or more sophisticated than iterative solutions. And tail recursion is never a better approach than a loop or other simple solution.

Summary

Tail call optimization is a feature of a programming language's compiler or interpreter that can be employed on recursive functions specifically written to be tail recursive. Tail recursive functions return the return value of the recursive function call as the last action in the recursive case. This allows the function to delete the current frame object and prevent the call stack from growing as new recursive function calls are made. If the call stack doesn't grow, the recursive function can't possibly cause a stack overflow.

Tail recursion is a workaround that allows some recursive algorithms to work with large arguments without crashing. However, this approach requires rearranging your code and possibly adding an accumulator parameter. This could make your code harder to understand. You may likely find that sacrificing code readability is not worth using a recursive algorithm over an iterative one.

Further Reading

Stack Overflow (the website, not the programming error) has a detailed discussion about the basics of tail recursion at *https://stackoverflow.com/questions/33923/what-is-tail-recursion*.

Van Rossum wrote about his decision not to use tail recursion in two blog posts at *https://neopythonic.blogspot.com.au/2009/04/tail-recursion-elimination.html* and *https://neopythonic.blogspot.com.au/2009/04/final-words-on-tail-calls.html*.

Python's standard library includes a module called inspect that allows you to view the frame objects on the call stack as a Python program is running. The official documentation for the inspect module is at *https://docs .python.org/3/library/inspect.html*, and a tutorial on Doug Hellmann's Python 3 Module of the Week blog is at *https://pymotw.com/3/inspect*.

Practice Questions

Test your comprehension by answering the following questions:

1. What does tail call optimization prevent?
2. What does the last action of a recursive function have to do so that the function can be tail recursive?
3. Do all compilers and interpreters implement tail call optimization?
4. What is an accumulator?
5. What is the disadvantage of tail recursion?
6. Can the quicksort algorithm (covered in Chapter 5) be rewritten to use tail call optimization?

9

DRAWING FRACTALS

Certainly, the most fun application of recursion is drawing fractals. *Fractals* are shapes that repeat themselves, sometimes chaotically, at different scales. The term was coined by the founder of fractal geometry, Benoit B. Mandelbrot, in 1975 and is derived from the Latin *frāctus*, meaning broken or fractured, like shattered glass. Fractals include many natural and artificial shapes. In nature, you might see them in the shapes of trees, fern leaves, mountain ranges, lightning bolts, coastlines, river networks, and snowflakes. Mathematicians, programmers, and artists can create elaborate geometric shapes based on a few recursive rules.

Recursion can produce elaborate fractal art using surprisingly few lines of code. This chapter covers Python's built-in turtle module for generating several common fractals with code. To create turtle graphics with JavaScript, you can use Greg Reimer's jtg library. For simplicity, this chapter presents only the Python fractal drawing programs and not the JavaScript equivalents. However, the jtg JavaScript library is covered in this chapter.

Turtle Graphics

Turtle graphics were a feature of the Logo programming language designed to help kids learn coding concepts. The feature has since been reproduced in many languages and platforms. Its central idea is an object called a *turtle*.

The turtle acts as a programmable pen that draws lines in a 2D window. Imagine an actual turtle holding a pen on the ground, drawing a line behind it as it moves around. The turtle can adjust the size and color of its pen, or "raise the pen" so that it does not draw as it moves. Turtle programs can produce intricate geometric drawings such as Figure 9-1.

When you put these instructions inside loops and functions, even small programs can create impressive geometric drawings. Consider the following *spiral.py* program:

Python
```
import turtle
turtle.tracer(1, 0) # Makes the turtle draw faster.
for i in range(360):
    turtle.forward(i)
    turtle.left(59)
turtle.exitonclick() # Pause until user clicks in the window.
```

When you run this program, the turtle window opens. The turtle (represented by a triangle) will trace the spiral pattern in Figure 9-1. While not a fractal, it is a beautiful drawing.

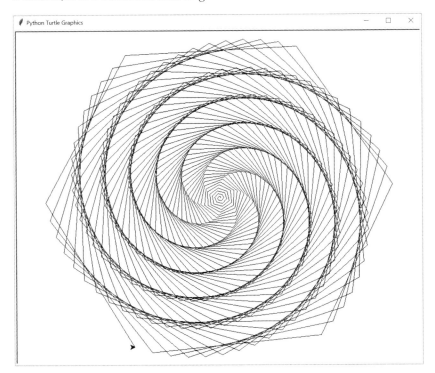

Figure 9-1: The spiral drawn by the program using Python's turtle module

The window in a turtle graphics system uses Cartesian x- and y-coordinates. The number for the horizontal x-coordinate increases going right and decreases going left, while the number for the vertical y-coordinate increases going up and decreases going down. These two coordinates together can provide a unique address for any point in the window. By default, the *origin* (the x, y coordinate point at 0, 0) is in the center of the window.

The turtle also has a *heading*, or direction, that is a number from 0 to 359 (a circle is split into 360 degrees). In Python's turtle module, a heading of 0 faces east (toward the right edge of the screen) and increases clockwise; a heading of 90 faces north, a heading of 180 faces west, and a heading of 270 faces south. In the JavaScript jtg library, this orientation is rotated so that 0 degrees faces north and increases counterclockwise. Figure 9-2 demonstrates the headings for the Python turtle module and the JavaScript jtg library.

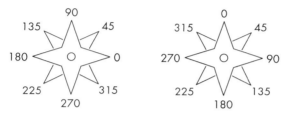

Figure 9-2: The headings in Python's turtle module (left) and the JavaScript jtg library (right)

In the JavaScript jtg library at *https://inventwithpython.com/jtg*, enter the following code into the text field at the bottom of the page:

JavaScript
```
for (let i = 0; i < 360; i++) { t.fd(i); t.lt(59) }
```

This draws the same spiral shown in Figure 9-1 on the main area of the web page.

Basic Turtle Functions

The most commonly used functions in turtle graphics cause the turtle to change heading and move forward or backward. The turtle.left() and turtle.right() functions rotate the turtle a certain number of degrees starting from its current heading, while the turtle.forward() and turtle.backward() functions move the turtle based on its current position.

Table 9-1 lists some of the turtle's functions. The first function (beginning with turtle.) is for Python, and the second (beginning with t.) is for JavaScript. The full Python documentation is available at *https://docs.python.org/3/library/turtle.html*. In the JavaScript jtg software, you can press F1 to display the help screen.

Table 9-1: Turtle Functions in Python's turtle Module and JavaScript's jtg Library

Python	JavaScript	Description
goto(*x*, *y*)	xy(*x*, *y*)	Moves the turtle to the x, y coordinates.
setheading(*deg*)	heading(*deg*)	Sets the turtle's heading. In Python, 0 degrees is east (right). In JavaScript, 0 degrees is north (up).
forward(*steps*)	fd(*steps*)	Moves the turtle a number of steps forward in the heading it is facing.
backward(*steps*)	bk(*steps*)	Moves the turtle a number of steps in the heading opposite from the one it is facing.
left(*deg*)	lt(*deg*)	Turns the turtle's heading to the left.
right(*deg*)	rt(*deg*)	Turns the turtle's heading to the right.
penup()	pu()	"Raises the pen" so that the turtle stops drawing as it moves.
pendown()	pd()	"Lowers the pen" so that the turtle starts drawing as it moves.
pensize(*size*)	thickness(*size*)	Changes the thickness of the lines the turtle draws. The default is 1.
pencolor(*color*)	color(*color*)	Changes the color of the lines the turtle draws. This can be a string of a common color such as red or white. The default is black.
xcor()	get.x()	Returns the turtle's current x position.
ycor()	get.y()	Returns the turtle's current y position.
heading()	get.heading()	Returns the turtle's current heading as a floating-point number from 0 to 359. In Python, 0 degrees is east (right). In JavaScript, 0 degrees is north (up).
reset()	reset()	Clears any drawn lines, and moves the turtle back to the original position and heading.
clear()	clean()	Clears any drawn lines but doesn't move the turtle.

The functions listed in Table 9-2 are available only in the Python turtle module.

Table 9-2: Python-Only Turtle Functions

Python	Description
begin_fill()	Begins drawing a filled-in shape. The lines drawn after this call will specify the perimeter of the filled-in shape.
end_fill()	Draws the filled-in shape that was started with the call to turtle.begin_fill().
fillcolor(*color*)	Sets the color used for filled-in shapes.
hideturtle()	Hides the triangle that represents the turtle.

Python	Description
showturtle()	Shows the triangle that represents the turtle.
tracer(*drawingUpdates*, *delay*)	Adjusts the speed of drawing. Pass 0 for *delay* for a delay of 0 milliseconds after each line the turtle draws. The larger the number passed for *drawingUpdates*, the faster the turtle draws by increasing the number of drawings before the module updates the screen.
update()	Draws any buffered lines (explained later in this section) to the screen. Call this after the turtle has completed drawing.
setworldcoordinates (*llx*, *lly*, *urx*, *ury*)	Readjusts which part of the coordinate plane the window shows. The first two arguments are the x, y coordinates for the lower-left corner of the window. The latter two arguments are the x, y coordinates for the upper-right corner of the window.
exitonclick()	Pauses the program and closes the window when the user clicks anywhere. Without this at the end of your program, the turtle graphics window may close as soon as the program ends.

In Python's turtle module, lines are displayed on the screen immediately. However, this can slow programs that draw thousands of lines. It's faster to *buffer*—that is, hold off displaying several lines and then display them all at once.

By calling turtle.tracer(1000, 0), you can instruct the turtle module to hold off displaying lines until 1,000 lines have been created by your program. After your program has finished calling line-drawing functions, make a final call to turtle.update() to display any remaining buffered lines to the screen. If your program is still taking too long to draw an image, pass a larger integer such as 2000 or 10000 as the first argument to turtle.tracer().

The Sierpiński Triangle

The easiest fractal to draw on paper is the *Sierpiński triangle*, introduced in Chapter 1. This fractal was described by Polish mathematician Wacław Sierpiński in 1915 (predating even the term *fractal*). However, the pattern is at least hundreds of years older.

To create a Sierpiński triangle, start by drawing an equilateral triangle—a triangle with equal-length sides, like the one on the left in Figure 9-3. Then draw an upside-down equilateral triangle inside the first triangle, as on the right in Figure 9-3. You'll form a shape that, if you're familiar with the *Legend of Zelda* video games, looks like the Triforce.

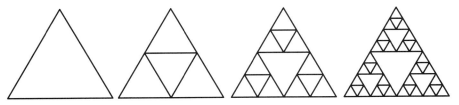

Figure 9-3: An equilateral triangle (left) with an upside-down triangle added to form a Sierpiński triangle, with additional triangles recursively added

An interesting thing happens when you draw the inner, upside-down triangle. You form three new, right-side-up equilateral triangles. Inside each of these three triangles, you can draw another upside-down triangle, which will create nine triangles. This recursion can continue forever mathematically, though in reality your pen won't be able to keep drawing tinier triangles.

This property, describing a full object that is similar to a part of itself, is called *self-similarity*. Recursive functions can produce these objects, since they "call" themselves again and again. Practically, this code must hit a base case eventually, but mathematically, these shapes have infinite resolution: you could theoretically zoom in on the shape forever.

Let's write a recursive program to create the Sierpiński triangle. The recursive drawTriangle() function will draw an equilateral triangle, and then recursively call this function three times to draw the inner equilateral triangles, as in Figure 9-4. The midpoint() function finds the point equidistant from two points passed to the function. This will be important as the inner triangles use these equidistant points for their vertices.

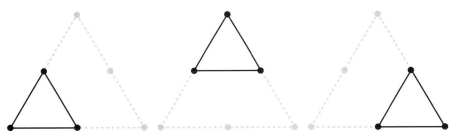

Figure 9-4: The three inner triangles, with midpoints shown with large dots

Note that this program calls turtle.setworldcoordinates(0, 0, 700, 700), which makes the 0, 0 origin at the lower-left corner of the window. The upper-right corner has the x, y coordinates 700, 700. The source code for *sierpinskiTriangle.py* is as follows:

```
import turtle
turtle.tracer(100, 0) # Increase the first argument to speed up the drawing.
turtle.setworldcoordinates(0, 0, 700, 700)
turtle.hideturtle()
```

```
MIN_SIZE = 4 # Try changing this to decrease/increase the amount of recursion.

def midpoint(startx, starty, endx, endy):
    # Return the x, y coordinate in the middle of the four given parameters.
    xDiff = abs(startx - endx)
    yDiff = abs(starty - endy)
    return (min(startx, endx) + (xDiff / 2.0), min(starty, endy) + (yDiff / 2.0))

def isTooSmall(ax, ay, bx, by, cx, cy):
    # Determine if the triangle is too small to draw.
    width = max(ax, bx, cx) - min(ax, bx, cx)
    height = max(ay, by, cy) - min(ay, by, cy)
    return width < MIN_SIZE or height < MIN_SIZE

def drawTriangle(ax, ay, bx, by, cx, cy):
    if isTooSmall(ax, ay, bx, by, cx, cy):
        # BASE CASE
        return
    else:
        # RECURSIVE CASE
        # Draw the triangle.
        turtle.penup()
        turtle.goto(ax, ay)
        turtle.pendown()
        turtle.goto(bx, by)
        turtle.goto(cx, cy)
        turtle.goto(ax, ay)
        turtle.penup()

        # Calculate midpoints between points A, B, and C.
        mid_ab = midpoint(ax, ay, bx, by)
        mid_bc = midpoint(bx, by, cx, cy)
        mid_ca = midpoint(cx, cy, ax, ay)

        # Draw the three inner triangles.
        drawTriangle(ax, ay, mid_ab[0], mid_ab[1], mid_ca[0], mid_ca[1])
        drawTriangle(mid_ab[0], mid_ab[1], bx, by, mid_bc[0], mid_bc[1])
        drawTriangle(mid_ca[0], mid_ca[1], mid_bc[0], mid_bc[1], cx, cy)
        return

# Draw an equilateral Sierpinski triangle.
drawTriangle(50, 50, 350, 650, 650, 50)

# Draw a skewed Sierpinski triangle.
#drawTriangle(30, 250, 680, 600, 500, 80)

turtle.exitonclick()
```

When you run this code, the output looks like Figure 9-5.

Figure 9-5: A standard Sierpiński triangle

Sierpiński triangles don't have to be drawn with equilateral triangles. As long as you use the midpoints of the outer triangle to draw the inner triangles, you can use any kind of triangle. Comment out the first `drawTriangle()` call and uncomment the second one (under the `# Draw a skewed Sierpinski triangle.` comment) and run the program again. The output will look like Figure 9-6.

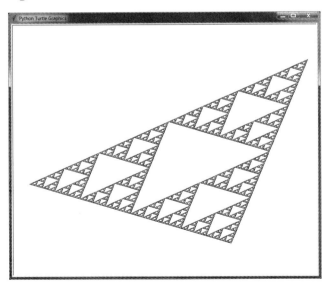

Figure 9-6: A skewed Sierpiński triangle

The `drawTriangle()` function takes six arguments corresponding to the x, y coordinates of the triangle's three points. Try experimenting with different values to adjust the shape of the Sierpiński triangle. You can also change the `MIN_SIZE` constant to a larger value to make the program reach the base case sooner and reduce the number of triangles drawn.

The Sierpiński Carpet

A fractal shape similar to the Sierpiński triangle can be drawn using rectangles instead. This pattern is known as the *Sierpiński carpet*. Imagine splitting a black rectangle into a 3 × 3 grid, then "cutting out" the center rectangle. Repeat this pattern in the surrounding eight rectangles of the grid. When this is done recursively, you end up with a pattern like Figure 9-7.

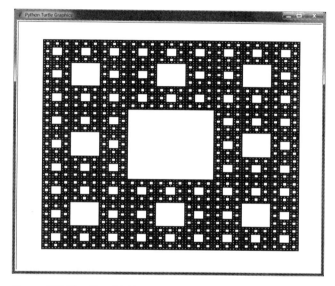

Figure 9-7: The Sierpiński carpet

The Python program that draws the carpet uses the `turtle.begin_fill()` and `turtle.end_fill()` functions to create solid, filled-in shapes. The lines that the turtle draws between these calls are used to draw the shape, as in Figure 9-8.

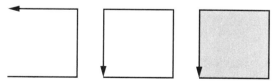

Figure 9-8: Calling turtle.begin_fill(), drawing a path, and calling turtle.end_fill() creates a filled-in shape.

The base case is reached when the rectangles of the 3×3 become smaller than six steps on a side. You can change the MIN_SIZE constant to a larger value to make the program reach the base case sooner. The source code for *sierpinskiCarpet.py* is as follows:

```
import turtle
turtle.tracer(10, 0) # Increase the first argument to speed up the drawing.
turtle.setworldcoordinates(0, 0, 700, 700)
turtle.hideturtle()

MIN_SIZE = 6 # Try changing this to decrease/increase the amount of recursion.
DRAW_SOLID = True

def isTooSmall(width, height):
    # Determine if the rectangle is too small to draw.
    return width < MIN_SIZE or height < MIN_SIZE

def drawCarpet(x, y, width, height):
    # The x and y are the lower-left corner of the carpet.

    # Move the pen into position.
    turtle.penup()
    turtle.goto(x, y)

    # Draw the outer rectangle.
    turtle.pendown()
    if DRAW_SOLID:
        turtle.fillcolor('black')
        turtle.begin_fill()
    turtle.goto(x, y + height)
    turtle.goto(x + width, y + height)
    turtle.goto(x + width, y)
    turtle.goto(x, y)
    if DRAW_SOLID:
        turtle.end_fill()
    turtle.penup()

    # Draw the inner rectangles.
    drawInnerRectangle(x, y, width, height)

def drawInnerRectangle(x, y, width, height):
    if isTooSmall(width, height):
        # BASE CASE
        return
    else:
        # RECURSIVE CASE

        oneThirdWidth = width / 3
        oneThirdHeight = height / 3
        twoThirdsWidth = 2 * (width / 3)
        twoThirdsHeight = 2 * (height / 3)
```

```
    # Move into position.
    turtle.penup()
    turtle.goto(x + oneThirdWidth, y + oneThirdHeight)

    # Draw the inner rectangle.
    if DRAW_SOLID:
        turtle.fillcolor('white')
        turtle.begin_fill()
    turtle.pendown()
    turtle.goto(x + oneThirdWidth, y + twoThirdsHeight)
    turtle.goto(x + twoThirdsWidth, y + twoThirdsHeight)
    turtle.goto(x + twoThirdsWidth, y + oneThirdHeight)
    turtle.goto(x + oneThirdWidth, y + oneThirdHeight)
    turtle.penup()
    if DRAW_SOLID:
        turtle.end_fill()

    # Draw the inner rectangles across the top.
    drawInnerRectangle(x, y + twoThirdsHeight, oneThirdWidth, oneThirdHeight)
    drawInnerRectangle(x + oneThirdWidth, y + twoThirdsHeight, oneThirdWidth,
oneThirdHeight)
    drawInnerRectangle(x + twoThirdsWidth, y + twoThirdsHeight, oneThirdWidth,
oneThirdHeight)

    # Draw the inner rectangles across the middle.
    drawInnerRectangle(x, y + oneThirdHeight, oneThirdWidth,
        oneThirdHeight)
    drawInnerRectangle(x + twoThirdsWidth, y + oneThirdHeight, oneThirdWidth,
        oneThirdHeight)

    # Draw the inner rectangles across the bottom.
    drawInnerRectangle(x, y, oneThirdWidth, oneThirdHeight)
    drawInnerRectangle(x + oneThirdWidth, y, oneThirdWidth, oneThirdHeight)
    drawInnerRectangle(x + twoThirdsWidth, y, oneThirdWidth,
        oneThirdHeight)

drawCarpet(50, 50, 600, 600)
turtle.exitonclick()
```

You can also set the DRAW_SOLID constant to False and run the program. This will skip the calls to turtle.begin_fill() and turtle.end_fill() so that only the outlines of the rectangles are drawn, as in Figure 9-9.

Try passing different arguments to drawCarpet(). The first two arguments are the x, y coordinates of the lower-left corner of the carpet, while the latter two arguments are the width and height. You can also change the MIN_SIZE constant to a larger value to make the program reach the base case sooner and reduce the number of rectangles drawn.

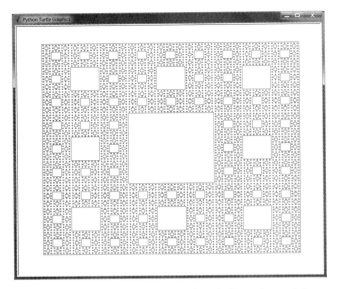

Figure 9-9: The Sierpiński carpet, with only the outlines of the rectangles drawn

Another 3D Sierpiński carpet uses cubes instead of squares. In this form, it is called a *Sierpiński cube*, or *Menger sponge*. It was first described by mathematician Karl Menger in 1926. Figure 9-10 shows a Menger sponge created in the video game *Minecraft*.

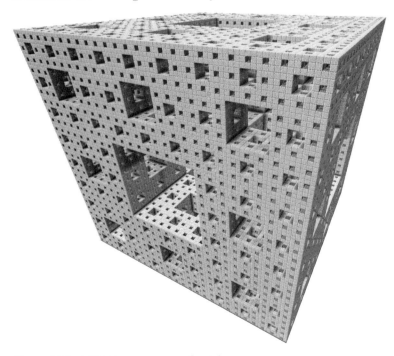

Figure 9-10: A 3D Menger sponge fractal

Fractal Trees

While the artificial fractals such as the Sierpiński triangle and carpet are perfectly self-similar, fractals can include shapes that do not have perfect self-similarity. Fractal geometry, as envisioned by mathematician Benoit B. Mandelbrot (whose middle initial recursively stands for Benoit B. Mandelbrot) included natural shapes such as mountains, coastlines, plants, blood vessels, and the clustering of galaxies as fractals. Upon close examination, these shapes continued to consist of "rougher" shapes not easily contained by the smooth curves and straight lines of simplified geometry.

As an example, we can use recursion to reproduce *fractal trees*, whether perfectly or imperfectly self-similar. Generating trees requires creating a branch with two child branches that issue from their parent at set angles and decrease at set lengths. The Y shape that they produce is recursively repeated to create a convincing drawing of a tree, as in Figures 9-11 and 9-12.

Figure 9-11: A perfectly self-similar fractal tree generated with the left and right branches using consistent angles and lengths

Movies and video games can use such recursive algorithms in *procedural generation*, the automatic (rather than manual) creation of 3D models such as trees, ferns, flowers, and other plants. Using algorithms, computers can quickly create entire forests consisting of millions of unique trees, saving an army of human 3D artists the painstaking effort.

Figure 9-12: A more realistic tree created using random changes to branch angle and lengths

Our fractal tree program displays a new, randomly generated tree every two seconds. The source code for *fractalTree.py* is as follows:

Python
```
import random
import time
import turtle
turtle.tracer(1000, 0) # Increase the first argument to speed up the drawing.
turtle.setworldcoordinates(0, 0, 700, 700)
turtle.hideturtle()

def drawBranch(startPosition, direction, branchLength):
    if branchLength < 5:
        # BASE CASE
        return

    # Go to the starting point & direction.
    turtle.penup()
    turtle.goto(startPosition)
    turtle.setheading(direction)

    # Draw the branch (thickness is 1/7 the length).
    turtle.pendown()
    turtle.pensize(max(branchLength / 7.0, 1))
    turtle.forward(branchLength)

    # Record the position of the branch's end.
    endPosition = turtle.position()
    leftDirection = direction + LEFT_ANGLE
    leftBranchLength = branchLength - LEFT_DECREASE
    rightDirection = direction - RIGHT_ANGLE
    rightBranchLength = branchLength - RIGHT_DECREASE
```

```
    # RECURSIVE CASE
    drawBranch(endPosition, leftDirection, leftBranchLength)
    drawBranch(endPosition, rightDirection, rightBranchLength)

seed = 0
while True:
    # Get pseudorandom numbers for the branch properties.
    random.seed(seed)
    LEFT_ANGLE      = random.randint(10,  30)
    LEFT_DECREASE   = random.randint( 8,  15)
    RIGHT_ANGLE     = random.randint(10,  30)
    RIGHT_DECREASE  = random.randint( 8,  15)
    START_LENGTH    = random.randint(80, 120)

    # Write out the seed number.
    turtle.clear()
    turtle.penup()
    turtle.goto(10, 10)
    turtle.write('Seed: %s' % (seed))

    # Draw the tree.
    drawBranch((350, 10), 90, START_LENGTH)
    turtle.update()
    time.sleep(2)

    seed = seed + 1
```

This program produces perfectly self-similar trees, as the LEFT_ANGLE, LEFT_DECREASE, RIGHT_ANGLE, and RIGHT_DECREASE variables are initially randomly chosen but stay constant for all the recursive calls. The random.seed() function sets a seed value for Python's random functions. The *random number seed value* causes the program to produce random-seeming numbers, but it uses the same sequence of random numbers for each branch of the tree. In other words, the same *seed* value reproduces the same *tree* each time you run the program. (I never apologize for my puns.)

To see this in action, enter the following into the Python interactive shell:

Python
```
>>> import random
>>> random.seed(42)
>>> [random.randint(0, 9) for i in range(20)]
[1, 0, 4, 3, 3, 2, 1, 8, 1, 9, 6, 0, 0, 1, 3, 3, 8, 9, 0, 8]
>>> [random.randint(0, 9) for i in range(20)]
[3, 8, 6, 3, 7, 9, 4, 0, 2, 6, 5, 4, 2, 3, 5, 1, 1, 6, 1, 5]
>>> random.seed(42)
>>> [random.randint(0, 9) for i in range(20)]
[1, 0, 4, 3, 3, 2, 1, 8, 1, 9, 6, 0, 0, 1, 3, 3, 8, 9, 0, 8]
```

In this example, we set the random seed to 42. When we generate 20 random integers, we get 1, 0, 4, 3, and so on. We can generate another 20 integers and continue to receive random integers. However, if we reset the seed to 42 and generate 20 random integers again, they'll be the same "random" integers as before.

If you'd like to create a more natural, less self-similar tree, replace the lines after the `# Record the position of the branch's end.` comment with the following lines. This generates new random angles and branch lengths for *every* recursive call, which is closer to the way trees grow in nature:

Python

```python
# Record the position of the branch's end.
endPosition = turtle.position()
leftDirection = direction + random.randint(10, 30)
leftBranchLength = branchLength - random.randint(8, 15)
rightDirection = direction - random.randint(10, 30)
rightBranchLength = branchLength - random.randint(8, 15)
```

You can experiment with different ranges for the `random.randint()` call, or try adding more recursive calls instead of just the two for the two branches.

How Long Is the Coast of Great Britain? The Koch Curve and Snowflake

Before I tell you about the Koch curve and snowflake, consider this question: how long is the coast of Great Britain? Look at Figure 9-13. The map on the left has a rough measure, which puts the coast at about 2,000 miles. But the map on the right has a more precise measure, which includes more nooks and crannies of the coast and comes to about 2,800 miles.

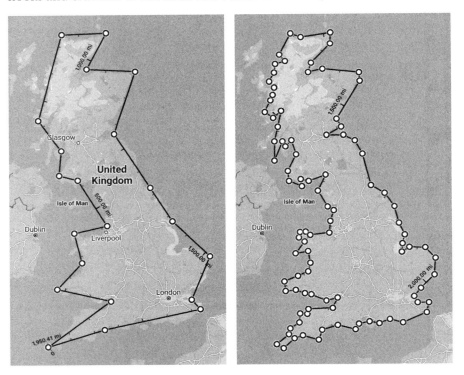

Figure 9-13: The island of Great Britain, with a rough measure (left) and more precise measure (right). Measuring the coast more precisely adds 800 miles to its length.

Mandelbrot's key insight about fractals such as the coastline of Britain is that you can continue to look closer and closer, and there will continue to be "roughness" at every scale. So, as your measurement gets finer and finer, the length of the coastline will get longer and longer. The "coast" will follow the Thames upriver, deep into the landmass along one bank and back out to the English Channel on the other bank. Thus, the answer to our question of Great Britain's coastline's length is, "It depends."

The *Koch curve* fractal has a similar property pertaining to the length of its coastline, or rather, perimeter. First introduced in 1902 by Swedish mathematician Helge von Koch, the Koch curve is one of the earliest fractals to be described mathematically. To construct it, take a line of length b and divide it into three equal parts, each of length $b / 3$. Replace the middle section with a "bump" whose sides are also of length $b / 3$. This bump causes the Koch curve to be longer than the original line, since we now have four line segments of length $b / 3$. (We'll exclude the original middle part of the line segment.) This bump creation can be repeated on the new four line segments. Figure 9-14 shows this construction.

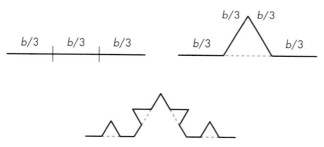

Figure 9-14: After splitting the line segment into three equal parts (left), add a bump to the middle part (right). We now have four segments of length b / 3, to which bumps can be added again (bottom).

To create the *Koch snowflake*, we start with an equilateral triangle and construct three Koch curves from its three sides, as in Figure 9-15.

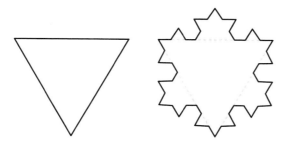

Figure 9-15: Creating three Koch curves on the three sides of an equilateral triangle to form a Koch snowflake

Each time you create a new bump, you are increasing the curve's length from three $b / 3$ lengths to four $b / 3$ lengths, or $4b / 3$. If you continue to do this with the three sides of an equilateral triangle, you'll create the Koch snowflake, as in Figure 9-16. (The small dotted patterns are artifacts, because slight rounding errors cause the turtle module to be unable to completely erase the middle $b / 3$ segment.) You can continue to create new bumps forever, though our program stops when they get smaller than a few pixels.

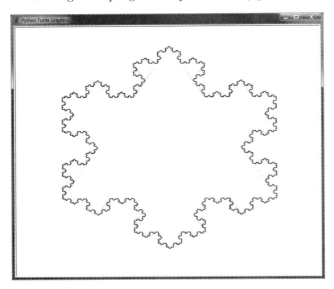

Figure 9-16: A Koch snowflake. Some of the interior lines remain because of small rounding errors.

The source code for *kochSnowflake.py* is as follows:

Python
```python
import turtle
turtle.tracer(10, 0) # Increase the first argument to speed up the drawing.
turtle.setworldcoordinates(0, 0, 700, 700)
turtle.hideturtle()
turtle.pensize(2)

def drawKochCurve(startPosition, heading, length):
    if length < 1:
        # BASE CASE
        return
    else:
        # RECURSIVE CASE
        # Move to the start position.
        recursiveArgs = []
        turtle.penup()
        turtle.goto(startPosition)
        turtle.setheading(heading)
        recursiveArgs.append({'position':turtle.position(),
                              'heading':turtle.heading()})

        # Erase the middle third.
        turtle.forward(length / 3)
        turtle.pencolor('white')
        turtle.pendown()
```

```
        turtle.forward(length / 3)

        # Draw the bump.
        turtle.backward(length / 3)
        turtle.left(60)
        recursiveArgs.append({'position':turtle.position(),
                              'heading':turtle.heading()})
        turtle.pencolor('black')
        turtle.forward(length / 3)
        turtle.right(120)
        recursiveArgs.append({'position':turtle.position(),
                              'heading':turtle.heading()})
        turtle.forward(length / 3)
        turtle.left(60)
        recursiveArgs.append({'position':turtle.position(),
                              'heading':turtle.heading()})

        for i in range(4):
            drawKochCurve(recursiveArgs[i]['position'],
                    recursiveArgs[i]['heading'],
                    length / 3)
        return

def drawKochSnowflake(startPosition, heading, length):
    # A Koch snowflake is three Koch curves in a triangle.

    # Move to the starting position.
    turtle.penup()
    turtle.goto(startPosition)
    turtle.setheading(heading)

    for i in range(3):
        # Record the starting position and heading.
        curveStartingPosition = turtle.position()
        curveStartingHeading = turtle.heading()
        drawKochCurve(curveStartingPosition,
                    curveStartingHeading, length)

        # Move back to the start position for this side.
        turtle.penup()
        turtle.goto(curveStartingPosition)
        turtle.setheading(curveStartingHeading)

        # Move to the start position of the next side.
        turtle.forward(length)
        turtle.right(120)

drawKochSnowflake((100, 500), 0, 500)
turtle.exitonclick()
```

The Koch snowflake is also sometimes called the *Koch island*. Its coastline would be literally infinitely long. While the Koch snowflake fits into the
finite area of a page of this book, the length of its perimeter is infinite, prov-
ing that, while it seems counterintuitive, the finite can contain the infinite!

The Hilbert Curve

A *space-filling curve* is a 1D line that curves around until it completely fills a 2D space without crossing over itself. German mathematician David Hilbert described his space-filling *Hilbert curve* in 1891. If you split a 2D area into a grid, the single, 1D line of the Hilbert curve can run through every cell in the grid.

Figure 9-17 contains the first three recursions of the Hilbert curve. The next recursion contains four copies of the previous recursion, and the dashed line shows how the four copies connect to one another.

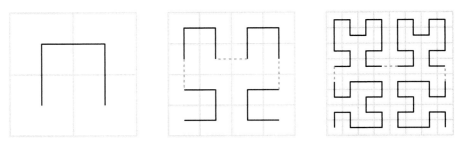

Figure 9-17: The first three recursions of the Hilbert space-filling curve

As the cells become infinitesimal points, the 1D curve can fill the entire 2D space the same way a 2D square does. Counterintuitively, this creates a 2D shape from a strictly 1D line!

The source code for *hilbertCurve.py* is as follows:

Python
```
import turtle
turtle.tracer(10, 0) # Increase the first argument to speed up the drawing.
turtle.setworldcoordinates(0, 0, 700, 700)
turtle.hideturtle()

LINE_LENGTH  = 5 # Try changing the line length by a little.
ANGLE = 90 # Try changing the turning angle by a few degrees.
LEVELS = 6 # Try changing the recursive level by a little.
DRAW_SOLID = False
#turtle.setheading(20) # Uncomment this line to draw the curve at an angle.

def hilbertCurveQuadrant(level, angle):
    if level == 0:
        # BASE CASE
        return
    else:
        # RECURSIVE CASE
        turtle.right(angle)
        hilbertCurveQuadrant(level - 1, -angle)
        turtle.forward(LINE_LENGTH)
```

```
        turtle.left(angle)
        hilbertCurveQuadrant(level - 1, angle)
        turtle.forward(LINE_LENGTH)
        hilbertCurveQuadrant(level - 1, angle)
        turtle.left(angle)
        turtle.forward(LINE_LENGTH)
        hilbertCurveQuadrant(level - 1, -angle)
        turtle.right(angle)
        return

def hilbertCurve(startingPosition):
    # Move to starting position.
    turtle.penup()
    turtle.goto(startingPosition)
    turtle.pendown()
    if DRAW_SOLID:
        turtle.begin_fill()

    hilbertCurveQuadrant(LEVELS, ANGLE) # Draw lower-left quadrant.
    turtle.forward(LINE_LENGTH)

    hilbertCurveQuadrant(LEVELS, ANGLE) # Draw lower-right quadrant.
    turtle.left(ANGLE)
    turtle.forward(LINE_LENGTH)
    turtle.left(ANGLE)

    hilbertCurveQuadrant(LEVELS, ANGLE) # Draw upper-right quadrant.
    turtle.forward(LINE_LENGTH)

    hilbertCurveQuadrant(LEVELS, ANGLE) # Draw upper-left quadrant.

    turtle.left(ANGLE)
    turtle.forward(LINE_LENGTH)
    turtle.left(ANGLE)
    if DRAW_SOLID:
        turtle.end_fill()

hilbertCurve((30, 350))
turtle.exitonclick()
```

Try experimenting with this code by decreasing LINE_LENGTH to shorten the line segments while increasing LEVELS to add more levels of recursion. Because this program uses only relative movements for the turtle, you can uncomment the turtle.setheading(20) line to draw the Hilbert curve at a 20-degree angle. Figure 9-18 shows the drawing produced with LINE_LENGTH of 10 and LEVELS of 5.

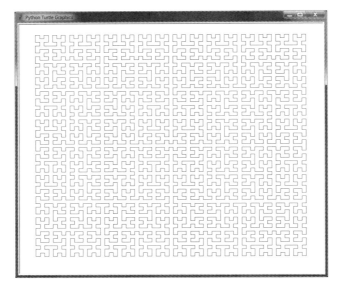

Figure 9-18: Five levels of the Hilbert curve, with line length 10

The Hilbert curve makes 90-degree (right-angle) turns. But try adjusting the ANGLE variable by a few degrees to 89 or 86, and run the program to view the changes. You can also set the DRAW_SOLID variable to True to produce a filled-in Hilbert curve, as in Figure 9-19.

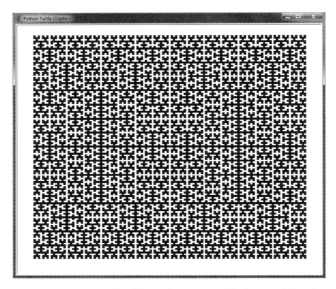

Figure 9-19: Six levels of the Hilbert curve, filled in, with line length 5

Summary

The incredibly wide field of fractals combines all the most interesting parts of programming and art, making this chapter the most fun to write. Mathematicians and computer scientists talk about the beauty and elegance that the advanced topics of their fields produce, but recursive fractals are able to turn this conceptual beauty into visual beauty that anyone can appreciate.

This chapter covered several fractals and the programs that draw them: the Sierpiński triangle, the Sierpiński carpet, procedurally generated fractal trees, the Koch curve and snowflake, and the Hilbert curve. All of these were drawn with Python's turtle module and functions that recursively call themselves.

Further Reading

To learn more about drawing with Python's turtle module, I've written a simple tutorial at *https://github.com/asweigart/simple-turtle-tutorial-for-python*. I also have a personal collection of turtle programs at *https://github.com/asweigart/art-of-turtle-programming*.

The question of Great Britain's coastline's length came from the title of a 1967 paper by Mandelbrot. The idea is summarized nicely on Wikipedia at *https://en.wikipedia.org/wiki/Coastline_paradox*. Khan Academy has more on the geometry of the Koch snowflake at *https://www.khanacademy.org/math/geometry-home/geometry-volume-surface-area/koch-snowflake/v/koch-snowflake-fractal*.

The 3Blue1Brown YouTube channel has excellent animations of fractals, particularly the "Fractals Are Typically Not Self-Similar" video at *https://youtu.be/gB9n2gHsHN4* and the "Fractal Charm: Space-Filling Curves" video at *https://youtu.be/RU0wScIj36o*.

Other space-filling curves require recursion to draw, such as the Peano curve, Gosper curve, and dragon curve, and they're worth researching on the web.

Practice Questions

Test your comprehension by answering the following questions:

1. What are fractals?
2. What do the x- and y-coordinates represent in a Cartesian coordinate system?
3. What are the origin coordinates in a Cartesian coordinate system?
4. What is procedural generation?
5. What is a seed value?
6. How long is the perimeter of a Koch snowflake?
7. What is a space-filling curve?

Practice Projects

For practice, write a program for each of the following tasks:

1. Create a turtle program that draws a box fractal as shown in Figure 9-20. This program is similar to the Sierpiński carpet program introduced in this chapter. Use the turtle.begin_fill() and turtle.end_fill() functions to draw the first large, black square. Then split this square into nine equal sections, and draw white squares in the top, left, right, and bottom squares. Repeat this process for the four corner squares and the center square.

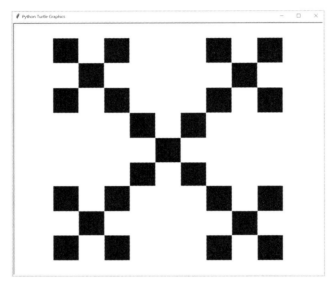

Figure 9-20: A box fractal, drawn to two levels

2. Create a turtle program that draws a Peano space-filling curve. This is similar to the Hilbert curve program in this chapter. Figure 9-21 shows the first three iterations of the Peano curve. While each Hilbert curve iteration is split across a 2×2 section (which is, in turn, split into 2×2 sections), the Peano curve is split across 3×3 sections.

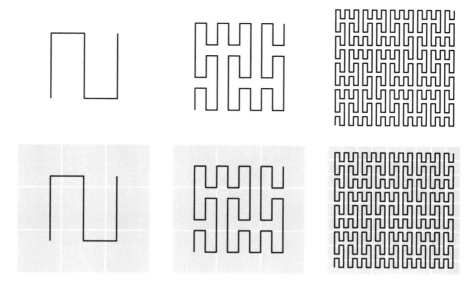

Figure 9-21: The first three iterations of the Peano curve, from left to right. The bottom row includes the 3 × 3 sections that each part of the curve is split across.

PART II

PROJECTS

10

FILE FINDER

In this chapter, you'll write your own recursive program to search for files according to custom needs. Your computer already has some file-searching commands and apps, but often they're limited to retrieving files based on a partial filename. What if you need to make esoteric, highly specific searches? For example, what if you need to find all files that have an even number of bytes, or files with names that contain every vowel?

You likely will never need to do these searches specifically, but you'll probably have odd search criteria someday. You'll be out of luck if you can't code this search yourself.

As you've learned, recursion is especially suited to problems that have a tree-like structure. The filesystem on your computer is like a tree, as you saw back in Figure 2-6. Each folder branches into subfolders, which in turn can branch into other subfolders. We'll write a recursive function to navigate this tree.

 Since browser-based JavaScript has no way to access the folders on your computer, the program for this chapter's project is written in Python only.

The Complete File-Search Program

Let's begin by taking a look at the complete source code for the recursive file-search program. The rest of this chapter explains each section of code individually. Copy the source code for the file-search program to a file named *fileFinder.py*:

```python
import os

def hasEvenByteSize(fullFilePath):
    """Returns True if fullFilePath has an even size in bytes,
    otherwise returns False."""
    fileSize = os.path.getsize(fullFilePath)
    return fileSize % 2 == 0


def hasEveryVowel(fullFilePath):
    """Returns True if the fullFilePath has a, e, i, o, and u,
    otherwise returns False."""
    name = os.path.basename(fullFilePath).lower()
    return ('a' in name) and ('e' in name) and ('i' in name) and ('o' in name) and ('u' in name)


def walk(folder, matchFunc):
    """Calls the match function with every file in the folder and its
    subfolders. Returns a list of files that the match function
    returned True for."""
    matchedFiles = [] # This list holds all the matches.
    folder = os.path.abspath(folder) # Use the folder's absolute path.

    # Loop over every file and subfolder in the folder:
    for name in os.listdir(folder):
        filepath = os.path.join(folder, name)
        if os.path.isfile(filepath):
            # Call the match function for each file:
            if matchFunc(filepath):
                matchedFiles.append(filepath)
        elif os.path.isdir(filepath):
            # Recursively call walk for each subfolder, extending
            # the matchedFiles with their matches:
            matchedFiles.extend(walk(filepath, matchFunc))
    return matchedFiles
```

```
print('All files with even byte sizes:')
print(walk('.', hasEvenByteSize))
print('All files with every vowel in their name:')
print(walk('.', hasEveryVowel))
```

The file-search program's main function is walk(), which "walks" across the entire span of files in a base folder and its subfolders. It calls one of two other functions that implement the custom search criteria it's looking for. In the context of this program, we'll call these *match functions*. A match function call returns True if the file matches the search criteria; otherwise, it returns False.

The job of the walk() function is to call the match function once for each file in the folders it walks across. Let's take a look at the code in more detail.

The Match Functions

In Python, you can pass functions themselves as arguments to a function call. In the following example, a callTwice() function calls its function argument twice, whether it's sayHello() or sayGoodbye():

Python
```
>>> def callTwice(func):
...     func()
...     func()
...
>>> def sayHello():
...     print('Hello!')
...
>>> def sayGoodbye():
...     print('Goodbye!')
...
>>> callTwice(sayHello)
Hello!
Hello!
>>> callTwice(sayGoodbye)
Goodbye!
Goodbye!
```

The callTwice() function calls whichever function was passed to it as the func parameter. Notice that we leave out the parentheses from the function argument, writing callTwice(sayHello) instead of callTwice(sayHello()). This is because we are passing the sayHello() function itself, and not calling sayHello() and passing its return value.

The walk() function accepts a match function argument for its search criteria. This lets us customize the behavior of the file search without modifying the code of the walk() function itself. We'll take a look at walk() later. First, let's look at the two sample match functions in the program.

Finding the Files with an Even Number of Bytes

The first matching function finds files with an even byte size:

Python
```
import os

def hasEvenByteSize(fullFilePath):
    """Returns True if fullFilePath has an even size in bytes,
    otherwise returns False."""
    fileSize = os.path.getsize(fullFilePath)
    return fileSize % 2 == 0
```

We import the os module, which is used throughout the program to get information about the files on your computer through functions such as getsize(), basename(), and others. Then we create a match function named hasEvenByteSize(). All match functions take a single string argument named fullFilePath, and return either True or False to signify a match or miss.

The os.path.getsize() function determines the size of the file in fullFilePath in bytes. Then we use the % modulus operator to determine whether this number is even. If it's even, the return statement returns True; if it's odd, it returns False. For example, let's consider the size of the Notepad application that comes with the Windows operating system (on macOS or Linux, try running this function on the */bin/ls* program):

Python
```
>>> import os
>>> os.path.getsize('C:/Windows/system32/notepad.exe')
211968
>>> 211968 % 2 == 0
True
```

The hasEvenByteSize() match function can use any Python function to find more information about the fullFilePath file. This gives you the powerful capability to write code for any search criteria you want. As walk() calls the match function for each file in the folder and subfolders it walks across, the match function returns True or False for each one. This tells walk() whether the file is a match.

Finding the Filenames That Contain Every Vowel

Let's take a look at the next match function:

```
def hasEveryVowel(fullFilePath):
    """Returns True if the fullFilePath has a, e, i, o, and u,
    otherwise returns False."""
    name = os.path.basename(fullFilePath).lower()
    return ('a' in name) and ('e' in name) and ('i' in name) and ('o' in name) and ('u' in
name)
```

We call os.path.basename() to remove the folder names from the filepath. Python does case-sensitive string comparisons, which ensures that hasEvery Vowel() doesn't miss any vowels in the filename because they are uppercase. For example, calling os.path.basename('C:/Windows/system32/notepad.exe') returns the string notepad.exe. This string's lower() method call returns a lowercase form of the string so that we have to check for only lowercase vowels in it. "Useful Python Standard Library Functions for Working with Files" later in this chapter explores some more functions for finding out information about files.

We use a return statement with a lengthy expression that evaluates to True if name contains a, e, i, o, or u, indicating the file matches the search criteria. Otherwise, the return statement returns False.

The Recursive walk() Function

While the match functions check whether a file matches the search criteria, the walk() function finds all the files to check. The recursive walk() function is passed the name of a base folder to search along with a match function to call for each file in the folder.

The walk() function also recursively calls itself for each subfolder in the base folder it's searching. These subfolders become the base folder in the recursive call. Let's ask the three questions about this recursive function:

What is the base case?   When the function has finished processing each file and subfolder in its given base folder.

What argument is passed to the recursive function call?   The base folder to search and the match function to use for finding matched files. For each subfolder in this folder, a recursive call is made with the subfolder as the new folder argument.

How does this argument become closer to the base case?   Eventually, the function either recursively calls itself on all the subfolders or encounters base folders that don't have any subfolders.

Figure 10-1 shows an example filesystem along with the recursive calls to walk(), which it makes with a base folder of C:\.

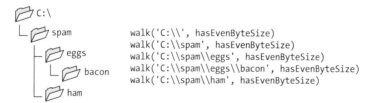

Figure 10-1: An example filesystem and the recursive walk() function calls over it

Let's take a look at the walk() function's code:

```
def walk(folder, matchFunc):
    """Calls the match function with every file in the folder and its
    subfolders. Returns a list of files that the match function
    returned True for."""
    matchedFiles = [] # This list holds all the matches.
    folder = os.path.abspath(folder) # Use the folder's absolute path.
```

The walk() function has two parameters: folder is a string of the base folder to search (we can pass '.' to refer to the current folder the Python program is run from), and matchFunc is a Python function that is passed a filename and returns True if the function says it is a search match. Otherwise, the function returns False.

The next part of the function examines the contents of folder:

Python
```
# Loop over every file and subfolder in the folder:
for name in os.listdir(folder):
    filepath = os.path.join(folder, name)
    if os.path.isfile(filepath):
```

The for loop calls os.listdir() to return a list of the contents of the folder folder. This list includes all files and subfolders. For each file, we create the full, absolute path by joining the folder with the name of the file or folder. If the name refers to a file, the os.path.isfile() function call returns True, and we'll check to see if the file is a search match:

Python
```
        # Call the match function for each file:
        if matchFunc(filepath):
            matchedFiles.append(filepath)
```

We call the match function, passing it the full absolute filepath of the for loop's current file. Note that matchFunc is the name of one of walk()'s parameters. If hasEvenByteSize(), hasEveryVowel(), or another function is passed as the argument for the matchFunc parameter, then that is the function walk() calls. If filepath contains a file that is a match according to the matching algorithm, it's added to the matches list:

Python
```
    elif os.path.isdir(filepath):
        # Recursively call walk for each subfolder, extending
        # the matchedFiles with their matches:
        matchedFiles.extend(walk(filepath, matchFunc))
```

Otherwise, if the for loop's file is a subfolder, the os.path.isdir() function call returns True. We then pass the subfolder to a recursive function call. The recursive call returns a list of all matching files in the subfolder (and its subfolders), which are then added to the matches list:

```
    return matchedFiles
```

After the for loop finishes, the matches list contains all the matching files in this folder (and in all its subfolders). This list becomes the return value for the walk() function.

Calling the walk() Function

Now that we've implemented the walk() function and some match functions, we can run our custom file search. We pass the '.' string, a special directory name meaning *the current directory*, for the first argument to walk() so that it uses the folder the program was run from as the base folder to search:

```python
print('All files with even byte sizes:')
print(walk('.', hasEvenByteSize))
print('All files with every vowel in their name:')
print(walk('.', hasEveryVowel))
```

The output of this program depends on what files are on your computer, but this demonstrates how you can write code for any search criteria you have. For example, the output could look like the following:

```
All files with even byte sizes:
['C:\\Path\\accesschk.exe', 'C:\\Path\\accesschk64.exe',
'C:\\Path\\AccessEnum.exe', 'C:\\Path\\ADExplorer.exe',
'C:\\Path\\Bginfo.exe', 'C:\\Path\\Bginfo64.exe',
'C:\\Path\\diskext.exe', 'C:\\Path\\diskext64.exe',
'C:\\Path\\Diskmon.exe', 'C:\\Path\\DiskView.exe',
'C:\\Path\\hex2dec64.exe', 'C:\\Path\\jpegtran.exe',
'C:\\Path\\Tcpview.exe', 'C:\\Path\\Testlimit.exe',
'C:\\Path\\wget.exe', 'C:\\Path\\whois.exe']
All files with every vowel in their name:
['C:\\Path\\recursionbook.bat']
```

Useful Python Standard Library Functions for Working with Files

Let's take a look at some functions that could help you as you write your own match functions. The standard library of modules that comes with Python features several useful functions for getting information about files. Many of these are in the os and shutil modules, so your program must run import os or import shutil before it can call these functions.

Finding Information About the File's Name

The full filepath passed to the match functions can be broken into the base name and directory name with the os.path.basename() and os.path.dirname() functions. You can also call os.path.split() to obtain these names as a tuple. Enter the following into Python's interactive shell. On macOS or Linux, try using /bin/ls as the filename:

```python
>>> import os
>>> filename = 'C:/Windows/system32/notepad.exe'
>>> os.path.basename(filename)
'notepad.exe'
>>> os.path.dirname(filename)
'C:/Windows/system32'
>>> os.path.split(filename)
('C:/Windows/system32', 'notepad.exe')
>>> folder, file = os.path.split(filename)
```

```
>>> folder
'C:/Windows/system32'
>>> file
'notepad.exe'
```

You can use any of Python's string methods on these string values to help evaluate the file against your search criteria, such as `lower()` in the `hasEveryVowel()` match function.

Finding Information About the File's Timestamps

Files have timestamps indicating when they were created, last modified, and last accessed. Python's `os.path.getctime()`, `os.path.getmtime()`, and `os.path.getatime()`, respectively, return these timestamps as floating-point values indicating the number of seconds since the *Unix epoch*, midnight on January 1, 1970, in the Coordinated Universal Time (UTC) time zone. Enter the following into the interactive shell:

Python
```
> import os
> filename = 'C:/Windows/system32/notepad.exe'
> os.path.getctime(filename)
1625705942.1165037
> os.path.getmtime(filename)
1625705942.1205275
> os.path.getatime(filename)
1631217101.8869188
```

These float values are easy for programs to use since they're just single numbers, but you'll need functions from Python's `time` module to make them simpler for humans to read. The `time.localtime()` function converts a Unix epoch timestamp into a `struct_time` object in the computer's time zone. A `struct_time` object has several attributes whose names begin with `tm_` for obtaining date and time information. Enter the following into the interactive shell:

Python
```
>>> import os
>>> filename = 'C:/Windows/system32/notepad.exe'
>>> ctimestamp = os.path.getctime(filename)
>>> import time
>>> time.localtime(ctimestamp)
time.struct_time(tm_year=2021, tm_mon=7, tm_mday=7, tm_hour=19,
tm_min=59, tm_sec=2, tm_wday=2, tm_yday=188, tm_isdst=1)
>>> st = time.localtime(ctimestamp)
>>> st.tm_year
2021
>>> st.tm_mon
7
>>> st.tm_mday
7
>>> st.tm_wday
2
>>> st.tm_hour
```

```
19
>>> st.tm_min
59
>>> st.tm_sec
2
```

Note that the tm_mday attribute is the day of the month, ranging from 1 to 31. The tm_wday attribute is the day of the week, starting at 0 for Monday, 1 for Tuesday, and so on, up to 6 for Sunday.

If you need a brief, human-readable string of the time_struct object, pass it to the time.asctime() function:

Python
```
>>> import os
>>> filename = 'C:/Windows/system32/notepad.exe'
>>> ctimestamp = os.path.getctime(filename)
>>> import time
>>> st = time.localtime(ctimestamp)
>>> time.asctime(st)
'Wed Jul  7 19:59:02 2021'
```

While the time.localtime() function returns a struct_time object in the local time zone, the time.gmtime() function returns a struct_time object in the UTC or Greenwich Mean time zone. Enter the following into the interactive shell:

Python
```
>>> import os
>>> filename = 'C:/Windows/system32/notepad.exe'
>>> ctimestamp = os.path.getctime(filename)
>>> import time
>>> ctimestamp = os.path.getctime(filename)
>>> time.localtime(ctimestamp)
time.struct_time(tm_year=2021, tm_mon=7, tm_mday=7, tm_hour=19,
tm_min=59, tm_sec=2, tm_wday=2, tm_yday=188, tm_isdst=1)
>>> time.gmtime(ctimestamp)
time.struct_time(tm_year=2021, tm_mon=7, tm_mday=8, tm_hour=0,
tm_min=59, tm_sec=2, tm_wday=3, tm_yday=189, tm_isdst=0)
```

The interaction between these os.path functions (which return Unix epoch timestamps) and time functions (which return struct_time objects) can be confusing. Figure 10-2 shows the chain of code starting from the filename string and ending with obtaining the individual parts of the timestamp.

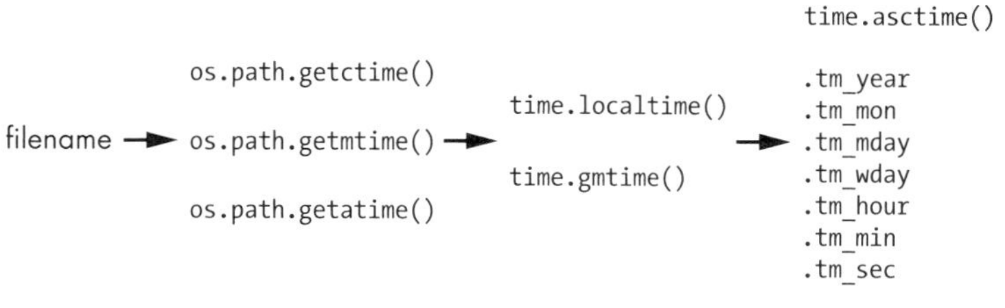

Figure 10-2: Going from the filename to the individual attributes of a timestamp

Finally, the `time.time()` function returns the number of seconds since the Unix epoch to the current time.

Modifying Your Files

After the `walk()` function returns a list of files matching your search criteria, you may want to rename, delete, or perform another operation on them. The `shutil` and `os` modules in the Python standard library have functions to do this. Further, the `send2trash` third-party module can also send files to your operating system's Recycle Bin, rather than permanently deleting them.

To move a file, call the `shutil.move()` function with two arguments. The first argument is the file to move, and the second is the folder to move it to. For example, you could call the following:

Python
```
>>> import shutil
>>> shutil.move('spam.txt', 'someFolder')
'someFolder\\spam.txt'
```

The `shutil.move()` function returns the string of the new filepath of the file. You can also specify a filename to move and rename the file at the same time:

Python
```
>>> import shutil
>>> shutil.move('spam.txt', 'someFolder\\newName.txt')
'someFolder\\newName.txt'
```

If the second argument lacks a folder, you can just specify a new name for the file to rename it in its current folder:

Python
```
>>> import shutil
>>> shutil.move('spam.txt', 'newName.txt')
'newName.txt'
```

Note that the `shutil.move()` function both moves and renames files, similar to the way the Unix and macOS `mv` command both moves and renames files. There is no separate `shutil.rename()` function.

To copy a file, call the `shutil.copy()` function with two arguments. The first argument is the filename of the file to copy, and the second argument is the new name of the copy. For example, you could call the following:

Python
```
>>> import shutil
>>> shutil.copy('spam.txt', 'spam-copy.txt')
'spam-copy.txt'
```

The `shutil.copy()` function returns the name of the copy. To delete a file, call the `os.unlink()` function and pass it the name of the file to delete:

Python
```
>>> import os
>>> os.unlink('spam.txt')
>>>
```

The name *unlink* is used instead of *delete* because of the technical detail that it removes the filename linked to the file. But since most files have only one linked filename, this unlinking also deletes the file. It's all right if you don't understand these filesystem concepts; just know that os.unlink() deletes a file.

Calling os.unlink() permanently deletes the file, which can be dangerous if a bug in your program causes the function to delete the wrong file. Instead, you can use the send2trash module's send2trash() function to put the file in your operating system's Recycle Bin. To install this module, run **run python -m pip install --user send2trash** from the command prompt on Windows or run **run python3 -m pip install** from the terminal on macOS or Linux. Once the module is installed, you'll be able to import it with import send2trash.

Enter the following into the interactive shell:

Python
```
>>> open('deleteme.txt', 'w').close() # Create a blank file.
>>> import send2trash
>>> send2trash.send2trash('deleteme.txt')
```

This example creates a blank file named *deleteme.txt*. After calling send2trash.send2trash() (the module and function share the same name), this file is removed to the Recycle Bin.

Summary

This chapter's file-search project uses recursion to "walk" across the contents of a folder and all its subfolders. The file-finder program's walk() function navigates these folders recursively, applying custom search criteria to every file in every subfolder. The search criteria are implemented as match functions, which are passed to the walk() function. This allows us to change the search criteria by writing new functions instead of modifying the code in walk().

Our project had two match functions, for finding files with an even byte file size or containing every vowel in its name, but you can write your own functions to pass to walk(). This is the power behind programming; you can create features for your own needs that are not available in commercial apps.

Further Reading

The documentation for Python's built-in os.walk() function (similar to the walk() function in the file-finder project) is at *https://docs.python.org/3/library/os.html#os.walk*. You can also learn more about your computer's filesystem and Python's file functions in Chapter 9 of my book *Automate the Boring Stuff with Python*, 2nd edition (No Starch Press, 2019) at *https://automatetheboring stuff.com/2e/chapter9*.

The datetime module in the Python standard library also has more ways to interact with timestamp data. You can learn more about it in Chapter 17 of *Automate the Boring Stuff with Python*, 2nd edition at *https://automatetheboring stuff.com/2e/chapter17*.

11

MAZE GENERATOR

Chapter 4 described a recursive algorithm that solves mazes, but another recursive algorithm generates mazes. In this chapter, we'll generate mazes in the same format as the maze-solver program in Chapter 4. So, whether you're a fan of solving mazes or creating them, you'll now have the power to apply programming to the task.

The algorithm works by visiting a starting space in the maze and then recursively visiting a neighboring space. The maze's hallways are "carved out" of the maze as the algorithm continues to visit neighbors. If the algorithm reaches a dead end that has no neighboring spaces, it backtracks to earlier spaces until it finds an unvisited neighbor and continues visiting from there. By the time the algorithm backtracks to the starting space, the entire maze has been generated.

The recursive backtracking algorithm we'll use here produces mazes that tend to have long hallways (the maze spaces that connect branching intersections) and are fairly simple to solve. However, this algorithm is easier to implement than many other maze-generation algorithms, such as Kruskal's algorithm or Wilson's algorithm, so it serves as a good introduction to the topic.

The Complete Maze-Generator Program

Let's begin by taking a look at the complete Python and JavaScript source code for the program, which uses the recursive backtracking algorithm for maze generation. The rest of this chapter explains each section of code individually.

Copy this Python code to a file named *mazeGenerator.py*:

Python
```
import random

WIDTH = 39 # Width of the maze (must be odd).
HEIGHT = 19 # Height of the maze (must be odd).
assert WIDTH % 2 == 1 and WIDTH >= 3
assert HEIGHT % 2 == 1 and HEIGHT >= 3
SEED = 1
random.seed(SEED)

# Use these characters for displaying the maze:
EMPTY = ' '
MARK = '@'
WALL = chr(9608) # Character 9608 is '█'
NORTH, SOUTH, EAST, WEST = 'n', 's', 'e', 'w'

# Create the filled-in maze data structure to start:
maze = {}
for x in range(WIDTH):
    for y in range(HEIGHT):
        maze[(x, y)] = WALL # Every space is a wall at first.

def printMaze(maze, markX=None, markY=None):
    """Displays the maze data structure in the maze argument. The
    markX and markY arguments are coordinates of the current
    '@' location of the algorithm as it generates the maze."""

    for y in range(HEIGHT):
        for x in range(WIDTH):
            if markX == x and markY == y:
                # Display the '@' mark here:
                print(MARK, end='')
            else:
                # Display the wall or empty space:
                print(maze[(x, y)], end='')
        print() # Print a newline after printing the row.


def visit(x, y):
    """"Carve out" empty spaces in the maze at x, y and then
    recursively move to neighboring unvisited spaces. This
    function backtracks when the mark has reached a dead end."""
```

```
        maze[(x, y)] = EMPTY # "Carve out" the space at x, y.
        printMaze(maze, x, y) # Display the maze as we generate it.
        print('\n\n')

        while True:
            # Check which neighboring spaces adjacent to
            # the mark have not been visited already:
            unvisitedNeighbors = []
            if y > 1 and (x, y - 2) not in hasVisited:
                unvisitedNeighbors.append(NORTH)

            if y < HEIGHT - 2 and (x, y + 2) not in hasVisited:
                unvisitedNeighbors.append(SOUTH)

            if x > 1 and (x - 2, y) not in hasVisited:
                unvisitedNeighbors.append(WEST)

            if x < WIDTH - 2 and (x + 2, y) not in hasVisited:
                unvisitedNeighbors.append(EAST)

            if len(unvisitedNeighbors) == 0:
                # BASE CASE
                # All neighboring spaces have been visited, so this is a
                # dead end. Backtrack to an earlier space:
                return
            else:
                # RECURSIVE CASE
                # Randomly pick an unvisited neighbor to visit:
                nextIntersection = random.choice(unvisitedNeighbors)

                # Move the mark to an unvisited neighboring space:

                if nextIntersection == NORTH:
                    nextX = x
                    nextY = y - 2
                    maze[(x, y - 1)] = EMPTY # Connecting hallway.
                elif nextIntersection == SOUTH:
                    nextX = x
                    nextY = y + 2
                    maze[(x, y + 1)] = EMPTY # Connecting hallway.
                elif nextIntersection == WEST:
                    nextX = x - 2
                    nextY = y
                    maze[(x - 1, y)] = EMPTY # Connecting hallway.
                elif nextIntersection == EAST:
                    nextX = x + 2
                    nextY = y
                    maze[(x + 1, y)] = EMPTY # Connecting hallway.

                hasVisited.append((nextX, nextY)) # Mark as visited.
                visit(nextX, nextY) # Recursively visit this space.


# Carve out the paths in the maze data structure:
hasVisited = [(1, 1)] # Start by visiting the top-left corner.
```

```
visit(1, 1)

# Display the final resulting maze data structure:
printMaze(maze)
```

Copy this JavaScript code to a file named *mazeGenerator.html*:

JavaScript

```javascript
<script type="text/javascript">

const WIDTH = 39; // Width of the maze (must be odd).
const HEIGHT = 19; // Height of the maze (must be odd).
console.assert(WIDTH % 2 == 1 && WIDTH >= 2);
console.assert(HEIGHT % 2 == 1 && HEIGHT >= 2);

// Use these characters for displaying the maze:
const EMPTY = " ";
const MARK = "@";
const WALL = "&#9608;"; // Character 9608 is '█'
const [NORTH, SOUTH, EAST, WEST] = ["n", "s", "e", "w"];

// Create the filled-in maze data structure to start:
let maze = {};
for (let x = 0; x < WIDTH; x++) {
    for (let y = 0; y < HEIGHT; y++) {
        maze[[x, y]] = WALL; // Every space is a wall at first.
    }
}


function printMaze(maze, markX, markY) {
    // Displays the maze data structure in the maze argument. The
    // markX and markY arguments are coordinates of the current
    // '@' location of the algorithm as it generates the maze.
    document.write('<code>');
    for (let y = 0; y < HEIGHT; y++) {
        for (let x = 0; x < WIDTH; x++) {
            if (markX === x && markY === y) {
                // Display the '@' mark here:
                document.write(MARK);
            } else {
                // Display the wall or empty space:
                document.write(maze[[x, y]]);
            }
        }
        document.write('<br />'); // Print a newline after printing the row.
    }
    document.write('</code>');
}


function visit(x, y) {
    // "Carve out" empty spaces in the maze at x, y and then
    // recursively move to neighboring unvisited spaces. This
    // function backtracks when the mark has reached a dead end.
```

```
    maze[[x, y]] = EMPTY; // "Carve out" the space at x, y.
    printMaze(maze, x, y); // Display the maze as we generate it.
    document.write('<br /><br /><br />');

while (true) {
    // Check which neighboring spaces adjacent to
    // the mark have not been visited already:
    let unvisitedNeighbors = [];
    if (y > 1 && !JSON.stringify(hasVisited).includes(JSON.stringify([x,
y - 2]))) {
        unvisitedNeighbors.push(NORTH);
    }
    if (y < HEIGHT - 2 &&
    !JSON.stringify(hasVisited).includes(JSON.stringify([x, y + 2]))) {
        unvisitedNeighbors.push(SOUTH);
    }
    if (x > 1 &&
    !JSON.stringify(hasVisited).includes(JSON.stringify([x - 2, y]))) {
        unvisitedNeighbors.push(WEST);
    }
    if (x < WIDTH - 2 &&
    !JSON.stringify(hasVisited).includes(JSON.stringify([x + 2, y]))) {
        unvisitedNeighbors.push(EAST);
    }

    if (unvisitedNeighbors.length === 0) {
        // BASE CASE
        // All neighboring spaces have been visited, so this is a
        // dead end. Backtrack to an earlier space:
        return;
    } else {
        // RECURSIVE CASE
        // Randomly pick an unvisited neighbor to visit:
        let nextIntersection = unvisitedNeighbors[
        Math.floor(Math.random() * unvisitedNeighbors.length)];

        // Move the mark to an unvisited neighboring space:
        let nextX, nextY;
        if (nextIntersection === NORTH) {
            nextX = x;
            nextY = y - 2;
            maze[[x, y - 1]] = EMPTY; // Connecting hallway.
        } else if (nextIntersection === SOUTH) {
            nextX = x;
            nextY = y + 2;
            maze[[x, y + 1]] = EMPTY; // Connecting hallway.
        } else if (nextIntersection === WEST) {
            nextX = x - 2;
            nextY = y;
            maze[[x - 1, y]] = EMPTY; // Connecting hallway.
        } else if (nextIntersection === EAST) {
            nextX = x + 2;
            nextY = y;
            maze[[x + 1, y]] = EMPTY; // Connecting hallway.
        }
```

```
                    hasVisited.push([nextX, nextY]); // Mark space as visited.
                    visit(nextX, nextY); // Recursively visit this space.
                }
            }
        }

    // Carve out the paths in the maze data structure:
    let hasVisited = [[1, 1]]; // Start by visiting the top-left corner.
    visit(1, 1);

    // Display the final resulting maze data structure:
    printMaze(maze);
    </script>
```

When you run this program, it produces a large amount of text that will fill the terminal window or browser with each step of the maze's construction. You'll have to scroll back up to the top to view the entire output.

The maze data structure begins as a completely filled-in 2D space. The recursive backtracker algorithm is given a starting point in this maze and then visits a previously unvisited neighboring space, "carving out" any hallway space in the process. Then it recursively calls itself on a neighboring space it hasn't visited before. If all the neighboring spaces have already been visited, the algorithm is at a dead end and backtracks to an earlier visited space to visit its unvisited neighbors. The program ends when the algorithm backtracks to its starting location.

You can see this algorithm in action by running the maze-generator program. As the maze is carved out, it displays the current x, y coordinates by using the @ character. The process looks like Figure 11-1. Notice that the fifth image in the top-right corner has backtracked to an earlier space after reaching a dead end to explore a new neighboring direction from that space.

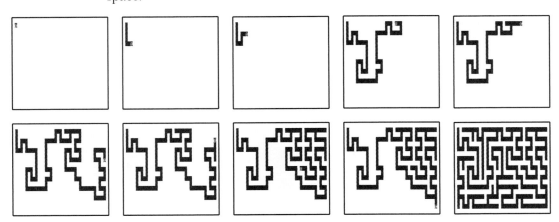

Figure 11-1: The maze as it gets "carved out" by the recursive backtracking algorithm

Let's take a look at the code in more detail.

Setting Up the Maze Generator's Constants

The maze generator uses several constants, which we can change before running the program to alter the size and appearance of the maze. The Python code for these constants is as follows:

Python

```python
import random

WIDTH = 39 # Width of the maze (must be odd).
HEIGHT = 19 # Height of the maze (must be odd).
assert WIDTH % 2 == 1 and WIDTH >= 3
assert HEIGHT % 2 == 1 and HEIGHT >= 3
SEED = 1
random.seed(SEED)
```

The JavaScript code is as follows:

JavaScript

```javascript
<script type="text/javascript">

const WIDTH = 39; // Width of the maze (must be odd).
const HEIGHT = 19; // Height of the maze (must be odd).
console.assert(WIDTH % 2 == 1 && WIDTH >= 3);
console.assert(HEIGHT % 2 == 1 && HEIGHT >= 3);
```

The constants WIDTH and HEIGHT dictate the size of the maze. They must be odd numbers, because our maze data structure requires walls between the visited spaces of the maze, leaving us with odd-numbered dimensions. To make sure the WIDTH and HEIGHT constants are set correctly, we use assertions to stop the program if the constants aren't odd or are too small.

The program relies on a random seed value to reproduce the same maze, given the same seed value. The Python version of this program lets us set this value by calling the random.seed() function. Unfortunately, JavaScript doesn't have a way to set the seed value explicitly and will generate different mazes each time we run the program.

NOTE *The "random" numbers the Python program generates are actually predictable, because they're based on a starting seed value; the program generates the same "random" maze given the same seed. This can be useful when trying to debug the program by having it reproduce the same maze as when we first noticed the bug.*

The Python code continues by setting a few more constants:

Python

```python
# Use these characters for displaying the maze:
EMPTY = ' '
MARK = '@'
WALL = chr(9608) # Character 9608 is '█'
NORTH, SOUTH, EAST, WEST = 'n', 's', 'e', 'w'
```

The JavaScript code for these constants is as follows:

JavaScript
```
// Use these characters for displaying the maze:
const EMPTY = " ";
const MARK = "@";
const WALL = "&#9608;"; // Character 9608 is '█'
const [NORTH, SOUTH, EAST, WEST] = ["n", "s", "e", "w"];
```

The EMPTY and WALL constants affect how the maze is displayed on the screen. The MARK constant is used to point out the position of the algorithm in the maze as it runs. The NORTH, SOUTH, EAST, and WEST constants represent the directions that the mark can move through the maze and are used to make the code more readable.

Creating the Maze Data Structure

The maze data structure is a Python dictionary or JavaScript object that has keys of Python tuples or JavaScript arrays of the x, y coordinates of every space in the maze. The value for these keys is a string in the WALL or EMPTY constant. This string notes whether this space is a blocking wall or a passable empty space in the maze.

For example, the maze in Figure 11-2 is represented by the following data structure:

```
{(0, 0): '█', (0, 1): '█', (0, 2): '█', (0, 3): '█', (0, 4): '█',
(0, 5): '█', (0, 6): '█', (1, 0): '█', (1, 1): ' ', (1, 2): ' ',
(1, 3): ' ', (1, 4): ' ', (1, 5): ' ', (1, 6): '█', (2, 0): '█',
(2, 1): '█', (2, 2): '█', (2, 3): '█', (2, 4): '█', (2, 5): ' ',
(2, 6): '█', (3, 0): '█', (3, 1): ' ', (3, 2): '█', (3, 3): ' ',
(3, 4): ' ', (3, 5): ' ', (3, 6): '█', (4, 0): '█', (4, 1): ' ',
(4, 2): '█', (4, 3): ' ', (4, 4): '█', (4, 5): '█', (4, 6): '█',
(5, 0): '█', (5, 1): ' ', (5, 2): ' ', (5, 3): ' ', (5, 4): ' ',
(5, 5): ' ', (5, 6): '█', (6, 0): '█', (6, 1): '█', (6, 2): '█',
(6, 3): '█', (6, 4): '█', (6, 5): '█', (6, 6): '█'}
```

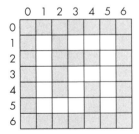

Figure 11-2: An example maze that can be represented by a data structure

The program must start with every space set to WALL. The recursive visit() function then carves out the hallways and intersections of the maze by setting spaces to EMPTY:

Python
```
# Create the filled-in maze data structure to start:
maze = {}
for x in range(WIDTH):
    for y in range(HEIGHT):
        maze[(x, y)] = WALL # Every space is a wall at first.
```

The corresponding JavaScript code is as follows:

JavaScript
```
// Create the filled-in maze data structure to start:
let maze = {};
for (let x = 0; x < WIDTH; x++) {
    for (let y = 0; y < HEIGHT; y++) {
        maze[[x, y]] = WALL; // Every space is a wall at first.
    }
}
```

We create the blank dictionary (in Python) or object (in JavaScript) in the maze global variable. The for loops loop over every possible x, y coordinate, setting each to WALL to create a completely filled-in maze. The call to visit() will carve out the hallways of the maze from this data structure by setting the spaces in it to EMPTY.

Printing the Maze Data Structure

To represent the maze as a data structure, the Python program uses a dictionary, and the JavaScript program uses an object. Within this structure, the keys are lists or arrays of two integers for the x- and y-coordinates, while the value is either the WALL or EMPTY single-character strings. Thus, we can access the wall or empty hallway space at the coordinates x, y in the maze as maze[(x, y)] in Python code and as maze[[x, y]] in JavaScript code.

The Python code for printMaze() starts as follows:

Python
```
def printMaze(maze, markX=None, markY=None):
    """Displays the maze data structure in the maze argument. The
    markX and markY arguments are coordinates of the current
    '@' location of the algorithm as it generates the maze."""

    for y in range(HEIGHT):
        for x in range(WIDTH):
```

The JavaScript code for printMaze() starts as follows:

JavaScript
```
function printMaze(maze, markX, markY) {
    // Displays the maze data structure in the maze argument. The
    // markX and markY arguments are coordinates of the current
    // '@' location of the algorithm as it generates the maze.
    document.write('<code>');
```

```
for (let y = 0; y < HEIGHT; y++) {
    for (let x = 0; x < WIDTH; x++) {
```

The printMaze() function prints the maze data structure it's passed as the maze parameter on the screen. Optionally, if markX and markY integer arguments are passed, the MARK constant (which we set to @) appears at these x, y coordinates in the printed maze. To make sure the maze is printed in a monospace font, the JavaScript version writes the HTML tag <code> before printing the maze itself. Without this HTML tag, the maze will appear distorted in the browser.

Within the function, nested for loops loop over every space in the maze data structure. These for loops iterate over each y-coordinate from 0 up to, but not including, HEIGHT, and each x-coordinate from 0 up to, but not including, WIDTH.

Inside the inner for loop, if the current x, y coordinates match the position of the mark (the location where the algorithm is currently carving), the program displays the @ in the MARK constant. The Python code does this as follows:

Python

```
if markX == x and markY == y:
    # Display the '@' mark here:
    print(MARK, end='')
else:
    # Display the wall or empty space:
    print(maze[(x, y)], end='')


print() # Print a newline after printing the row.
```

The JavaScript code is as follows:

JavaScript

```
if (markX === x && markY === y) {
    // Display the '@' mark here:
    document.write(MARK);
} else {
    // Display the wall or empty space:
    document.write(maze[[x, y]]);
}
}
document.write('<br />'); // Print a newline after printing the row.
}
document.write('</code>');
}
```

Otherwise, the program displays either the WALL or EMPTY constant's character at this x, y coordinate in the maze data structure by printing maze[(x, y)] in Python and maze[[x, y]] in JavaScript. After the inner for loop is done looping over the x-coordinates, we print a newline at the end of the row in preparation for the next row.

Using the Recursive Backtracker Algorithm

The visit() function implements the recursive backtracker algorithm. The function has a list (in Python) or array (in JavaScript) that keeps track of the x, y coordinates that have already been visited by previous visit() function calls. It also in-place modifies the global maze variable that stores the maze data structure. The Python code for visit() begins as follows:

Python
```python
def visit(x, y):
    """"Carve out" empty spaces in the maze at x, y and then
    recursively move to neighboring unvisited spaces. This
    function backtracks when the mark has reached a dead end."""
    maze[(x, y)] = EMPTY # "Carve out" the space at x, y.
    printMaze(maze, x, y) # Display the maze as we generate it.
    print('\n\n')
```

The JavaScript code for visit() begins as follows:

JavaScript
```javascript
function visit(x, y) {
    // "Carve out" empty spaces in the maze at x, y and then
    // recursively move to neighboring unvisited spaces. This
    // function backtracks when the mark has reached a dead end.

    maze[[x, y]] = EMPTY; // "Carve out" the space at x, y.
    printMaze(maze, x, y); // Display the maze as we generate it.
    document.write('<br /><br /><br />');
```

The visit() function accepts x, y coordinates as arguments for the place in the maze the algorithm is visiting. Then the function changes the data structure in maze at this location to an empty space. To let the user see the progression of the maze generation, it calls printMaze(), passing the x and y arguments as the current position of the mark.

Next, the recursive backtracker calls visit() with the coordinates of a previously unvisited neighboring space. The Python code continues as follows:

Python
```python
while True:
    # Check which neighboring spaces adjacent to
    # the mark have not been visited already:
    unvisitedNeighbors = []
    if y > 1 and (x, y - 2) not in hasVisited:
        unvisitedNeighbors.append(NORTH)

    if y < HEIGHT - 2 and (x, y + 2) not in hasVisited:
        unvisitedNeighbors.append(SOUTH)

    if x > 1 and (x - 2, y) not in hasVisited:
        unvisitedNeighbors.append(WEST)

    if x < WIDTH - 2 and (x + 2, y) not in hasVisited:
        unvisitedNeighbors.append(EAST)
```

The JavaScript code continues as follows:

```
while (true) {
    // Check which neighboring spaces adjacent to
    // the mark have not been visited already:
    let unvisitedNeighbors = [];
    if (y > 1 && !JSON.stringify(hasVisited).includes(JSON.stringify([x, y - 2]))) {
        unvisitedNeighbors.push(NORTH);
    }
    if (y < HEIGHT - 2 && !JSON.stringify(hasVisited).includes(JSON.stringify([x, y + 2])))
{
        unvisitedNeighbors.push(SOUTH);
    }
    if (x > 1 && !JSON.stringify(hasVisited).includes(JSON.stringify([x - 2, y]))) {
        unvisitedNeighbors.push(WEST);
    }
    if (x < WIDTH - 2 && !JSON.stringify(hasVisited).includes(JSON.stringify([x + 2, y])))
{
        unvisitedNeighbors.push(EAST);
    }
```

The while loop continues to loop as long as unvisited neighbors remain for this location in the maze. We create a list or array of unvisited neighboring spaces in the unvisitedNeighbors variables. Four if statements check that the current x, y position is not on the border of the maze (so that we still have a neighboring space to check) and whether the neighboring space's x, y coordinates don't appear in the hasVisited list or array already.

If all the neighbors have been visited, the function returns so that it can backtrack to an earlier space. The Python code continues on to check for the base case:

Python
```
    if len(unvisitedNeighbors) == 0:
        # BASE CASE
        # All neighboring spaces have been visited, so this is a
        # dead end. Backtrack to an earlier space:
        return
```

The JavaScript code does so as follows:

JavaScript
```
    if (unvisitedNeighbors.length === 0) {
        // BASE CASE
        // All neighboring spaces have been visited, so this is a
        // dead end. Backtrack to an earlier space:
        return;
```

The base case for the recursive backtracking algorithm occurs when no unvisited neighbors remain to visit next. In this case, the function simply returns. The visit() function itself has no return value. Rather, the recursive function calls visit() to modify the maze data structure in the global maze variable as a side effect. When the original function call to maze() returns, the maze global variable contains the completely generated maze.

The Python code continues on to the recursive case like this:

Python

```python
    else:
        # RECURSIVE CASE
        # Randomly pick an unvisited neighbor to visit:
        nextIntersection = random.choice(unvisitedNeighbors)

        # Move the mark to an unvisited neighboring space:

        if nextIntersection == NORTH:
            nextX = x
            nextY = y - 2
            maze[(x, y - 1)] = EMPTY # Connecting hallway.
        elif nextIntersection == SOUTH:
            nextX = x
            nextY = y + 2
            maze[(x, y + 1)] = EMPTY # Connecting hallway.
        elif nextIntersection == WEST:
            nextX = x - 2
            nextY = y
            maze[(x - 1, y)] = EMPTY # Connecting hallway.
        elif nextIntersection == EAST:
            nextX = x + 2
            nextY = y
            maze[(x + 1, y)] = EMPTY # Connecting hallway.

        hasVisited.append((nextX, nextY)) # Mark space as visited.
        visit(nextX, nextY) # Recursively visit this space.
```

The JavaScript code continues as follows:

JavaScript

```javascript
    } else {
        // RECURSIVE CASE
        // Randomly pick an unvisited neighbor to visit:
        let nextIntersection = unvisitedNeighbors[
        Math.floor(Math.random() * unvisitedNeighbors.length)];

        // Move the mark to an unvisited neighboring space:
        let nextX, nextY;
        if (nextIntersection === NORTH) {
            nextX = x;
            nextY = y - 2;
            maze[[x, y - 1]] = EMPTY; // Connecting hallway.
        } else if (nextIntersection === SOUTH) {
            nextX = x;
            nextY = y + 2;
            maze[[x, y + 1]] = EMPTY; // Connecting hallway.
        } else if (nextIntersection === WEST) {
            nextX = x - 2;
            nextY = y;
            maze[[x - 1, y]] = EMPTY; // Connecting hallway.
        } else if (nextIntersection === EAST) {
            nextX = x + 2;
            nextY = y;
```

```
            maze[[x + 1, y]] = EMPTY;    // Connecting hallway.
        }
        hasVisited.push([nextX, nextY]); // Mark space as visited.
        visit(nextX, nextY);             // Recursively visit this space.
      }
    }
  }
```

The unvisitedNeighbors list or array contains one or more of the NORTH, SOUTH, WEST, and EAST constants. We choose one of these directions for the next recursive call to visit(), and then set the nextX and nextY variables with the coordinates of the neighboring space in this direction.

After this, we add the x, y coordinates of nextX and nextY to the hasVisited list or array before making the recursive call for this neighboring space. In this way, the visit() function continues to visit neighboring spaces, carving out the maze hallways by setting locations in maze to EMPTY. The connecting hallway between the current space and neighboring space is also set to EMPTY.

When no neighbors exist, the base case simply returns to an earlier location. In the visit() function, the execution jumps back to the start of the while loop. The code in the while loop again checks which neighboring spaces haven't been visited and makes a recursive visit() call on one of them, or returns if all neighboring spaces have already been visited.

As the maze fills up with hallways and each space has been visited, the recursive calls will continue to return until the original visit() function call returns. At this point, the maze variable contains the completely generated maze.

Starting the Chain of Recursive Calls

The recursive visit() uses two global variables, maze and hasVisited. The hasVisited variable is a list or array containing the x, y coordinates of every space the algorithm has visited and begins with (1, 1) since that is the maze starting point. The Python code for this is as follows:

Python
```
# Carve out the paths in the maze data structure:
hasVisited = [(1, 1)] # Start by visiting the top-left corner.
visit(1, 1)

# Display the final resulting maze data structure:
printMaze(maze)
```

The JavaScript code for this is as follows:

JavaScript
```
// Carve out the paths in the maze data structure:
let hasVisited = [[1, 1]]; // Start by visiting the top-left corner.
visit(1, 1);

// Display the final resulting maze data structure:
printMaze(maze);
```

After setting up `hasVisited` to include the x, y coordinates of 1, 1 (the top-left corner of the maze), we call `visit()` with these coordinates. This function call will result in all the recursive function calls that generate the hallways of the maze. By the time this function call returns, `hasVisited` will contain every x, y coordinate of the maze, and `maze` will contain the completely generated maze.

Summary

As you just learned, we can use recursion to not only solve mazes (by traversing them as tree data structures) but also generate them using the recursive backtracker algorithm. The algorithm "carves out" hallways in the maze, backtracking to earlier points when it encounters a dead end. Once the algorithm is forced to backtrack to the starting point, the maze is completely generated.

We can represent a well-connected maze with no loops as a DAG—that is, a tree data structure. The recursive backtracker algorithm makes use of the idea that recursive algorithms are well suited to problems involving tree-like data structures and backtracking.

Further Reading

Wikipedia has an entry on maze generation in general, with a section on the recursive backtracker algorithm, at *https://en.wikipedia.org/wiki/Maze _generation_algorithm#Recursive_backtracker*. I've created a browser-based animation of the recursive backtracker algorithm that shows the "carving" of hallways in action at *https://scratch.mit.edu/projects/17358777*.

If maze generation interests you, you should read *Mazes for Programmers: Code Your Own Twisty Little Passages* by Jamis Buck (Pragmatic Bookshelf, 2015).

12

SLIDING-TILE SOLVER

A *sliding-tile puzzle*, or *15-puzzle*, is a small puzzle game implemented as a set of 15 numbered sliding tiles on a 4 × 4 board. One tile is missing, allowing adjacent tiles to slide into the empty space on the board. The player's goal is to move the tiles into numeric order, as in Figure 12-1. Some versions of this game have fragments of a picture on the tiles that create a whole image when the puzzle is complete.

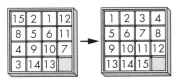

Figure 12-1: Solving a numeric
sliding-tile puzzle from its
scrambled state (left) to its
solved, ordered state (right)

Incidentally, mathematicians have proven that even the hardest 15-puzzle
can be solved in 80 moves.

Solving 15-Puzzles Recursively

The algorithm that solves 15-puzzles is similar to the maze-solving algorithm. Each state of the board (that is, one arrangement of tiles) can be
thought of as a maze intersection with four hallways to go down. In the case
of 15-puzzles, sliding a tile in one of the four directions is like picking a
hallway to follow to the next intersection.

Just as you can turn a maze into a DAG, you can convert a 15-puzzle
into a tree graph, as in Figure 12-2. The board states are nodes with up to
four edges (representing a direction to slide a tile) to other nodes (representing the resultant state). The root node is the starting state of the
15-puzzle. The solved-state node is the one in which the tiles are ordered
correctly. The path from the root node to the solved state details the slides
needed to solve the puzzle.

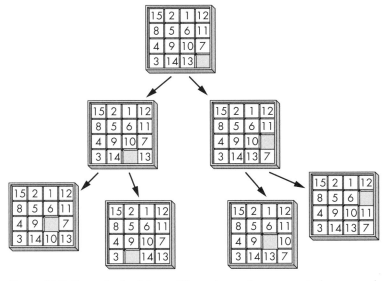

Figure 12-2: The task of solving a 15-puzzle can be represented as a graph
with tile states as nodes and slides as edges.

Clever algorithms are available for solving 15-puzzles, but we could also just recursively explore the entire tree graph until we find a path from the root node to the solution node. This puzzle's tree can be searched with a depth-first search (DFS) algorithm. However, unlike a well-connected maze, the 15-puzzle's tree graph is not a DAG. Rather, the graph's nodes are *undirected*, because you can traverse both directions of an edge by undoing the previous slide you made.

Figure 12-3 shows an example of the undirected edges between two nodes. Because it is possible to go back and forth between these two nodes forever, our 15-puzzle algorithm could encounter a stack overflow before it finds a solution.

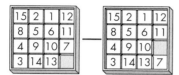

Figure 12-3: The 15-puzzle has undirected edges (drawn without an arrowhead) between its nodes because slides can be undone by performing the opposite slide.

To optimize our algorithm, we'll avoid slides that undo the previous slide. However, this optimization alone won't save the algorithm from a stack overflow. While it makes the *edges* in the tree graph directed, it doesn't turn the puzzle-solver algorithm into a DAG, because it has cycles, or loops, from lower nodes to higher ones. These loops happen if you slide the tiles in a circular pattern, as in Figure 12-4.

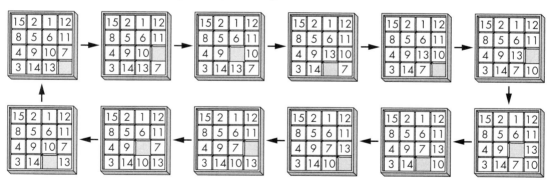

Figure 12-4: An example of a loop in the 15-puzzle's graph

Cycles in the graph mean that the later nodes at the bottom could loop back to a node at the top. Our solving algorithm could get "stuck" following this loop and never explore the branch that has the actual solution. In practice, this infinite loop would result in a stack overflow.

We can still use recursion to solve a 15-puzzle. We just need to add our own base case for the maximum number of moves in order to avoid causing a stack overflow. Then, when the maximum number of slide moves is reached, the algorithm will begin backtracking to earlier nodes. If the 15-puzzle solver project can't find a solution in every possible combination of 10 slides, it will try again using a maximum of 11 slides. If the puzzle can't be solved in 11 moves, the project tries 12 moves, and so on. This prevents the algorithm from getting stuck exploring the moves of an infinite loop instead of exploring possible solutions of fewer moves.

The Complete Sliding-Tile Solver Program

Let's begin by taking a look at the complete source code for the sliding-tile puzzle solver program. The rest of this chapter explains each section of code individually.

Copy the Python version of the code to a file named *slidingTileSolver.py*:

Python
```python
import random, time

DIFFICULTY = 40 # How many random slides a puzzle starts with.
SIZE = 4 # The board is SIZE x SIZE spaces.
random.seed(1) # Select which puzzle to solve.

BLANK = 0
UP = 'up'
DOWN = 'down'
LEFT = 'left'
RIGHT = 'right'


def displayBoard(board):
    """Display the tiles stored in `board` on the screen."""
    for y in range(SIZE): # Iterate over each row.
        for x in range(SIZE): # Iterate over each column.
            if board[y * SIZE + x] == BLANK:
                print('__ ', end='') # Display blank tile.
            else:
                print(str(board[y * SIZE + x]).rjust(2) + ' ', end='')
        print() # Print a newline at the end of the row.


def getNewBoard():
    """Return a list that represents a new tile puzzle."""
    board = []
    for i in range(1, SIZE * SIZE):
        board.append(i)
    board.append(BLANK)
    return board


def findBlankSpace(board):
    """Return an [x, y] list of the blank space's location."""
    for x in range(SIZE):
```

```
        for y in range(SIZE):
            if board[y * SIZE + x] == BLANK:
                return [x, y]


def makeMove(board, move):
    """Modify `board` in place to carry out the slide in `move`."""
    bx, by = findBlankSpace(board)
    blankIndex = by * SIZE + bx

    if move == UP:
        tileIndex = (by + 1) * SIZE + bx
    elif move == LEFT:
        tileIndex = by * SIZE + (bx + 1)
    elif move == DOWN:
        tileIndex = (by - 1) * SIZE + bx
    elif move == RIGHT:
        tileIndex = by * SIZE + (bx - 1)

    # Swap the tiles at blankIndex and tileIndex:
    board[blankIndex], board[tileIndex] = board[tileIndex], board[blankIndex]


def undoMove(board, move):
    """Do the opposite move of `move` to undo it on `board`."""
    if move == UP:
        makeMove(board, DOWN)
    elif move == DOWN:
        makeMove(board, UP)
    elif move == LEFT:
        makeMove(board, RIGHT)
    elif move == RIGHT:
        makeMove(board, LEFT)


def getValidMoves(board, prevMove=None):
    """Returns a list of the valid moves to make on this board. If
    prevMove is provided, do not include the move that would undo it."""

    blankx, blanky = findBlankSpace(board)

    validMoves = []
    if blanky != SIZE - 1 and prevMove != DOWN:
        # Blank space is not on the bottom row.
        validMoves.append(UP)

    if blankx != SIZE - 1 and prevMove != RIGHT:
        # Blank space is not on the right column.
        validMoves.append(LEFT)

    if blanky != 0 and prevMove != UP:
        # Blank space is not on the top row.
        validMoves.append(DOWN)
```

```python
        if blankx != 0 and prevMove != LEFT:
            # Blank space is not on the left column.
            validMoves.append(RIGHT)

    return validMoves


def getNewPuzzle():
    """Get a new puzzle by making random slides from the solved state."""
    board = getNewBoard()
    for i in range(DIFFICULTY):
        validMoves = getValidMoves(board)
        makeMove(board, random.choice(validMoves))
    return board


def solve(board, maxMoves):
    """Attempt to solve the puzzle in `board` in at most `maxMoves`
    moves. Returns True if solved, otherwise False."""
    print('Attempting to solve in at most', maxMoves, 'moves...')
    solutionMoves = [] # A list of UP, DOWN, LEFT, RIGHT values.
    solved = attemptMove(board, solutionMoves, maxMoves, None)

    if solved:
        displayBoard(board)
        for move in solutionMoves:
            print('Move', move)
            makeMove(board, move)
            print() # Print a newline.
            displayBoard(board)
            print() # Print a newline.

        print('Solved in', len(solutionMoves), 'moves:')
        print(', '.join(solutionMoves))
        return True # Puzzle was solved.
    else:
        return False # Unable to solve in maxMoves moves.


def attemptMove(board, movesMade, movesRemaining, prevMove):
    """A recursive function that attempts all possible moves on `board`
    until it finds a solution or reaches the `maxMoves` limit.
    Returns True if a solution was found, in which case `movesMade`
    contains the series of moves to solve the puzzle. Returns False
    if `movesRemaining` is less than 0."""

    if movesRemaining < 0:
        # BASE CASE - Ran out of moves.
        return False

    if board == SOLVED_BOARD:
        # BASE CASE - Solved the puzzle.
        return True

    # RECURSIVE CASE - Attempt each of the valid moves:
```

```
            for move in getValidMoves(board, prevMove):
                # Make the move:
                makeMove(board, move)
                movesMade.append(move)

                if attemptMove(board, movesMade, movesRemaining - 1, move):
                    # If the puzzle is solved, return True:
                    undoMove(board, move) # Reset to the original puzzle.
                    return True

                # Undo the move to set up for the next move:
                undoMove(board, move)
                movesMade.pop() # Remove the last move since it was undone.
            return False # BASE CASE - Unable to find a solution.


        # Start the program:
        SOLVED_BOARD = getNewBoard()
        puzzleBoard = getNewPuzzle()
        displayBoard(puzzleBoard)
        startTime = time.time()

        maxMoves = 10
        while True:
            if solve(puzzleBoard, maxMoves):
                break # Break out of the loop when a solution is found.
            maxMoves += 1
        print('Run in', round(time.time() - startTime, 3), 'seconds.')
```

Copy the JavaScript version of the code to a file named *slidingTile Solver.html*:

```
<script type="text/javascript">
const DIFFICULTY = 40; // How many random slides a puzzle starts with.
const SIZE = 4; // The board is SIZE x SIZE spaces.

const BLANK = 0;
const UP = "up";
const DOWN = "down";
const LEFT = "left";
const RIGHT = "right";


function displayBoard(board) {
    // Display the tiles stored in `board` on the screen.
    document.write("<pre>");
    for (let y = 0; y < SIZE; y++) { // Iterate over each row.
        for (let x = 0; x < SIZE; x++) { // Iterate over each column.
            if (board[y * SIZE + x] == BLANK) {
                document.write('__ '); // Display blank tile.
            } else {
                document.write(board[y * SIZE + x].toString().padStart(2) + " ");
            }
        }
    }
```

```
        document.write("<br />"); // Print a newline at the end of the row.
    }
    document.write("</pre>");
}


function getNewBoard() {
    // Return a list that represents a new tile puzzle.
    let board = [];
    for (let i = 1; i < SIZE * SIZE; i++) {
        board.push(i);
    }
    board.push(BLANK);
    return board;
}


function findBlankSpace(board) {
    // Return an [x, y] array of the blank space's location.
    for (let x = 0; x < SIZE; x++) {
        for (let y = 0; y < SIZE; y++) {
            if (board[y * SIZE + x] === BLANK) {
                return [x, y];
            }
        }
    }
}


function makeMove(board, move) {
    // Modify `board` in place to carry out the slide in `move`.
    let bx, by;
    [bx, by] = findBlankSpace(board);
    let blankIndex = by * SIZE + bx;

    let tileIndex;
    if (move === UP) {
        tileIndex = (by + 1) * SIZE + bx;
    } else if (move === LEFT) {
        tileIndex = by * SIZE + (bx + 1);
    } else if (move === DOWN) {
        tileIndex = (by - 1) * SIZE + bx;
    } else if (move === RIGHT) {
        tileIndex = by * SIZE + (bx - 1);
    }

    // Swap the tiles at blankIndex and tileIndex:
    [board[blankIndex], board[tileIndex]] = [board[tileIndex], board[blankIndex]];
}


function undoMove(board, move) {
    // Do the opposite move of `move` to undo it on `board`.
```

```
        if (move === UP) {
            makeMove(board, DOWN);
        } else if (move === DOWN) {
            makeMove(board, UP);
        } else if (move === LEFT) {
            makeMove(board, RIGHT);
        } else if (move === RIGHT) {
            makeMove(board, LEFT);
        }
    }


    function getValidMoves(board, prevMove) {
        // Returns a list of the valid moves to make on this board. If
        // prevMove is provided, do not include the move that would undo it.

        let blankx, blanky;
        [blankx, blanky] = findBlankSpace(board);

        let validMoves = [];
        if (blanky != SIZE - 1 && prevMove != DOWN) {
            // Blank space is not on the bottom row.
            validMoves.push(UP);
        }
        if (blankx != SIZE - 1 && prevMove != RIGHT) {
            // Blank space is not on the right column.
            validMoves.push(LEFT);
        }
        if (blanky != 0 && prevMove != UP) {
            // Blank space is not on the top row.
            validMoves.push(DOWN);
        }
        if (blankx != 0 && prevMove != LEFT) {
            // Blank space is not on the left column.
            validMoves.push(RIGHT);
        }
        return validMoves;
    }


    function getNewPuzzle() {
        // Get a new puzzle by making random slides from the solved state.
        let board = getNewBoard();
        for (let i = 0; i < DIFFICULTY; i++) {
            let validMoves = getValidMoves(board);
            makeMove(board, validMoves[Math.floor(Math.random() * validMoves.length)]);
        }
        return board;
    }

    function solve(board, maxMoves) {
        // Attempt to solve the puzzle in `board` in at most `maxMoves`
        // moves. Returns true if solved, otherwise false.
        document.write("Attempting to solve in at most " + maxMoves + " moves...<br />");
        let solutionMoves = []; // A list of UP, DOWN, LEFT, RIGHT values.
```

```
        let solved = attemptMove(board, solutionMoves, maxMoves, null);

    if (solved) {
        displayBoard(board);
        for (let move of solutionMoves) {
            document.write("Move " + move + "<br />");
            makeMove(board, move);
            document.write("<br />"); // Print a newline.
            displayBoard(board);
            document.write("<br />"); // Print a newline.
        }
        document.write("Solved in " + solutionMoves.length + " moves:<br />");
        document.write(solutionMoves.join(", ") + "<br />");
        return true; // Puzzle was solved.
    } else {
        return false; // Unable to solve in maxMoves moves.
    }
}


function attemptMove(board, movesMade, movesRemaining, prevMove) {
    // A recursive function that attempts all possible moves on `board`
    // until it finds a solution or reaches the `maxMoves` limit.
    // Returns true if a solution was found, in which case `movesMade`
    // contains the series of moves to solve the puzzle. Returns false
    // if `movesRemaining` is less than 0.

    if (movesRemaining < 0) {
        // BASE CASE - Ran out of moves.
        return false;
    }

    if (JSON.stringify(board) == SOLVED_BOARD) {
        // BASE CASE - Solved the puzzle.
        return true;
    }

    // RECURSIVE CASE - Attempt each of the valid moves:
    for (let move of getValidMoves(board, prevMove)) {
        // Make the move:
        makeMove(board, move);
        movesMade.push(move);

        if (attemptMove(board, movesMade, movesRemaining - 1, move)) {
            // If the puzzle is solved, return true:
            undoMove(board, move); // Reset to the original puzzle.
            return true;
        }

        // Undo the move to set up for the next move:
        undoMove(board, move);
        movesMade.pop(); // Remove the last move since it was undone.
    }
    return false; // BASE CASE - Unable to find a solution.
}
```

```
// Start the program:
const SOLVED_BOARD = JSON.stringify(getNewBoard());
let puzzleBoard = getNewPuzzle();
displayBoard(puzzleBoard);
let startTime = Date.now();

let maxMoves = 10;
while (true) {
    if (solve(puzzleBoard, maxMoves)) {
        break; // Break out of the loop when a solution is found.
    }
    maxMoves += 1;
}
document.write("Run in " + Math.round((Date.now() - startTime) / 100) / 10 + " seconds.<br
/>");
</script>
```

The program's output looks like the following:

```
 7  1  3  4
 2  5 10  8
 __  6  9 11
13 14 15 12
Attempting to solve in at most 10 moves...
Attempting to solve in at most 11 moves...
Attempting to solve in at most 12 moves...
--snip--
 1  2  3  4
 5  6  7  8
 9 10 11 __
13 14 15 12

Move up

 1  2  3  4
 5  6  7  8
 9 10 11 12
13 14 15 __

Solved in 18 moves:
left, down, right, down, left, up, right, up, left, left, down,
right, right, up, left, left, left, up
Run in 39.519 seconds.
```

Note that when JavaScript runs in a browser, the code must complete before it displays any output. Until then, it may appear to have frozen, and your browser might ask if you'd like to prematurely stop it. You can ignore this warning and let the program keep working until it has solved the puzzle.

The program's recursive `attemptMove()` function solves sliding-tile puzzles by trying every possible combination of slides. The function is given a move to try. If this solves the puzzle, the function returns a Boolean `True` value. Otherwise, it calls `attemptMove()` with all the other possible moves it can make and returns a Boolean `False` value if none of them find a solution before exceeding the maximum number of moves. We'll explore this function in more detail later.

The data structure we use to represent a sliding-tile board is a list (in Python) or array (in JavaScript) of integers, with 0 representing the blank space. In our program, this data structure is often stored in a variable named `board`. The values at `board[y * SIZE + x]` match the tile at the x, y coordinates on the board, as depicted in Figure 12-5. For example, if the `SIZE` constant is 4, the value at the x, y coordinates 3, 1 can be found at `board[1 * 4 + 3]`.

This small calculation enables us to use a 1D array or list to store the values of a 2D tile board. This programming technique is useful not just in our project but for any 2D data structure that must be stored in an array or list, such as a 2D image stored as a stream of bytes.

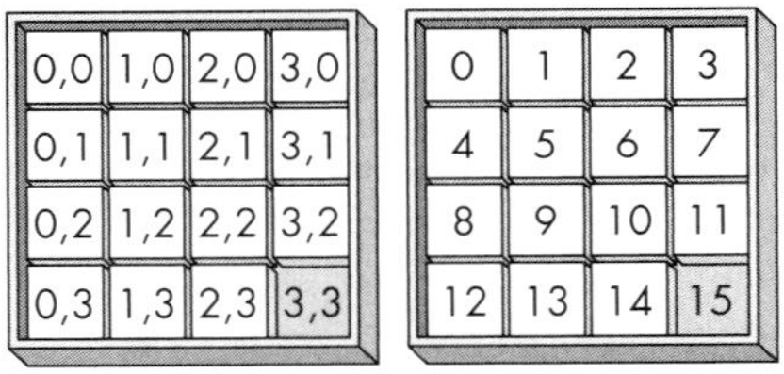

Figure 12-5: The x, y coordinates for each space on the board (left) and the corresponding data structure index (right)

Let's look at some example data structures. The board with mixed-up tiles shown previously on the left side of Figure 12-1 would be represented by the following:

    [15, 2, 1, 12, 8, 5, 6, 11, 4, 9, 10, 7, 3, 14, 13, 0]

The solved, ordered puzzle on the right side of Figure 12-1 would be represented by this:

    [1, 2, 3, 4, 5, 6, 7, 8, 9, 10, 11, 12, 13, 14, 15, 0]

All the functions in our program will expect board data structures that follow this format.

Unfortunately, the 4 × 4 version of the sliding-tile puzzle has so many possible moves that it would take a normal laptop weeks to solve. You can change the `SIZE` constant from 4 to 3 to solve a simpler 3 × 3 version of the puzzle. The finished, ordered 3 × 3 puzzle's data structure would look like this:

    [1, 2, 3, 4, 5, 6, 7, 8, 0].

Setting Up the Program's Constants

At the beginning of the source code, the program uses a few constants to make the code more readable. The Python code is as follows:

Python

```python
import random, time

DIFFICULTY = 40 # How many random slides a puzzle starts with.
SIZE = 4 # The board is SIZE x SIZE spaces.
random.seed(1) # Select which puzzle to solve.

BLANK = 0
UP = 'up'
DOWN = 'down'
LEFT = 'left'
RIGHT = 'right'
```

The JavaScript code is as follows:

JavaScript

```javascript
<script type="text/javascript">
const DIFFICULTY = 40; // How many random slides a puzzle starts with.
const SIZE = 4; // The board is SIZE x SIZE spaces.

const BLANK = 0;
const UP = "up";
const DOWN = "down";
const LEFT = "left";
const RIGHT = "right";
```

To have reproducible random numbers, the Python program sets the random number seed to 1. The same seed value will always reproduce the same random puzzle, which is useful for debugging. You can change the seed value to any other integer to create different puzzles. JavaScript has no way to set its random seed value, and *slidingtilesolver.html* doesn't have an equivalent feature.

The SIZE constant sets the size of the square board. You can change this size to anything, but 4 × 4 boards are standard, while 3 × 3 boards are useful for testing, because the program is quick to solve them. The BLANK constant is used in the puzzle data structure to represent the blank space and must be kept at 0. The UP, DOWN, LEFT, and RIGHT constants are used to make the code readable, similar to the NORTH, SOUTH, WEST, and EAST constants in the maze-generator project in Chapter 11.

Representing the Sliding-Tile Puzzle as Data

The sliding-tile board's data structure is just a list or array of integers. What makes it representative of an actual puzzle board is the way it's used by the functions in the program. The displayBoard(), getNewBoard(), findBlankSpace(), and other functions in this program all deal with this data structure.

Displaying the Board

The first function, displayBoard(), prints the board data structure on the screen. The Python code for the displayBoard() function is as follows:

```python
def displayBoard(board):
    """Display the tiles stored in `board` on the screen."""
    for y in range(SIZE): # Iterate over each row.
        for x in range(SIZE): # Iterate over each column.
            if board[y * SIZE + x] == BLANK:
                print('__ ', end='') # Display blank tile.
            else:
                print(str(board[y * SIZE + x]).rjust(2) + ' ', end='')
        print() # Print a newline at the end of the row.
```

The JavaScript code for the displayBoard() function is as follows:

```javascript
function displayBoard(board) {
    // Display the tiles stored in `board` on the screen.
    document.write("<pre>");
    for (let y = 0; y < SIZE; y++) { // Iterate over each row.
        for (let x = 0; x < SIZE; x++) { // Iterate over each column.
            if (board[y * SIZE + x] == BLANK) {
                document.write('__ '); // Display blank tile.
            } else {
                document.write(board[y * SIZE + x].toString().padStart(2) + " ");
            }
        }
        document.write("<br />");
    }
    document.write("</pre>");
}
```

The pair of nested for loops iterate over every row and column on the board. The first for loop loops over the y-coordinates, and the second for loop loops over the x-coordinates. This is because the program needs to print all the columns of a single row before printing a newline character to move on to the next row.

The if statement checks whether the tile at the current x, y coordinates is the blank tile. If it is, the program prints two underscores with a trailing space. Otherwise, the code in the else block prints the tile number with a trailing space. The trailing space is what separates the tile numbers from one another on the screen. If the tile number is a single digit, the rjust() or padStart() method will insert an extra space so that the tile number is aligned with the two-digit numbers on the screen.

For example, say the scrambled puzzle on the left side of Figure 12-1 is represented by this data structure:

[15, 2, 1, 12, 8, 5, 6, 11, 4, 9, 10, 7, 3, 14, 13, 0]

When the data structure is passed to displayBoard(), it prints the following text:

```
15  2  1 12
 8  5  6 11
 4  9 10  7
 3 14 13 __
```

Creating a New Board Data Structure

Next, the getNewBoard() function returns a new board data structure with the tiles in their ordered, solved places. The Python code for the getNewBoard() function is as follows:

Python
```python
def getNewBoard():
    """Return a list that represents a new tile puzzle."""
    board = []
    for i in range(1, SIZE * SIZE):
        board.append(i)
    board.append(BLANK)
    return board
```

The JavaScript code for the getNewBoard() function is as follows:

JavaScript
```javascript
function getNewBoard() {
    // Return a list that represents a new tile puzzle.
    let board = [];
    for (let i = 1; i < SIZE * SIZE; i++) {
        board.push(i);
    }
    board.push(BLANK);
    return board;
}
```

The getNewBoard() function returns a board data structure appropriate to the integer in the SIZE constant (either 3 × 3 or 4 × 4). The for loop generates this list or array with the integers from 1 up to, but not including, SIZE squared, with a 0 (the value stored in the BLANK constant) at the end to represent the blank space in the lower-right corner.

Finding the Coordinates of the Blank Space

Our program uses the findBlankSpace() function to find the x, y coordinates of the blank space on the board. The Python code is as follows:

Python
```python
def findBlankSpace(board):
    """Return an [x, y] list of the blank space's location."""
    for x in range(SIZE):
        for y in range(SIZE):
            if board[y * SIZE + x] == BLANK:
                return [x, y]
```

The JavaScript code is as follows:

```javascript
function findBlankSpace(board) {
    // Return an [x, y] array of the blank space's location.
    for (let x = 0; x < SIZE; x++) {
        for (let y = 0; y < SIZE; y++) {
            if (board[y * SIZE + x] === BLANK) {
                return [x, y];
            }
        }
    }
}
```

Like the displayBoard() function, the findBlankSpace() function has a pair of nested for loops. These for loops will loop over every position in the board data structure. When the board[y * SIZE + x] code finds the blank space, it returns the x- and y-coordinates as two integers in a Python list or JavaScript array.

Making a Move

Next, the makeMove() function accepts two arguments: a board data structure and an UP, DOWN, LEFT, or RIGHT direction to slide a tile on that board. This code is fairly repetitive, so the short variable names bx and by are used to represent the x- and y-coordinates of the blank space.

To make a move, the board data structure swaps the value of the moved tile with the 0 of the blank tile. The Python code for the makeMove() function is as follows:

```python
def makeMove(board, move):
    """Modify `board` in place to carry out the slide in `move`."""
    bx, by = findBlankSpace(board)
    blankIndex = by * SIZE + bx

    if move == UP:
        tileIndex = (by + 1) * SIZE + bx
    elif move == LEFT:
        tileIndex = by * SIZE + (bx + 1)
    elif move == DOWN:
        tileIndex = (by - 1) * SIZE + bx
    elif move == RIGHT:
        tileIndex = by * SIZE + (bx - 1)

    # Swap the tiles at blankIndex and tileIndex:
    board[blankIndex], board[tileIndex] = board[tileIndex], board[blankIndex]
```

The JavaScript code for the makeMove() function is as follows:

```javascript
function makeMove(board, move) {
    // Modify `board` in place to carry out the slide in `move`.
    let bx, by;
    [bx, by] = findBlankSpace(board);
    let blankIndex = by * SIZE + bx;
```

```
    let tileIndex;
    if (move === UP) {
        tileIndex = (by + 1) * SIZE + bx;
    } else if (move === LEFT) {
        tileIndex = by * SIZE + (bx + 1);
    } else if (move === DOWN) {
        tileIndex = (by - 1) * SIZE + bx;
    } else if (move === RIGHT) {
        tileIndex = by * SIZE + (bx - 1);
    }

    // Swap the tiles at blankIndex and tileIndex:
    [board[blankIndex], board[tileIndex]] = [board[tileIndex], board[blankIndex]];
}
```

The if statements determine the index of the tile to move based on the move parameter. The function then "slides" a tile by swapping the BLANK value at board[blankindex] with the numbered tile at board[tileIndex]. The makeMove() function doesn't return anything. Instead, it modifies the board data structure in place.

Python has the a, b = b, a syntax to swap the value of two variables. For JavaScript, we need to envelop them in an array, such as [a, b] = [b, a] to perform the swap. We use this syntax at the end of the function to swap the values in board[blankIndex] and board[tileIndex] with each other.

Undoing a Move

Next, as part of the backtracking in the recursive algorithm, our program needs to undo moves. This is as simple as making a move in the opposite direction as the initial move. The Python code for the undoMove() function is as follows:

Python
```
def undoMove(board, move):
    """Do the opposite move of `move` to undo it on `board`."""
    if move == UP:
        makeMove(board, DOWN)
    elif move == DOWN:
        makeMove(board, UP)
    elif move == LEFT:
        makeMove(board, RIGHT)
    elif move == RIGHT:
        makeMove(board, LEFT)
```

The JavaScript code for the undoMove() function is as follows:

JavaScript
```
function undoMove(board, move) {
    // Do the opposite move of `move` to undo it on `board`.
    if (move === UP) {
        makeMove(board, DOWN);
    } else if (move === DOWN) {
        makeMove(board, UP);
    } else if (move === LEFT) {
        makeMove(board, RIGHT);
```

```
    } else if (move === RIGHT) {
        makeMove(board, LEFT);
    }
}
```

We've already programmed the swapping logic into the makeMove() function, so undoMove() can just call that function for the direction opposite of the move argument. This way, a hypothetical someMove move made on a hypothetical someBoard data structure by the makeMove(someBoard, someMove) function call can be undone by calling undoMove(someBoard, someMove).

Setting Up a New Puzzle

To create a new, scrambled puzzle, we cannot simply put the tiles in random places, because some configurations of tiles produce invalid, unsolvable puzzles. Instead, we need to start from a solved puzzle and make many random moves. Solving the puzzle becomes a matter of figuring out which slides will undo these random slides to get back to the original, ordered configuration.

But it's not always possible to make moves in each of the four directions. For example, if the blank space is in the bottom-right corner, as in Figure 12-6, tiles can slide only down or right because no tiles can slide left or up. Furthermore, if sliding the 7 tile in Figure 12-6 up was the previous move, then sliding it down is removed as a valid move because it would undo the previous move.

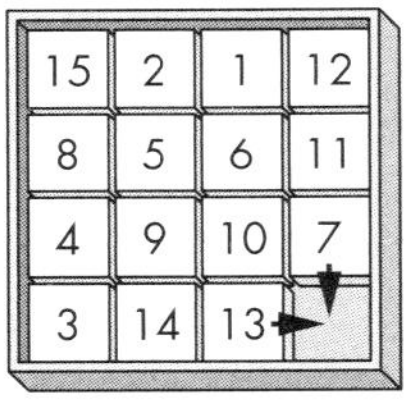

Figure 12-6: If the blank space is in the bottom-right corner, down and right are the only valid slide directions.

To help us, we need a getValidMoves() function that can tell us which slide directions are possible on a given board data structure:

Python
```python
def getValidMoves(board, prevMove=None):
    """Returns a list of the valid moves to make on this board. If
    prevMove is provided, do not include the move that would undo it."""

    blankx, blanky = findBlankSpace(board)

    validMoves = []
```

```
    if blanky != SIZE - 1 and prevMove != DOWN:
        # Blank space is not on the bottom row.
        validMoves.append(UP)

    if blankx != SIZE - 1 and prevMove != RIGHT:
        # Blank space is not on the right column.
        validMoves.append(LEFT)

    if blanky != 0 and prevMove != UP:
        # Blank space is not on the top row.
        validMoves.append(DOWN)

    if blankx != 0 and prevMove != LEFT:
        # Blank space is not on the left column.
        validMoves.append(RIGHT)

    return validMoves
```

The JavaScript code for this function is as follows:

JavaScript
```javascript
function getValidMoves(board, prevMove) {
    // Returns a list of the valid moves to make on this board. If
    // prevMove is provided, do not include the move that would undo it.

    let blankx, blanky;
    [blankx, blanky] = findBlankSpace(board);

    let validMoves = [];
    if (blanky != SIZE - 1 && prevMove != DOWN) {
        // Blank space is not on the bottom row.
        validMoves.push(UP);
    }
    if (blankx != SIZE - 1 && prevMove != RIGHT) {
        // Blank space is not on the right column.
        validMoves.push(LEFT);
    }
    if (blanky != 0 && prevMove != UP) {
        // Blank space is not on the top row.
        validMoves.push(DOWN);
    }
    if (blankx != 0 && prevMove != LEFT) {
        // Blank space is not on the left column.
        validMoves.push(RIGHT);
    }
    return validMoves;
}
```

The first thing the getValidMoves() function does is call findBlankSpace() and store the x, y coordinates of the blank space in the variables blankx and blanky. Next, the function sets up the validMoves variable with an empty Python list or empty JavaScript array to hold all the valid directions for a slide.

Looking back at Figure 12-5, a y-coordinate of 0 represents the top edge of the board. If blanky, the blank space's y-coordinate, is not 0, then we know the blank space is not on the top edge. If the previous move was also not DOWN, then *up* is a valid move, and the code adds UP to validMoves.

Similarly, the left edge has an x-coordinate of 0, the bottom edge has a y-coordinate of SIZE - 1, and the right edge has an x-coordinate of SIZE - 1. Using the expression SIZE - 1 ensures that this code works no matter whether the board is 3×3, 4×4, or any other size. The getValidMoves() function does these checks for all four directions and then returns validMoves.

Next, the getNewPuzzle() function returns the data structure of a scrambled board for the program to solve. Tiles can't simply be randomly placed on the board, because some configurations of tiles produce puzzles that are impossible to solve. To avoid this, the getNewPuzzle() function starts with an ordered, solved board and then applies a large number of random slides to it. Solving this puzzle is, in effect, figuring out the moves that undo these slides. The Python code for the getNewPuzzle() function is as follows:

Python

```
def getNewPuzzle():
    """Get a new puzzle by making random slides from the solved state."""
    board = getNewBoard()
    for i in range(DIFFICULTY):
        validMoves = getValidMoves(board)
        makeMove(board, random.choice(validMoves))
    return board
```

The JavaScript code is as follows:

```
function getNewPuzzle() {
    // Get a new puzzle by making random slides from the solved state.
    let board = getNewBoard();
    for (let i = 0; i < DIFFICULTY; i++) {
        let validMoves = getValidMoves(board);
        makeMove(board, validMoves[Math.floor(Math.random() * validMoves.length)]);
    }
    return board;
}
```

The call to getNewBoard() obtains a board data structure in the ordered, solved state. The for loop calls getValidMoves() to obtain a list of valid moves, given the current state of the board, and then calls makeMove() with a randomly selected move from the list. The random.choice() function in Python and the Math.floor() and Math.random() functions in JavaScript will handle the random selection from the validMoves list or array, no matter what combination of UP, DOWN, LEFT, and RIGHT values it contains.

The DIFFICULTY constant determines how many random slides from make Move() the for loop applies. The higher the integer in DIFFICULTY, the more scrambled the puzzle becomes. Even though this results in some moves that undo earlier moves by pure chance, such as sliding left and then immediately sliding right, with enough slides the function produces a thoroughly scrambled board. For testing purposes, DIFFICULTY is set to 40, allowing the program to produce a solution in about a minute. For a more realistic 15-puzzle, you should change DIFFICULTY to 200.

After the board data structure in board is created and scrambled, the getNewPuzzle() function returns it.

Recursively Solving the Sliding-Tile Puzzle

Now that we have the functions for creating and manipulating the puzzle data structure, let's create the functions that solve the puzzle by recursively sliding the tiles in each possible direction and checking whether this produces a finished, ordered board.

The attemptMove() function performs a single slide on a board data structure, then recursively calls itself once for each of the valid moves the board can make. Multiple base cases exist. If the board data structure is in a solved state, the function returns a Boolean True value; if the maximum number of moves has been reached, it returns a Boolean False value. Also, if a recursive call has returned True, then attemptMove() should return True, and if recursive calls for all the valid moves have returned False, then attempt Move() should return False.

The solve() Function

The solve() function takes a board data structure and maximum number of moves the algorithm should attempt before backtracking. Then it performs the first call to attemptMove(). If this first call to attemptMove() returns True, the code in solve() displays the series of steps that solves the puzzle. If it returns False, the code in solve() tells the user no solution was found with this maximum number of moves.

The Python code for solve() begins as follows:

Python
```
def solve(board, maxMoves):
    """Attempt to solve the puzzle in `board` in at most `maxMoves`
    moves. Returns True if solved, otherwise False."""
    print('Attempting to solve in at most', maxMoves, 'moves...')
    solutionMoves = [] # A list of UP, DOWN, LEFT, RIGHT values.
    solved = attemptMove(board, solutionMoves, maxMoves, None)
```

The JavaScript code for solve() begins as follows:

```
function solve(board, maxMoves) {
    // Attempt to solve the puzzle in `board` in at most `maxMoves`
    // moves. Returns true if solved, otherwise false.
    document.write("Attempting to solve in at most " + maxMoves + " moves...<br />");
    let solutionMoves = []; // A list of UP, DOWN, LEFT, RIGHT values.
    let solved = attemptMove(board, solutionMoves, maxMoves, null);
```

The solve() function has two parameters: board contains the data structure of the puzzle to solve, and maxMoves is the maximum number of moves the function should make to try to solve the puzzle. The solutionMoves list or array contains the sequence of UP, DOWN, LEFT, and RIGHT values that produce the solved state. The attemptMove() function modifies this list or array in place as it makes recursive calls. If the initial attemptMove() function finds a solution and returns True, solutionMoves contains the sequence of moves for the solution.

The solve() function then makes the initial call to attemptMove(), and stores the True or False it returns in the solved variable. The rest of the solve() function handles these two cases:

Python

```python
if solved:
    displayBoard(board)
    for move in solutionMoves:
        print('Move', move)
        makeMove(board, move)
        print() # Print a newline.
        displayBoard(board)
        print() # Print a newline.

    print('Solved in', len(solutionMoves), 'moves:')
    print(', '.join(solutionMoves))
    return True # Puzzle was solved.
else:
    return False # Unable to solve in maxMoves moves.
```

The JavaScript code is as follows:

JavaScript

```javascript
if (solved) {
    displayBoard(board);
    for (let move of solutionMoves) {
        document.write("Move " + move + "<br />");
        makeMove(board, move);
        document.write("<br />"); // Print a newline.
        displayBoard(board);
        document.write("<br />"); // Print a newline.
    }
    document.write("Solved in " + solutionMoves.length + " moves:<br />");
    document.write(solutionMoves.join(", ") + "<br />");
    return true; // Puzzle was solved.
} else {
    return false; // Unable to solve in maxMoves moves.
}
}
```

If attemptMove() finds a solution, the program runs through all the moves gathered in the solutionMoves list or array and displays the board after each slide. This proves to the user that the moves collected by attemptMove() are the real solution to the puzzle. Finally, the solve() function itself returns True. If attemptMove() is unable to find a solution, the solve() function simply returns False.

The attemptMove() Function

Let's take a look at attemptMove(), the core recursive function behind our tile-solving algorithm. Remember the tree graph that a sliding-tile puzzle produces; calling attemptMove() for a certain direction is like traveling down that edge of this graph to the next node. A recursive attemptMove() call moves further down the tree. When this recursive attemptMove() call returns, it backtracks to a previous node. When attemptMove() has backtracked all the way to the root node, the program execution has returned to the solve() function.

The Python code for attemptMove() begins as follows:

Python
```python
def attemptMove(board, movesMade, movesRemaining, prevMove):
    """A recursive function that attempts all possible moves on `board`
    until it finds a solution or reaches the `maxMoves` limit.
    Returns True if a solution was found, in which case `movesMade`
    contains the series of moves to solve the puzzle. Returns False
    if `movesRemaining` is less than 0."""

    if movesRemaining < 0:
        # BASE CASE - Ran out of moves.
        return False

    if board == SOLVED_BOARD:
        # BASE CASE - Solved the puzzle.
        return True
```

The JavaScript code for attemptMove() begins as follows:

JavaScript
```javascript
function attemptMove(board, movesMade, movesRemaining, prevMove) {
    // A recursive function that attempts all possible moves on `board`
    // until it finds a solution or reaches the `maxMoves` limit.
    // Returns true if a solution was found, in which case `movesMade`
    // contains the series of moves to solve the puzzle. Returns false
    // if `movesRemaining` is less than 0.

    if (movesRemaining < 0) {
        // BASE CASE - Ran out of moves.
        return false;
    }

    if (JSON.stringify(board) == SOLVED_BOARD) {
        // BASE CASE - Solved the puzzle.
        return true;
    }
```

The attemptMove() function has four parameters. The board parameter contains a tile puzzle board data structure to solve. The movesMade parameter contains a list or array that attemptMove() modifies in place, adding the UP, DOWN, LEFT, and RIGHT values that the recursive algorithm has made. If attemptMove() solves the puzzle, movesMade will contain the moves that led to the solution. This list or array is also what the solutionMoves variable in the solve() function refers to.

The solve() function uses its maxMoves variable as the movesRemaining parameter in the initial call to attemptMove(). Each recursive call passes max Moves - 1 for the next value of maxMoves, causing it to decrease as more recursive calls are made. When it becomes less than 0, the attemptMove() function stops making additional recursive calls and returns False.

Finally, the prevMove parameter contains the UP, DOWN, LEFT, or RIGHT value that the previous call to attemptMove() made so that it doesn't undo that move. For the initial call to attemptMove(), the solve() function passes Python's None or JavaScript's null value for this parameter, since no previous move exists.

The beginning of the attemptMove() code checks for two base cases, returning False if movesRemaining has become less than 0, and returning True if board is in the solved state. The SOLVED_BOARD constant contains a board in the solved state that we can compare to the data structure in board.

The next part of attemptMove() performs each of the valid moves it can do on this board. The Python code is as follows:

Python

```
# RECURSIVE CASE - Attempt each of the valid moves:
for move in getValidMoves(board, prevMove):
    # Make the move:
    makeMove(board, move)
    movesMade.append(move)

    if attemptMove(board, movesMade, movesRemaining - 1, move):
        # If the puzzle is solved, return True:
        undoMove(board, move) # Reset to the original puzzle.
        return True
```

The JavaScript code is as follows:

JavaScript

```
// RECURSIVE CASE - Attempt each of the valid moves:
for (let move of getValidMoves(board, prevMove)) {
    // Make the move:
    makeMove(board, move);
    movesMade.push(move);

    if (attemptMove(board, movesMade, movesRemaining - 1, move)) {
        // If the puzzle is solved, return True:
        undoMove(board, move); // Reset to the original puzzle.
        return true;
    }
```

The for loop sets the move variable to each of the directions returned by getValidMoves(). For each move, we call makeMove() to modify the board data structure with the move and to add the move to the list or array in movesMade.

Next, the code recursively calls attemptMove() to explore the range of all possible future moves within the depth set by movesRemaining. The board and movesMade variables are forwarded to this recursive call. The code sets the recursive call's movesRemaining parameter to movesRemaining - 1 so that it decreases by one. It also sets the prevMode parameter to move so that it doesn't immediately undo the move just made.

If the recursive call returns True, a solution exists and is recorded in the movesMade list or array. We call the undoMove() function so that board will contain the original puzzle after the execution returns to solve() and then return True to indicate a solution has been found.

The Python code for attemptMove() continues as follows:

Python

```python
    # Undo the move to set up for the next move:
    undoMove(board, move)
    movesMade.pop() # Remove the last move since it was undone.
return False # BASE CASE - Unable to find a solution.
```

The JavaScript code is as follows:

JavaScript

```javascript
    // Undo the move to set up for the next move:
    undoMove(board, move);
    movesMade.pop(); // Remove the last move since it was undone.
  }
  return false; // BASE CASE - Unable to find a solution.
}
```

If attemptMove() returns False, no solution is found. In that case, we call undoMove() and remove the latest move from the movesMade list or array.

All of this is done for each of the valid directions. If none of the calls to attemptMove() for these directions finds a solution before reaching the maximum number of moves, the attemptMove() function returns False.

Starting the Solver

The solve() function is useful for kicking off the initial call to attemptMove(), but the program still needs to do some setup. The Python code for this is as follows:

Python

```python
# Start the program:
SOLVED_BOARD = getNewBoard()
puzzleBoard = getNewPuzzle()
displayBoard(puzzleBoard)
startTime = time.time()
```

The JavaScript code for this setup is as follows:

JavaScript

```javascript
// Start the program:
const SOLVED_BOARD = JSON.stringify(getNewBoard());
let puzzleBoard = getNewPuzzle();
displayBoard(puzzleBoard);
let startTime = Date.now();
```

First, the SOLVED_BOARD constant is set to an ordered, solved board as returned by getNewBoard(). This constant isn't set at the top of the source code because the getNewBoard() function needs to be defined before it can be called.

Next, a random puzzle is returned from getNewPuzzle() and stored in the puzzleBoard variable. This variable contains the puzzle board data structure that will be solved. If you want to solve a specific 15-puzzle instead of a random one, you can replace the call to getNewPuzzle() with a list or array containing the puzzle you do want to solve.

The board in puzzleBoard is displayed to the user, and the current time is stored in startTime so that the program can calculate the runtime of the algorithm. The Python code continues as follows:

```python
maxMoves = 10
while True:
    if solve(puzzleBoard, maxMoves):
        break # Break out of the loop when a solution is found.
    maxMoves += 1
print('Run in', round(time.time() - startTime, 3), 'seconds.')
```

The JavaScript code is as follows:

```javascript
let maxMoves = 10;
while (true) {
    if (solve(puzzleBoard, maxMoves)) {
        break; // Break out of the loop when a solution is found.
    }
    maxMoves += 1;
}
document.write("Run in " + Math.round((Date.now() - startTime) / 100) / 10 + " seconds.<br
/>");
</script>
```

The program begins trying to solve the puzzle in puzzleBoard in a maximum of 10 moves. The infinite while loop calls solve(). If a solution is found, solve() prints the solution on the screen and returns True. In that case, the code here can break out of the infinite while loop and print the total runtime of the algorithm.

Otherwise, if solve() returns False, maxMoves is incremented by 1 and the loop calls solve() again. This lets the program try progressively longer combinations of moves to solve the puzzle. This pattern continues until solve() finally returns True.

Summary

A 15-puzzle is a good example of adapting the principles of recursion to a real-world problem. Recursion can perform a depth-first search on the tree graph of states that a 15-puzzle produces to find the path to a solution state. However, a purely recursive algorithm won't work, which was why we had to make certain adjustments.

The problem arises because a 15-puzzle has a massive number of possible states and doesn't form a DAG. The edges in this graph are undirected, and the graph contains loops, or cycles. Our solving algorithm needs to ensure that it doesn't make moves that immediately undo the previous move, so that it traverses the graph in one direction. It also needs to have a maximum number of moves the algorithm is willing to make before it begins to backtrack; otherwise, the loops guarantee that the algorithm will eventually recurse too much and cause a stack overflow.

Recursion isn't necessarily the best approach for solving sliding-tile puzzles. All but the easiest puzzles simply have too many combinations for a typical laptop to solve within a reasonable amount of time. However, I like the 15-puzzle as an exercise in recursion because it connects the theoretical ideas of DAGs and DFS into a real-world problem. While 15-puzzles were invented over a century ago, the advent of computers provides a rich tool for exploring techniques to solve these amusing toys.

Further Reading

The Wikipedia entry for 15-puzzles at *https://en.wikipedia.org/wiki/15_puzzle* details their history and mathematical background.

You can find the Python source code for a playable version of the sliding-tile puzzle game in my book *The Big Book of Small Python Projects* (No Starch Press, 2021) and online at *https://inventwithpython.com/bigbookpython/project68.html*.

13

FRACTAL ART MAKER

Chapter 9 introduced you to programs that draw many well-known fractals with the turtle Python module, but you can also make your own fractal art with the project in this chapter. The Fractal Art Maker program uses Python's turtle module to turn simple shapes into complex designs with minimal additional code.

The project in this chapter comes with nine example fractals, although you can also write new functions to create fractals of your design. Modify the example fractals to produce radically different artwork or write code from scratch to implement your own creative vision.

NOTE *For a thorough explanation of the functions in the* turtle *module, return to Chapter 9.*

The Built-in Fractals

You can direct your computer to create an unlimited number of fractals. Figure 13-1 shows the nine fractals that come with the Fractal Art Maker program that we'll use in this chapter. These are produced from functions that draw a simple square or equilateral triangle as the base shape, then introduce slight differences in their recursive configuration to produce completely different images.

Four Corners	Spiral Squares	Double Spiral Squares
Triangle Spiral	Conway's Game of Life Glider	Sierpiński Triangle
Wave	Horn	Snowflake

Figure 13-1: The nine example fractals that come with the Fractal Art Maker program

You can produce all of these fractals by setting the DRAW_FRACTAL constant at the top of the program to an integer from 1 to 9 and then running the Fractal Art Maker program. You can also set DRAW_FRACTAL to 10 or 11 to draw the basic square and triangle shapes, respectively, that compose these fractals, as shown in Figure 13-2.

Figure 13-2: The results of calling drawFilledSquare() *(left) and* drawTriangleOutline() *(right) on their own*

These shapes are fairly simple: a square filled with either white or gray, and a simple outline of a triangle. The drawFractal() function uses these basic shapes to create amazing fractals.

The Fractal Art Maker Algorithm

The Fractal Art Maker's algorithm has two major components: a shape-drawing function and the recursive drawFractal() function.

The shape-drawing function draws a basic shape. The Fractal Art Maker program comes with the two shape-drawing functions shown previously in Figure 13-2, drawFilledSquare() and drawTriangleOutline(), but you can also create your own. We pass a shape-drawing function to the drawFractal() function as an argument, just as we passed the match functions to the file finder's walk() function in Chapter 10.

The drawFractal() function also has a parameter indicating changes to the size, position, and angle of the shapes between recursive calls to drawFractal(). We'll cover these specific details later in this chapter, but let's look at one example: fractal 7, which draws a wave-like image.

The program produces the Wave fractal by calling the drawTriangle Outline() shape-drawing function, which creates a single triangle. The additional arguments to drawFractal() tell it to make three recursive calls to drawFractal(). Figure 13-3 shows the triangle produced by the original call to drawFractal() and the triangles produced by the three recursive calls.

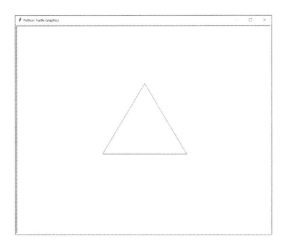 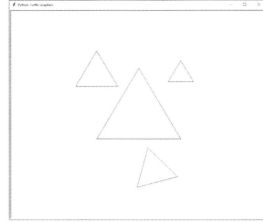

Figure 13-3: The triangle produced by the first call to drawFractal() (left) and the first set of three recursive calls (right)

The first recursive call tells drawFractal() to call drawTriangleOutline() but with a triangle that is half the size and positioned to the top left of the previous triangle. The second recursive call produces a triangle to the top right of the previous triangle that is 30 percent of its size. The third recursive call produces a triangle below the previous triangle that is half its size and rotated 15 degrees compared to it.

Each of these three recursive calls to drawFractal() makes three more recursive calls to drawFractal(), producing nine new triangles. The new triangles have the same changes to their size, position, and angle relative to their previous triangle. The top-left triangle is always half the size of the previous triangle, while the bottom triangle is always rotated 15 degrees more. Figure 13-4 shows the triangles produced by the first and second levels of recursion.

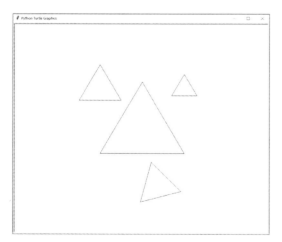 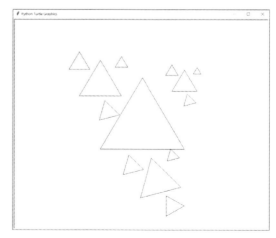

Figure 13-4: The first level of recursive calls to drawFractal() (left) and the nine new triangles of the second level of recursive calls (right)

The nine calls to drawFractal() that produce these nine new triangles each make three recursive calls to drawFractal(), producing 27 new triangles at the next level of recursion. As this pattern of recursion continues, eventually the triangles become so small that drawFractal() stops making new recursive calls. This is one of the base cases for the recursive drawFractal() function. The other occurs when the recursive depth reaches a specified level. Either way, these recursive calls produce the final Wave fractal in Figure 13-5.

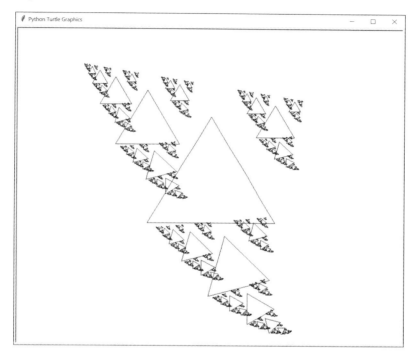

Figure 13-5: The final Wave fractal after each triangle recursively generates three more triangles

The nine example fractals in Figure 13-1 that come with the Fractal Art Maker are made with just two shape-drawing functions and a few changes to the arguments to drawFractal(). Let's take a look at the Fractal Art Maker's code to see how it accomplishes this.

The Complete Fractal Art Maker Program

Enter the following code into a new file and save it as *fractalArtMaker.py*. This program relies on Python's built-in turtle module, so no JavaScript code is used for this chapter's project:

Python
```
import turtle, math

DRAW_FRACTAL = 1 # Set to 1 through 11 and run the program.
```

```
turtle.tracer(5000, 0) # Increase the first argument to speed up the drawing.
turtle.hideturtle()

def drawFilledSquare(size, depth):
    size = int(size)

    # Move to the top-right corner before drawing:
    turtle.penup()
    turtle.forward(size // 2)
    turtle.left(90)
    turtle.forward(size // 2)
    turtle.left(180)
    turtle.pendown()

    # Alternate between white and gray (with black border):
    if depth % 2 == 0:
        turtle.pencolor('black')
        turtle.fillcolor('white')
    else:
        turtle.pencolor('black')
        turtle.fillcolor('gray')

    # Draw a square:
    turtle.begin_fill()
    for i in range(4): # Draw four lines.
        turtle.forward(size)
        turtle.right(90)
    turtle.end_fill()


def drawTriangleOutline(size, depth):
    size = int(size)

    # Move the turtle to the top of the equilateral triangle:
    height = size * math.sqrt(3) / 2
    turtle.penup()
    turtle.left(90) # Turn to face upward.
    turtle.forward(height * (2/3)) # Move to the top corner.
    turtle.right(150) # Turn to face the bottom-right corner.
    turtle.pendown()

    # Draw the three sides of the triangle:
    for i in range(3):
        turtle.forward(size)
        turtle.right(120)


def drawFractal(shapeDrawFunction, size, specs, maxDepth=8, depth=0):
    if depth > maxDepth or size < 1:
        return # BASE CASE

    # Save the position and heading at the start of this function call:
    initialX = turtle.xcor()
    initialY = turtle.ycor()
    initialHeading = turtle.heading()
```

```python
        # Call the draw function to draw the shape:
        turtle.pendown()
        shapeDrawFunction(size, depth)
        turtle.penup()

        # RECURSIVE CASE
        for spec in specs:
            # Each dictionary in specs has keys 'sizeChange', 'xChange',
            # 'yChange', and 'angleChange'. The size, x, and y changes
            # are multiplied by the size parameter. The x change and y
            # change are added to the turtle's current position. The angle
            # change is added to the turtle's current heading.
            sizeCh = spec.get('sizeChange', 1.0)
            xCh = spec.get('xChange', 0.0)
            yCh = spec.get('yChange', 0.0)
            angleCh = spec.get('angleChange', 0.0)

            # Reset the turtle to the shape's starting point:
            turtle.goto(initialX, initialY)
            turtle.setheading(initialHeading + angleCh)
            turtle.forward(size * xCh)
            turtle.left(90)
            turtle.forward(size * yCh)
            turtle.right(90)

            # Make the recursive call:
            drawFractal(shapeDrawFunction, size * sizeCh, specs, maxDepth,
            depth + 1)


if DRAW_FRACTAL == 1:
    # Four Corners:
    drawFractal(drawFilledSquare, 350,
        [{'sizeChange': 0.5, 'xChange': -0.5, 'yChange': 0.5},
         {'sizeChange': 0.5, 'xChange': 0.5, 'yChange': 0.5},
         {'sizeChange': 0.5, 'xChange': -0.5, 'yChange': -0.5},
         {'sizeChange': 0.5, 'xChange': 0.5, 'yChange': -0.5}], 5)
elif DRAW_FRACTAL == 2:
    # Spiral Squares:
    drawFractal(drawFilledSquare, 600, [{'sizeChange': 0.95,
        'angleChange': 7}], 50)
elif DRAW_FRACTAL == 3:
    # Double Spiral Squares:
    drawFractal(drawFilledSquare, 600,
        [{'sizeChange': 0.8, 'yChange': 0.1, 'angleChange': -10},
         {'sizeChange': 0.8, 'yChange': -0.1, 'angleChange': 10}])
elif DRAW_FRACTAL == 4:
    # Triangle Spiral:
    drawFractal(drawTriangleOutline, 20,
        [{'sizeChange': 1.05, 'angleChange': 7}], 80)
elif DRAW_FRACTAL == 5:
    # Conway's Game of Life Glider:
    third = 1 / 3
    drawFractal(drawFilledSquare, 600,
        [{'sizeChange': third, 'yChange': third},
```

```
                {'sizeChange': third, 'xChange': third},
                {'sizeChange': third, 'xChange': third, 'yChange': -third},
                {'sizeChange': third, 'yChange': -third},
                {'sizeChange': third, 'xChange': -third, 'yChange': -third}])
elif DRAW_FRACTAL == 6:
    # Sierpiński Triangle:
    toMid = math.sqrt(3) / 6
    drawFractal(drawTriangleOutline, 600,
        [{'sizeChange': 0.5, 'yChange': toMid, 'angleChange': 0},
         {'sizeChange': 0.5, 'yChange': toMid, 'angleChange': 120},
         {'sizeChange': 0.5, 'yChange': toMid, 'angleChange': 240}])
elif DRAW_FRACTAL == 7:
    # Wave:
    drawFractal(drawTriangleOutline, 280,
        [{'sizeChange': 0.5, 'xChange': -0.5, 'yChange': 0.5},
         {'sizeChange': 0.3, 'xChange': 0.5, 'yChange': 0.5},
         {'sizeChange': 0.5, 'yChange': -0.7, 'angleChange': 15}])
elif DRAW_FRACTAL == 8:
    # Horn:
    drawFractal(drawFilledSquare, 100,
        [{'sizeChange': 0.96, 'yChange': 0.5, 'angleChange': 11}], 100)
elif DRAW_FRACTAL == 9:
    # Snowflake:
    drawFractal(drawFilledSquare, 200,
        [{'xChange': math.cos(0 * math.pi / 180),
          'yChange': math.sin(0 * math.pi / 180), 'sizeChange': 0.4},
         {'xChange': math.cos(72 * math.pi / 180),
          'yChange': math.sin(72 * math.pi / 180), 'sizeChange': 0.4},
         {'xChange': math.cos(144 * math.pi / 180),
          'yChange': math.sin(144 * math.pi / 180), 'sizeChange': 0.4},
         {'xChange': math.cos(216 * math.pi / 180),
          'yChange': math.sin(216 * math.pi / 180), 'sizeChange': 0.4},
         {'xChange': math.cos(288 * math.pi / 180),
          'yChange': math.sin(288 * math.pi / 180), 'sizeChange': 0.4}])
elif DRAW_FRACTAL == 10:
    # The filled square shape:
    turtle.tracer(1, 0)
    drawFilledSquare(400, 0)
elif DRAW_FRACTAL == 11:
    # The triangle outline shape:
    turtle.tracer(1, 0)
    drawTriangleOutline(400, 0)
else:
    assert False, 'Set DRAW_FRACTAL to a number from 1 to 11.'

turtle.exitonclick() # Click the window to exit.
```

When you run this program, it will show the first of nine fractal images from Figure 13-1. You can change the DRAW_FRACTAL constant at the beginning of the source code to any integer from 1 to 9 and run the program again to see a new fractal. After learning how the program works, you'll also be able to create your own shape-drawing functions and call drawFractal() to produce fractals of your own design.

Setting Up Constants and the Turtle Configuration

The first lines of the program cover basic setup steps for our turtle-based program:

Python

```
import turtle, math

DRAW_FRACTAL = 1 # Set to 1 through 11 and run the program.

turtle.tracer(5000, 0) # Increase the first argument to speed up the drawing.
turtle.hideturtle()
```

The program imports the `turtle` module for drawing. It also imports the `math` module for the `math.sqrt()` function, which the Sierpiński Triangle fractal will use, and the `math.cos()` and `math.sin()` functions, for the Snowflake fractal.

The `DRAW_FRACTAL` constant can be set to any integer from 1 to 9 to draw one of the nine built-in fractals the program produces. You can also set it to 10 or 11 to show the output of the square or triangle shape-drawing function, respectively.

We also call some turtle functions to prepare for drawing. The `turtle.tracer(5000, 0)` call speeds up the drawing of the fractal. The 5000 argument tells the `turtle` module to wait until 5,000 turtle drawing instructions have been processed before rendering the drawing on the screen, and the 0 argument tells it to pause for 0 milliseconds after each drawing instruction. Otherwise, the `turtle` module would render the image after each drawing instruction, which significantly slows the program if we want only the final image.

You can change this call to `turtle.tracer(1, 10)` if you want to slow the drawing and watch the lines as they're produced. This can be useful when making your own fractals to debug any problems with the drawing.

The `turtle.hideturtle()` call hides the triangle shape on the screen that represents the turtle's current position and heading. (*Heading* is another term for *direction*.) We call this function so that the marker doesn't appear in the final image.

Working with the Shape-Drawing Functions

The `drawFractal()` function uses a shape-drawing function passed to it to draw the individual parts of the fractal. This is usually a simple shape, such as a square or triangle. The beautiful complexity of the fractals emerges from `drawFractal()` recursively calling this function for each individual component of the whole fractal.

The shape-drawing functions for the Fractal Art Maker have two parameters: size and depth. The size parameter is the length of the sides of the square or triangle it draws. The shape-drawing functions should always use arguments to `turtle.forward()` that are based on size so that the lengths will be proportionate to size at each level of recursion. Avoid code like `turtle.forward(100)` or `turtle.forward(200)`; instead, use code that is based on the size parameter, like turtle.forward(size) or turtle.forward(size * 2). In Python's turtle module, turtle.forward(1) moves the turtle by one *unit*, which is not necessarily the same as one pixel.

The shape-drawing functions' second parameter is the recursive depth of drawFractal(). The original call to drawFractal() has the depth parameter set to 0. Recursive calls to drawFractal() use depth + 1 as the depth parameter. In the Wave fractal, the first triangle in the center of the window has a depth argument of 0. The three triangles created next have a depth of 1. The nine triangles around those three triangles have a depth of 2, and so on.

Your shape-drawing function can ignore this argument, but using it can cause interesting variations to the basic shape. For example, the drawFilledSquare() shape-drawing function uses depth to alternate between drawing white squares and gray squares. Keep this in mind if you'd like to create your own shape-drawing functions for the Fractal Art Maker program, as they must accept a size and depth argument.

The drawFilledSquare() Function

The drawFilledSquare() function draws a filled-in square with sides of length size. To color the square, we use the turtle module's turtle.begin_fill() and turtle.end_fill() functions to make the square either white or gray, with a black border, depending on whether the depth argument is even or odd. Because these squares are filled in, any squares drawn on top of them later will cover them.

Like all shape-drawing functions for the Fractal Art Maker program, drawFilledSquare() accepts a size and depth parameter:

```
def drawFilledSquare(size, depth):
    size = int(size)
```

The size argument could be a floating-point number with a fractional part, which sometimes causes the turtle module to make slightly asymmetrical and uneven drawings. To prevent this, the first line of the function rounds size down to an integer.

When the function draws the square, it assumes the turtle is in the center of the square. Thus, the turtle must first move to the top-right corner of the square, relative to its initial heading:

Python

```
# Move to the top-right corner before drawing:
turtle.penup()
turtle.forward(size // 2)
turtle.left(90)
turtle.forward(size // 2)
turtle.left(180)
turtle.pendown()
```

The drawFractal() function always has the pen down and ready to draw when the shape-drawing function is called, so drawFilledSquare() must call turtle.penup() to avoid drawing a line as it moves to the starting position. To find the starting position relative to the middle of the square, the turtle must first move half of the square's length (that is, size // 2) forward, to the future right edge of the square. Next the turtle turns 90 degrees to face up and then moves size // 2 units forward to the top-right corner. The turtle is now facing the wrong way, so it turns around 180 degrees and places the pen down so that it can begin drawing.

Note that *top-right* and *up* are relative to the direction the turtle is originally facing. This code works just as well if the turtle begins facing to the right at 0 degrees or has a heading of 90, 42, or any other number of degrees. When you create your own shape-drawing functions, stick to the relative turtle movement functions like turtle.forward(), turtle.left(), and turtle.right() instead of absolute turtle movement functions like turtle.goto().

Next, the depth argument tells the function whether it should draw a white square or a gray one:

Python

```
# Alternate between white and gray (with black border):
if depth % 2 == 0:
    turtle.pencolor('black')
    turtle.fillcolor('white')
else:
    turtle.pencolor('black')
    turtle.fillcolor('gray')
```

If depth is even, the depth % 2 == 0 condition is True, and the square's *fill color* is white. Otherwise, the code sets the fill color to gray. Either way, the border of the square, determined by the *pen color*, is set to black. To change either of these colors, use strings of common color names, like red or yellow, or an HTML color code comprising a hash mark and six hexadecimal digits, like #24FF24 for lime green or #AD7100 for brown.

The website *https://html-color.codes* has charts for many HTML color codes. The fractals in this black-and-white book lack color, but your computer can render your own fractals in a bright range of colors!

With the colors set, we can finally draw the four lines of the actual square:

Python

```
# Draw a square:
turtle.begin_fill()
for i in range(4): # Draw four lines.
    turtle.forward(size)
    turtle.right(90)
turtle.end_fill()
```

To tell the turtle module that we intend to draw a filled-in shape and not just the outline, we call the turtle.begin_fill() function. Next is a for loop that draws a line of length size and turns the turtle 90 degrees to the right. The for loop repeats this four times to create the square. When the function finally calls turtle.end_fill(), the filled-in square appears on the screen.

The drawTriangleOutline() Function

The second shape-drawing function draws the outline of an equilateral triangle whose sides have a length of size. The function draws the triangle oriented with one corner at the top and two corners at the bottom. Figure 13-6 illustrates the various dimensions of an equilateral triangle.

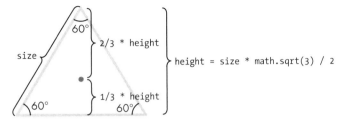

Figure 13-6: The measurements of an equilateral triangle with sides the length of size

Before we begin drawing, we must determine the triangle's height based on the length of its sides. Geometry tells us that, for equilateral triangles with sides of length L, the height h of the triangle is L times the square root of 3 divided by 2. In our function, L corresponds to the size parameter, so our code sets the height variable as follows:

```
height = size * math.sqrt(3) / 2
```

Geometry also tells us that the center of the triangle is one-third of the height from the bottom side and two-thirds of the height from the top point. This gives us the information we need to move the turtle to its starting position:

```
Python   def drawTriangleOutline(size, depth):
             size = int(size)

             # Move the turtle to the top of the equilateral triangle:
             height = size * math.sqrt(3) / 2
             turtle.penup()
             turtle.left(90) # Turn to face upward.
             turtle.forward(height * (2/3)) # Move to the top corner.
             turtle.right(150) # Turn to face the bottom-right corner.
             turtle.pendown()
```

To reach the top corner, we turn the turtle 90 degrees left to face up (relative to the turtle's original heading right at 0 degrees) and then move forward a number of units equal to height * (2/3). The turtle is still facing up, so to begin drawing the line on the right side, the turtle must turn 90 degrees right to face rightward, then an additional 60 degrees to face the bottom-right corner of the triangle. This is why we call turtle.right(150).

At this point, the turtle is ready to start drawing the triangle, so we lower the pen by calling turtle.pendown(). A for loop will handle drawing the three sides:

Python

```
# Draw the three sides of the triangle:
for i in range(3):
    turtle.forward(size)
    turtle.right(120)
```

Drawing the actual triangle is a matter of moving forward by size units, and then turning 120 degrees to the right, three separate times. The third and final 120-degree turn leaves the turtle facing its original direction. You can see these movements and turns in Figure 13-7.

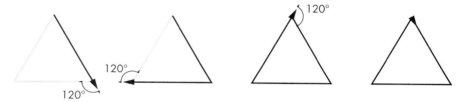

Figure 13-7: Drawing an equilateral triangle involves three forward movements and three 120-degree turns.

The drawTriangleOutline() function draws only the outline and not a filled-in shape, so it doesn't call turtle.begin_fill() and turtle.end_fill() as drawFilledSquare() does.

Using the Fractal Drawing Function

Now that we have two sample drawing functions to work with, let's examine the main function in the Fractal Art Maker project, drawFractal(). This function has three required parameters and one optional one: shapeDrawFunction, size, specs, and maxDepth.

The shapeDrawFunction parameter expects a function, like drawFilledSquare() or drawTriangleOutline(). The size parameter expects the starting size passed to the drawing function. Often, a value between 100 and 500 is a good starting size, though this depends on the code in your shape-drawing function, and finding the right value may require experimentation.

The specs parameter expects a list of dictionaries that specify how the recursive shapes should change their size, position, and angle as drawFractal() recursively calls itself. These specifications are described later in this section.

To prevent drawFractal() from recursing until it causes a stack overflow, the maxDepth parameter holds the number of times drawFractal() should recursively call itself. By default, maxDepth has a value of 8, but you can provide a different value if you want more or fewer recursive shapes.

A fifth parameter, depth, is handled by drawFractal()'s recursive call to itself and defaults to 0. You don't need to specify it when you call drawFractal().

Setting Up the Function

The first thing the drawFractal() function does is check for its two base cases:

Python
```
def drawFractal(shapeDrawFunction, size, specs, maxDepth=8, depth=0):
    if depth > maxDepth or size < 1:
        return # BASE CASE
```

If depth is greater than maxDepth, the function will stop the recursion and return. The other base case occurs if size is less than 1, at which point the shapes being drawn would be too small to be seen on the screen and so the function should simply return.

We keep track of the turtle's original position and heading in three variables: initialX, initialY, and initialHeading. This way, no matter where the shape-drawing function leaves the turtle positioned or what direction it is headed, drawFractal() can revert the turtle back to the original position and heading for the next recursive call:

Python
```
# Save the position and heading at the start of this function call:
initialX = turtle.xcor()
initialY = turtle.ycor()
initialHeading = turtle.heading()
```

The turtle.xcor() and turtle.ycor() functions return the absolute x- and y-coordinates of the turtle on the screen. The turtle.heading() function returns the direction in which the turtle is pointed in degrees.

The next few lines call the shape-drawing function passed to the shapeDrawFunction parameter:

Python
```
# Call the draw function to draw the shape:
turtle.pendown()
shapeDrawFunction(size, depth)
turtle.penup()
```

Because the value passed as the argument for the shapeDrawFunction parameter is a function, the code shapeDrawFunction(size, depth) calls this function with the values in size and depth. The pen is lowered before and raised after the shapeDrawFunction() call to ensure that the shape-drawing function can consistently expect the pen to be down when the drawing begins.

Using the Specifications Dictionary

After the call to shapeDrawFunction(), the rest of drawFractal()'s code is devoted to making recursive calls to drawFractal() based on the specification in the specs list's dictionaries. For each dictionary, drawFractal() makes one recursive call to drawFractal(). If specs is a list with one dictionary, every call to drawFractal() results in only one recursive call to drawFractal(). If specs is a list with three dictionaries, every call to drawFractal() results in three recursive calls to drawFractal().

The dictionaries in the specs parameter provide specifications for each recursive call. Each of these dictionaries has the keys sizeChange, xChange, yChange, and angleChange. These dictate how the size of the fractal, the position of the turtle, and the heading of the turtle change for a recursive drawFractal() call. Table 13-1 describes the four keys in a specification.

Table 13-1: Keys in the Specification Dictionaries

Key	Default value	Description
sizeChange	1.0	The next recursive shape's size value is the current size multiplied by this value.
xChange	0.0	The next recursive shape's x-coordinate is the current x-coordinate plus the current size multiplied by this value.
yChange	0.0	The next recursive shape's y-coordinate is the current y-coordinate plus the current size multiplied by this value.
angleChange	0.0	The next recursive shape's starting angle is the current starting angle plus this value.

Let's take a look at the specification dictionary for the Four Corners fractal, which produces the top-left image shown previously in Figure 13-1. The call to drawFractal() for the Four Corners fractal passes the following list of dictionaries for the specs parameter:

Python
```
[{'sizeChange': 0.5, 'xChange': -0.5, 'yChange': 0.5},
 {'sizeChange': 0.5, 'xChange': 0.5, 'yChange': 0.5},
 {'sizeChange': 0.5, 'xChange': -0.5, 'yChange': -0.5},
 {'sizeChange': 0.5, 'xChange': 0.5, 'yChange': -0.5}]
```

The specs list has four dictionaries, so each call to drawFractal() that draws a square will, in turn, recursively call drawFractal() four more times to draw four more squares. Figure 13-8 shows this progression of squares (which alternate between white and gray).

To determine the size of the next square to be drawn, the value for the sizeChange key is multiplied by the current size parameter. The first dictionary in the specs list has a sizeChange value of 0.5, which makes the next recursive call have a size argument of 350 * 0.5, or 175 units. This makes the next square half the size of the previous square. A sizeChange value of 2.0 would, for example, double the size of the next square. If the dictionary has no sizeChange key, the value defaults to 1.0 for no change to the size.

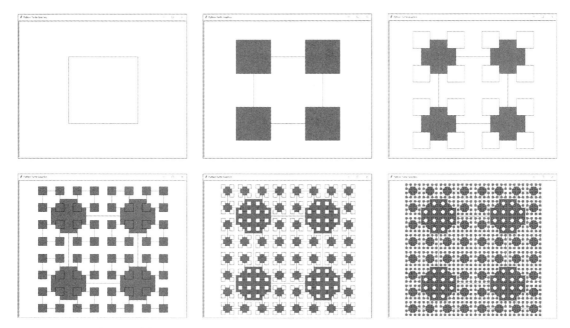

Figure 13-8: Each step of the Four Corners example from left to right, top to bottom. Each square recursively produces four more squares at its corners, with colors alternating between white and gray.

To determine the x-coordinate of the next square, the first dictionary's xChange value, -0.5 in this case, is multiplied by the size. When size is 350, this means the next square has an x-coordinate of -175 units relative to the turtle's current position. This xChange value and the yChange key's value of 0.5 places the next square's position a distance of 50 percent of the current square's size, to the left and above the current square's position. This happens to center it on the top-left corner of the current square.

If you look at the three other dictionaries in the specs list, you'll notice they all have a sizeChange value of 0.5. The difference between them is that their xChange and yChange values place them in the other three corners of the current square. As a result, the next four squares are drawn centered on the four corners of the current square.

The dictionaries in the specs list for this example don't have an angleChange value, so this value defaults to 0.0 degrees. A positive angleChange value indicates a counterclockwise rotation, while a negative value indicates a clockwise rotation.

Each dictionary represents a separate square to be drawn each time the recursive function is called. If we were to remove the first dictionary from the specs list, each drawFractal() call would produce only three squares, as in Figure 13-9.

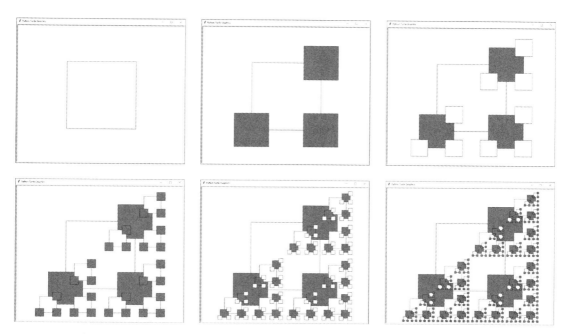

Figure 13-9: The Four Corners fractal with the first dictionary removed from the specs list

Applying the Specifications

Let's look at how the code in drawFractal() actually does everything we've described:

Python
```
# RECURSIVE CASE
for spec in specs:
    # Each dictionary in specs has keys 'sizeChange', 'xChange',
    # 'yChange', and 'angleChange'. The size, x, and y changes
    # are multiplied by the size parameter. The x change and y
    # change are added to the turtle's current position. The angle
    # change is added to the turtle's current heading.
    sizeCh = spec.get('sizeChange', 1.0)
    xCh = spec.get('xChange', 0.0)
    yCh = spec.get('yChange', 0.0)
    angleCh = spec.get('angleChange', 0.0)
```

The for loop assigns an individual specification dictionary in the specs list to the loop variable spec on each iteration of the loop. The get() dictionary method calls pull the values for the sizeChange, xChange, yChange, and angleChange keys from this dictionary and assign them to the shorter-named sizeCh, xCh, yCh, and angleCh variables. The get() method substitutes a default value if the key doesn't exist in the dictionary.

Next, the turtle's position and heading are reset to the values indicated when drawFractal() was first called. This ensures that the recursive calls from previous loop iterations don't leave the turtle in some other place. Then the heading and position are changed according to the angleCh, xCh, and yCh variables:

Python

```python
# Reset the turtle to the shape's starting point:
turtle.goto(initialX, initialY)
turtle.setheading(initialHeading + angleCh)

turtle.forward(size * xCh)
turtle.left(90)
turtle.forward(size * yCh)
turtle.right(90)
```

The x-change and y-change positions are expressed relative to the turtle's current heading. If the turtle's heading is 0, the turtle's relative x-axis is the same as the actual x-axis on the screen. However, if the turtle's heading is, say, 45, the turtle's relative x-axis is at a 45-degree tilt. Moving "right" along the turtle's relative x-axis would then move at an up-right angle.

This is why moving forward by size * xCh moves the turtle along its relative x-axis. If xCh is negative, turtle.forward() moves left along the turtle's relative x-axis. The turtle.left(90) call points the turtle along the turtle's relative y-axis, and turtle.forward(size * yCh) moves the turtle to the next shape's starting position. However, the turtle.left(90) call changed the turtle's heading, so turtle.right(90) is called to reset it back to its original direction.

Figure 13-10 shows how these four lines of code move the turtle to the right along its relative x-axis and up along its relative y-axis and leave it in the correct heading, no matter what its initial heading was.

 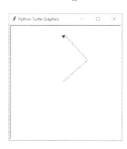  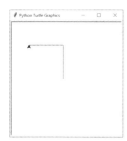

Figure 13-10: In each of these four images, the turtle always moves 100 units "right" and "up" along the relative x-axis and y-axis of its initial heading.

Finally, with the turtle in the correct position and heading for the next shape, we make the recursive call to drawFractal():

Python

```python
# Make the recursive call:
drawFractal(shapeDrawFunction, size * sizeCh, specs, maxDepth,
    depth + 1)
```

The shapeDrawFunction, specs, and maxDepth arguments are passed to the recursive drawFractal() call unchanged. However, size * sizeCh is passed for the next size parameter to reflect the change in the size of the recursive shape, and depth + 1 is passed for the depth parameter to increment it for the next shape-drawing function call.

Creating the Example Fractals

Now that we've covered how the shape-drawing functions and recursive draw Fractal() function work, let's look at the nine example fractals that come with the Fractal Art Maker. You can see these examples in Figure 13-1.

Four Corners

The first fractal is *Four Corners*, which begins as a large square. As the function calls itself, the fractal's specifications cause four smaller squares to be drawn in the four corners of the square:

Python
```
if DRAW_FRACTAL == 1:
    # Four Corners:
    drawFractal(drawFilledSquare, 350,
        [{'sizeChange': 0.5, 'xChange': -0.5, 'yChange': 0.5},
         {'sizeChange': 0.5, 'xChange': 0.5, 'yChange': 0.5},
         {'sizeChange': 0.5, 'xChange': -0.5, 'yChange': -0.5},
         {'sizeChange': 0.5, 'xChange': 0.5, 'yChange': -0.5}], 5)
```

The call to drawFractal() here limits the maximum depth to 5, as any more tends to make the fractal so dense that the fine detail becomes hard to see. This fractal appears in Figure 13-8.

Spiral Squares

The *Spiral Squares fractal* also starts as a large square, but it creates just one new square on each recursive call:

Python
```
elif DRAW_FRACTAL == 2:
    # Spiral Squares:
    drawFractal(drawFilledSquare, 600, [{'sizeChange': 0.95,
        'angleChange': 7}], 50)
```

This square is slightly smaller and rotated by 7 degrees. The centers of all the squares are unchanged, so there's no need to add xChange and yChange keys to the specification. The default maximum depth of 8 is too small to get an interesting fractal, so we increase it to 50 to produce a hypnotic spiral pattern.

Double Spiral Squares

The *Double Spiral Squares fractal* is similar to Spiral Squares, except each square creates two smaller squares. This creates an interesting fan effect, as the second square is drawn later and tends to cover up previously drawn squares:

Python
```
elif DRAW_FRACTAL == 3:
    # Double Spiral Squares:
    drawFractal(drawFilledSquare, 600,
        [{'sizeChange': 0.8, 'yChange': 0.1, 'angleChange': -10},
         {'sizeChange': 0.8, 'yChange': -0.1, 'angleChange': 10}])
```

The squares are created slightly higher or lower than their previous square and rotated either 10 or -10 degrees.

Triangle Spiral

The *Triangle Spiral fractal*, another variation of Spiral Squares, uses the draw-TriangleOutline() shape-drawing function instead of drawFilledSquare():

Python
```
elif DRAW_FRACTAL == 4:
    # Triangle Spiral:
    drawFractal(drawTriangleOutline, 20,
        [{'sizeChange': 1.05, 'angleChange': 7}], 80)
```

Unlike the Spiral Squares fractal, the Triangle Spiral fractal begins at the small size of 20 units and slightly increases in size for each level of recursion. The sizeChange key is greater than 1.0, so the shapes are always increasing in size. This means the base case occurs when the recursion reaches a depth of 80, because the base case of size becoming less than 1 is never reached.

Conway's Game of Life Glider

Conway's Game of Life is a famous example of cellular automata. The game's simple rules cause interesting and wildly chaotic patterns to emerge on a 2D grid. One such pattern is a *Glider* consisting of five cells in a 3×3 space:

Python
```
elif DRAW_FRACTAL == 5:
    # Conway's Game of Life Glider:
    third = 1 / 3
    drawFractal(drawFilledSquare, 600,
        [{'sizeChange': third, 'yChange': third},
         {'sizeChange': third, 'xChange': third},
         {'sizeChange': third, 'xChange': third, 'yChange': -third},
         {'sizeChange': third, 'yChange': -third},
         {'sizeChange': third, 'xChange': -third, 'yChange': -third}])
```

The Glider fractal here has additional Gliders drawn inside each of its five cells. The third variable helps precisely set the position of the recursive shapes in the 3×3 space.

You can find a Python implementation of Conway's Game of Life in my book *The Big Book of Small Python Projects* (No Starch Press, 2021) and online at *https://inventwithpython.com/bigbookpython/project13.html*. Tragically, John Conway, the mathematician and professor who developed Conway's Game of Life, passed away of complications from COVID-19 in April 2020.

Sierpiński Triangle

We created the *Sierpiński Triangle fractal* in Chapter 9, but our Fractal Art Maker can re-create it as well by using the drawTriangleOutline() shape function. After all, a Sierpiński triangle is an equilateral triangle with three smaller equilateral triangles drawn in its interior:

Python
```
elif DRAW_FRACTAL == 6:
    # Sierpiński Triangle:
    toMid = math.sqrt(3) / 6
    drawFractal(drawTriangleOutline, 600,
        [{'sizeChange': 0.5, 'yChange': toMid, 'angleChange': 0},
         {'sizeChange': 0.5, 'yChange': toMid, 'angleChange': 120},
         {'sizeChange': 0.5, 'yChange': toMid, 'angleChange': 240}])
```

The center of these smaller triangles is size * math.sqrt(3) / 6 units from the center of the previous triangle. The three calls adjust the heading of the turtle to 0, 120, and 240 degrees before moving up on the turtle's relative y-axis.

Wave

We discussed the *Wave fractal* at the start of this chapter, and you can see it in Figure 13-5. This relatively simple fractal creates three smaller and distinct recursive triangles:

Python
```
elif DRAW_FRACTAL == 7:
    # Wave:
    drawFractal(drawTriangleOutline, 280,
        [{'sizeChange': 0.5, 'xChange': -0.5, 'yChange': 0.5},
         {'sizeChange': 0.3, 'xChange': 0.5, 'yChange': 0.5},
         {'sizeChange': 0.5, 'yChange': -0.7, 'angleChange': 15}])
```

Horn

The *Horn fractal* resembles a ram's horn:

Python
```
elif DRAW_FRACTAL == 8:
    # Horn:
    drawFractal(drawFilledSquare, 100,
        [{'sizeChange': 0.96, 'yChange': 0.5, 'angleChange': 11}], 100)
```

This simple fractal is made up of squares, each of which is slightly smaller, moved up, and rotated 11 degrees from the previous square. We increase the maximum recursion depth to 100 to extend the horn into a tight spiral.

Snowflake

The final fractal, *Snowflake*, is composed of squares laid out in a pentagon pattern. This is similar to the Four Corners fractal, but it uses five evenly spaced recursive squares instead of four:

Python
```
elif DRAW_FRACTAL == 9:
    # Snowflake:
    drawFractal(drawFilledSquare, 200,
        [{'xChange': math.cos(0 * math.pi / 180),
          'yChange': math.sin(0 * math.pi / 180), 'sizeChange': 0.4},
         {'xChange': math.cos(72 * math.pi / 180),
          'yChange': math.sin(72 * math.pi / 180), 'sizeChange': 0.4},
         {'xChange': math.cos(144 * math.pi / 180),
          'yChange': math.sin(144 * math.pi / 180), 'sizeChange': 0.4},
         {'xChange': math.cos(216 * math.pi / 180),
          'yChange': math.sin(216 * math.pi / 180), 'sizeChange': 0.4},
         {'xChange': math.cos(288 * math.pi / 180),
          'yChange': math.sin(288 * math.pi / 180), 'sizeChange': 0.4}])
```

This fractal uses the cosine and sine functions from trigonometry, implemented in Python's math.cos() and math.sin() functions, to determine how to shift the squares along the x-axis and y-axis. A full circle has 360 degrees, so to evenly space out the five recursive squares in this circle, we place them at intervals of 0, 72, 144, 216, and 288 degrees. The math.cos() and math.sin() functions expect the angle argument to be in radians instead of degrees, so we must multiply these numbers by math.pi / 180.

The end result is that each square is surrounded by five other squares, which are surrounded by five other squares, and so on, to form a crystal-like fractal that resembles a snowflake.

Producing a Single Square or Triangle

For completion, you can also set DRAW_FRACTAL to 10 or 11 to view what a single call to drawFilledSquare() and drawTriangleOutline() produce in the turtle window. These shapes are drawn with a size of 600:

Python
```
elif DRAW_FRACTAL == 10:
    # The filled square shape:
    turtle.tracer(1, 0)
    drawFilledSquare(400, 0)
elif DRAW_FRACTAL == 11:
    # The triangle outline shape:
    turtle.tracer(1, 0)
    drawTriangleOutline(400, 0)
turtle.exitonclick() # Click the window to exit.
```

After drawing the fractal or shape based on the value in DRAW_FRACTAL, the program calls turtle.exitonclick() so that the turtle window stays open until the user clicks it. Then the program terminates.

Creating Your Own Fractals

You can create your own fractals by changing the specification passed to the drawFractal() function. Start by thinking about how many recursive calls you'd like each call to drawFractal() to generate, and how the size, position, and heading of the shapes should change. You can use the existing shape-drawing functions or create your own.

For example, Figure 13-11 shows the nine built-in fractals, except the square and triangle functions have been swapped. Some of these produce bland shapes, but others can result in unexpected beauty.

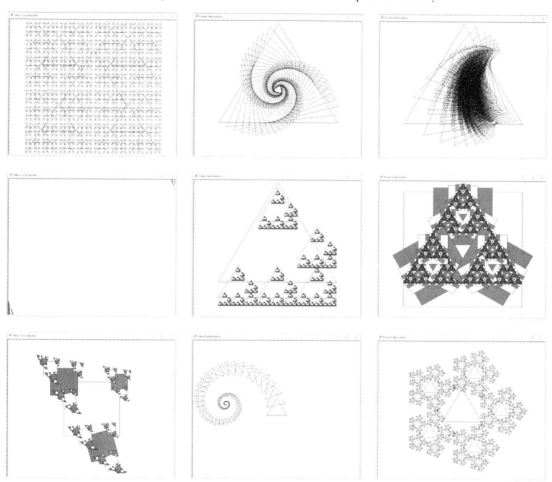

Figure 13-11: The nine fractals that come with Fractal Art Maker, with the shape-drawing functions swapped

Summary

The Fractal Art Maker projects demonstrate the endless possibilities of recursion. A simple recursive drawFractal() function, paired with a shape-drawing function, can create a large variety of detailed geometric art.

At the core of Fractal Art Maker is the recursive drawFractal() function, which accepts another function as an argument. This second function draws a basic shape repeatedly by using the size, position, and heading given in the list of specification dictionaries.

You can test an unlimited number of shape-drawing functions and specification settings. Let your creativity drive your fractal projects as you experiment with the code in this program.

Further Reading

There are websites that allow you to create fractals. Interactive Fractal Tree at *https://www.visnos.com/demos/fractal* has sliders to change a binary tree fractal's angle and size parameters. Procedural Snowflake at *https://procedural-snowflake.glitch.me* generates new snowflakes in your browser. Nico's Fractal Machine at *https://sciencevsmagic.net/fractal* creates animated drawings of fractals. You can find others by searching the web for *fractal maker* or *fractal generator online*.

14

DROSTE MAKER

The *Droste effect* is a recursive art technique named after a 1904 illustration on a tin of Droste's Cacao, a Dutch brand of cocoa. Shown in Figure 14-1, the tin features an image of a nurse holding a meal tray containing a tin of Droste cocoa, which itself bears the illustration.

In this chapter we'll create a Droste Maker program that can generate similar recursive images from any photograph or drawing you have, whether it be a museum patron looking at an exhibit of themself, a cat in front of a computer monitor of a cat in front of a computer monitor, or something else entirely.

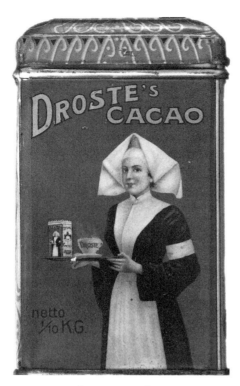

Figure 14-1: The recursive illustration on a tin of Droste's Cacao

Using a graphics program such as Microsoft Paint or Adobe Photoshop, you'll prepare the image by covering an area of it with a pure magenta color, indicating where to place the recursive image. The Python program uses the Pillow image library to read this image data and produce a recursive image.

First, we'll cover how to install the Pillow library and how the Droste Maker algorithm works. Next, we'll present the Python source code for the program with accompanying explanation of the code.

Installing the Pillow Python Library

This chapter's project requires the Pillow image library. This library allows your Python programs to create and modify image files including PNGs, JPEGs, and GIFs. It has several functions to perform resizing, copying, cropping, and other common actions on images.

To install this library on Windows, open a command prompt window and run `py -m pip install --user pillow`. To install this library on macOS or Linux, open a Terminal window and run `python3 -m pip install --user pillow`. This command makes Python use the pip installer program to download the module from the official Python Package Index at *https://pypi.org*.

To verify that the installation worked, open a Python terminal and run `from PIL import Image`. (While the library's name is Pillow, the Python module installed is named PIL, in capital letters.) If no error appears, the library was installed correctly.

The official documentation for Pillow can be found at *https://pillow.readthedocs.io*.

Painting Your Image

The next step is to prepare an image by setting a portion of it to the RGB (red, green, blue) color value (255, 0, 255). Computer graphics often use magenta to mark which pixels of an image should be rendered as transparent. Our program will treat these magenta pixels like a green screen in video production, replacing them with a resized version of the initial image. Of course, this resized image will have its own smaller magenta area, which the program will replace with another resized image. The base case occurs when the final image has no more magenta pixels, at which point the algorithm is done.

Figure 14-2 shows the progression of images created as the resized image is recursively applied to the magenta pixels. In this example, a model stands in front of an art museum exhibit that has been replaced with magenta pixels, turning the photograph itself into the exhibit. You can download this base image from *https://inventwithpython.com/museum.png*.

Be sure you use only the pure (255, 0, 255) magenta color for painting the magenta area in your image. Some tools may have a fading effect that produces a more natural look. For example, Photoshop's Brush tool will produce faded magenta pixels on the outline of the painted area, so you will need to use the Pencil tool instead, which paints using only the precise pure magenta color you've selected. If your graphics program doesn't allow you to specify the precise RGB color for drawing, you can copy and paste the colors from the PNG image at *https://inventwithpython.com/magenta.png*.

The magenta area in the image can be of any size or shape; it does not have to be an exact, contiguous rectangle. You can see that in Figure 14-2, the museum visitor cuts into the magenta rectangle, placing them in front of the recursive image.

If you make your own images with Droste Maker, you should use the PNG image file format instead of JPEG. JPEG images use *lossy* compression techniques to keep the file size small that introduce slight imperfections. These are usually imperceptible to the human eye and don't affect overall image quality. However, this lossy compression will replace the pure (255, 0, 255) magenta pixels with slightly different shades of magenta. The *lossless* image compression of PNG images ensures this won't happen.

Figure 14-2: Recursive applications of the image to the magenta pixels. If you are viewing the black-and-white image printed in this book, the magenta area is the rectangle in front of the museum visitor.

The Complete Droste Maker Program

The following is the source code for *drostemaker.py*; because this program relies on the Python-only Pillow library, there is no JavaScript equivalent for this project in this book:

```python
from PIL import Image

def makeDroste(baseImage, stopAfter=10):
    # If baseImage is a string of an image filename, load that image:
    if isinstance(baseImage, str):
        baseImage = Image.open(baseImage)

    if stopAfter == 0:
        # BASE CASE
        return baseImage
    # The magenta color has max red/blue/alpha, zero green:
    if baseImage.mode == 'RGBA':
        magentaColor = (255, 0, 255, 255)
    elif baseImage.mode == 'RGB':
        magentaColor = (255, 0, 255)

    # Find the dimensions of the base image and its magenta area:
    baseImageWidth, baseImageHeight = baseImage.size
    magentaLeft = None
    magentaRight = None
    magentaTop = None
    magentaBottom = None

    for x in range(baseImageWidth):
        for y in range(baseImageHeight):
            if baseImage.getpixel((x, y)) == magentaColor:
                if magentaLeft is None or x < magentaLeft:
                    magentaLeft = x
                if magentaRight is None or x > magentaRight:
                    magentaRight = x
                if magentaTop is None or y < magentaTop:
                    magentaTop = y
                if magentaBottom is None or y > magentaBottom:
                    magentaBottom = y

    if magentaLeft is None:
        # BASE CASE - No magenta pixels are in the image.
        return baseImage

    # Get a resized version of the base image:
    magentaWidth = magentaRight - magentaLeft + 1
    magentaHeight = magentaBottom - magentaTop + 1
    baseImageAspectRatio = baseImageWidth / baseImageHeight
    magentaAspectRatio = magentaWidth / magentaHeight

    if baseImageAspectRatio < magentaAspectRatio:
        # Make the resized width match the width of the magenta area:
        widthRatio = magentaWidth / baseImageWidth
        resizedImage = baseImage.resize((magentaWidth,
        int(baseImageHeight * widthRatio) + 1), Image.NEAREST)
    else:
        # Make the resized height match the height of the magenta area:
        heightRatio =  magentaHeight / baseImageHeight
```

```
    resizedImage = baseImage.resize((int(baseImageWidth *
    heightRatio) + 1, magentaHeight), Image.NEAREST)

    # Replace the magenta pixels with the smaller, resized image:
    for x in range(magentaLeft, magentaRight + 1):
        for y in range(magentaTop, magentaBottom + 1):
            if baseImage.getpixel((x, y)) == magentaColor:
                pix = resizedImage.getpixel((x - magentaLeft, y - magentaTop))
                baseImage.putpixel((x, y), pix)

    # RECURSIVE CASE:
    return makeDroste(baseImage, stopAfter=stopAfter - 1)


recursiveImage = makeDroste('museum.png')
recursiveImage.save('museum-recursive.png')
recursiveImage.show()
```

Before you run this program, place your image file in the same folder as *drostemaker.py*. The program will save the recursive image as *museum-recursive.png* and then open an image viewer to display it. If you want to run the program on your own image that you've added a magenta area to, replace makeDroste('museum.png') at the end of the source code with the name of your image file and save('museum-recursive.png') with the name you'd like to use to save the recursive image.

Setting Up

The Droste Maker program has only one function, makeDroste(), which accepts a Pillow Image object or a string of an image's filename. The function returns a Pillow Image object with any magenta pixels recursively replaced by a version of the same image:

Python
```
from PIL import Image


def makeDroste(baseImage, stopAfter=10):
    # If baseImage is a string of an image filename, load that image:
    if isinstance(baseImage, str):
        baseImage = Image.open(baseImage)
```

The program begins by importing the Image class from the Pillow library (named PIL as a Python module). Within the makeDroste() function, we check whether the baseImage parameter is a string, and if so, we replace it with a Pillow Image object loaded from the corresponding image file.

Next, we check whether the stopAfter parameter is 0. If it is, we've reached one of the algorithm's base cases and the function returns the Pillow Image object of the base image:

Python

```python
if stopAfter == 0:
    # BASE CASE
    return baseImage
```

The `stopAfter` parameter is 10 by default if the function call doesn't provide one. The recursive call to `makeDroste()` later in this function passes `stopAfter - 1` as the argument for this parameter so that it decreases with each recursive call and approaches the base case of 0.

For example, passing 0 for `stopAfter` results in the function immediately returning a recursive image identical to the base image. Passing 1 for `stopAfter` replaces the magenta area with a recursive image once, makes one recursive call, reaches the base case, and immediately returns. Passing 2 for `stopAfter` causes two recursive calls, and so on.

This parameter prevents the function from recursing until it causes a stack overflow in cases when the magenta area is particularly large. It also lets us pass a smaller argument than 10 to limit the number of recursive images placed in the base image. For example, the four images in Figure 14-2 were created by passing 0, 1, 2, and 3 for the `stopAfter` parameter.

Next, we check the color mode of the base image. This can be either RGB for an image with red-green-blue pixels or RGBA for an image that has an alpha channel for its pixels. The *alpha value* tells a pixel's level of transparency. Here's the code:

Python

```python
# The magenta color has max red/blue/alpha, zero green:
if baseImage.mode == 'RGBA':
    magentaColor = (255, 0, 255, 255)
elif baseImage.mode == 'RGB':
    magentaColor = (255, 0, 255)
```

The Droste Maker needs to know the color mode so that it can find magenta pixels. The values for each channel range from 0 to 255, and magenta pixels have a maximum amount of red and blue but no green. Further, if an alpha channel exists, it would be set to 255 for a completely opaque color and 0 for a completely transparent one. The `magentaColor` variable is set to the correct tuple value for a magenta pixel depending on the image's color mode given in `baseImage.mode`.

Finding the Magenta Area

Before the program can recursively insert the image into the magenta area, it must find the boundaries of the magenta area in the image. This involves finding the leftmost, rightmost, topmost, and bottommost magenta pixels in the image.

While the magenta area itself doesn't need to be a perfect rectangle, the program needs to know the rectangular boundaries of the magenta in order to properly resize the image for insertion. For example, Figure 14-3 shows a base image of the *Mona Lisa* with the magenta area outlined in white. The magenta pixels are replaced to produce the recursive image.

Figure 14-3: The base image with a magenta area outlined in white (left) and the recursive image it produces (right)

To calculate the resizing and placement of the resized image, the program retrieves the width and height of the base image from the size attribute of the Pillow Image object in baseImage. The following lines initialize four variables for the four edges of the magenta area—magentaLeft, magentaRight, magentaTop, and magentaBottom—to the None value:

Python

```
# Find the dimensions of the base image and its magenta area:
baseImageWidth, baseImageHeight = baseImage.size
magentaLeft = None
magentaRight = None
magentaTop = None
magentaBottom = None
```

These edge variable values are replaced by integer x and y coordinates in the code that comes next:

Python

```python
for x in range(baseImageWidth):
    for y in range(baseImageHeight):
        if baseImage.getpixel((x, y)) == magentaColor:
            if magentaLeft is None or x < magentaLeft:
                magentaLeft = x
            if magentaRight is None or x > magentaRight:
                magentaRight = x
            if magentaTop is None or y < magentaTop:
                magentaTop = y
            if magentaBottom is None or y > magentaBottom:
                magentaBottom = y
```

These nested for loops iterate the x and y variables over every possible x, y coordinate in the base image. We check whether the pixel at each coordinate is the pure magenta color stored in magentaColor, then update the magentaLeft variable if the coordinates of the magenta pixel are further left than currently recorded in magentaLeft, and so on for the other three directions.

By the time the nested for loops are finished, magentaLeft, magentaRight, magentaTop, and magentaBottom will describe the boundaries of the magenta pixels in the base image. If the image has no magenta pixels, these variables will remain set to their initial None value:

Python

```python
if magentaLeft is None:
    # BASE CASE - No magenta pixels are in the image.
    return baseImage
```

If magentaLeft (or really, any of the four variables) is still set to None after the nested for loops complete, no magenta pixels are in the image. This is a base case for our recursive algorithm because the magenta area becomes smaller and smaller with each recursive call to makeDroste(). At this point, the function returns the Pillow Image object in baseImage.

Resizing the Base Image

We need to resize the base image to cover the entire magenta area and no more. Figure 14-4 shows the complete resized image overlaid transparently on the original base image. This resized image is cropped so that only the parts over magenta pixels are copied over to the final image.

Figure 14-4: The base image with the magenta area in the monitor (top), the resized image over the base image (middle), and the final recursive image that replaces only the magenta pixels (bottom)

We cannot simply resize the base image to the dimensions of the magenta area because it's unlikely the two share the same *aspect ratio*, or proportion of the width divided by the height. Doing so results in a recursive image that looks stretched or squished, like Figure 14-5.

Instead, we must make the resized image large enough to completely cover the magenta area but still retain the image's original aspect ratio. This means either setting the width of the resized image to the width of the magenta area such that the height of the resized image is equal to or larger than the height of the magenta area, or setting the height of the resized image to the height of the magenta area such that the width of the resized image is equal to or larger than the width of the magenta area.

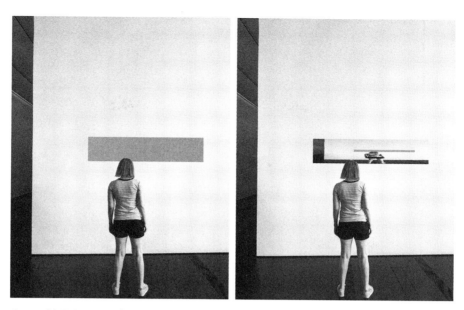

Figure 14-5: Resizing the image to the dimensions of the magenta area can result in a different aspect ratio, causing it to look stretched or squished.

To calculate the correct resizing dimensions, the program needs to determine the aspect ratio of both the base image and the magenta area:

Python

```
# Get a resized version of the base image:
magentaWidth = magentaRight - magentaLeft + 1
magentaHeight = magentaBottom - magentaTop + 1
baseImageAspectRatio = baseImageWidth / baseImageHeight
magentaAspectRatio = magentaWidth / magentaHeight
```

From `magentaRight` and `magentaLeft`, we can calculate the width of the magenta area. The `+ 1` accounts for a small, necessary adjustment: if the right side of the magenta area was the x-coordinate of 11 and the left side was 10, the width would be two pixels. This is correctly calculated by (`magentaRight - magentaLeft + 1`), not (`magentaRight - magentaLeft`).

Because the aspect ratio is the width divided by the height, images with large aspect ratios are taller than they are wide, and those with small aspect ratios are wider than they are tall. An aspect ratio of 1.0 describes a perfect square. The next lines set the dimensions of the resized image after comparing the aspect ratios of the base image and the magenta area:

```
if baseImageAspectRatio < magentaAspectRatio:
    # Make the resized width match the width of the magenta area:
    widthRatio = magentaWidth / baseImageWidth
    resizedImage = baseImage.resize((magentaWidth,
    int(baseImageHeight * widthRatio) + 1), Image.NEAREST)
```

```
else:
    # Make the resized height match the height of the magenta area:
    heightRatio =  magentaHeight / baseImageHeight
    resizedImage = baseImage.resize((int(baseImageWidth *
    heightRatio) + 1, magentaHeight), Image.NEAREST)
```

If the base image's aspect ratio is less than the magenta area's aspect ratio, the resized image's width should match the width of the magenta area. If the base image's aspect ratio is greater, the resized image's height should match the height of the magenta area. We then determine the other dimension by multiplying the base image's height by the width ratio, or the base image's width by the height ratio. This ensures that the resized image both completely covers the magenta area and remains proportional to its original aspect ratio.

We call the resize() method once to produce a new Pillow Image object resized to match either the width of the base image or the height of the base image. The first argument is a (width, height) tuple for the new image's size. The second argument is the Image.NEAREST constant from the Pillow library that tells the resize() method to use the nearest neighbor algorithm when resizing the image. This prevents the resize() method from blending the colors of the pixels to produce a smooth image.

We don't want this, because it could blur the magenta pixels with neighboring non-magenta pixels in the resized image. Our makeDroste() function relies on detecting magenta pixels with the exact RGB color of (255, 0, 255) and would ignore these slightly off magenta pixels. The end result would be a pinkish outline around the magenta areas that would ruin our image. The nearest neighbor algorithm doesn't do this blurring, leaving our magenta pixels exactly at the (255, 0, 255) magenta color.

Recursively Placing the Image Within the Image

Once the base image has been resized, we can place the resized image over the base image. But the pixels from the resized image should be placed over only magenta pixels in the base image. The resized image will be placed such that the top-left corner of the resized image is at the top-left corner of the magenta area:

Python
```
# Replace the magenta pixels with the smaller, resized image:
for x in range(magentaLeft, magentaRight + 1):
    for y in range(magentaTop, magentaBottom + 1):
        if baseImage.getpixel((x, y)) == magentaColor:
            pix = resizedImage.getpixel((x - magentaLeft, y - magentaTop))
            baseImage.putpixel((x, y), pix)
```

Two nested for loops iterate over every pixel in the magenta area. Remember that the magenta area does not have to be a perfect rectangle, so we check whether the pixel at the current coordinates is magenta. If so, we get the pixel color from the corresponding coordinates in the resized image and place it on the base image. After the two nested for loops have finished looping, the magenta pixels in the base image will have been replaced by pixels from the resized image.

However, the resized image itself could have magenta pixels, and if so, these will now become part of the base image, as in the top-right image of Figure 14-2. We'll need to pass the modified base image to a recursive makeDroste() call:

Python
```
# RECURSIVE CASE:
return makeDroste(baseImage, stopAfter - 1)
```

This line is the recursive call in our recursive algorithm, and it's the last line of code in the makeDroste() function. This recursion handles the new magenta area copied from the resized image. Note that the value passed for the stopAfter parameter is stopAfter - 1, ensuring that it comes closer to the base case of 0.

Finally, the Droste Maker program begins by passing 'museum.png' to makeDroste() to get the Pillow Image object of the recursive image. We save this as a new image file named *museum-recursive.png* and display the recursive image in a new window for the user to view:

Python
```
recursiveImage = makeDroste('museum.png')
recursiveImage.save('museum-recursive.png')
recursiveImage.show()
```

You can change these filenames to whichever image on your computer you'd like to use with the program.

Does the makeDroste() function need to be implemented with recursion? Simply put, no. Notice that no tree-like structure is involved in the problem, and the algorithm does no backtracking, which is a sign that recursion may be an overengineered approach to this code.

Summary

This chapter's project was a program that produces recursive Droste effect images, just like the illustration on old tins of Droste's Cacao. The program works by using pure magenta pixels with RGB values of (255, 0, 255) to mark the parts of the image that should be replaced by a smaller version. Since this smaller version will also have its own smaller magenta area, the replacements will repeat until the magenta area is gone to produce a recursive image.

The base case for our recursive algorithm occurs when no more magenta pixels remain in the image to place the smaller recursive image in, or when the stopAfter counter reaches 0. Otherwise, the recursive case passes the image to the makeDroste() function to continue to replace the magenta area with even smaller recursive images.

You can modify your own photos to add magenta pixels and then run them through the Droste Maker. The museum patron looking at an exhibit of themself, the cat in front of a computer monitor of the cat in front of a computer monitor, and the faceless *Mona Lisa* images are just a few examples of the surreal possibilities you can create with this recursive program.

Further Reading

The Wikipedia article for the Droste effect at *https://en.wikipedia.org/wiki/Droste_effect* has examples of products other than Droste's Cacao that use the Droste effect. Dutch artist M.C. Escher's *Print Gallery* is a famous example of a scene that also contains itself, and you can learn more about it at *https://en.wikipedia.org/wiki/Print_Gallery_(M._C._Escher)*.

In a video titled "The Neverending Story (and Droste Effect)" on the Numberphile YouTube channel, Dr. Clifford Stoll discusses recursion and the Droste's Cacao box art at *https://youtu.be/EeuLDnOupCI*.

Chapter 19 of my book *Automate the Boring Stuff with Python*, 2nd edition (No Starch Press, 2019) provides a basic tutorial of the Pillow library at *https://automatetheboringstuff.com/2e/chapter19*.

INDEX

V

vertices, 72

W

wedding seating chart, 126
Wilander, John, xx
Wilson's maze algorithm, 216

X

xcor() turtle function, 178
xkcd comic, 4
xy() jtg function, 178

Y

ycor() turtle function, 178

RESOURCES

Visit *https://nostarch.com/recursive-book-recursion* for errata and more information.

More no-nonsense books from **NO STARCH PRESS**

BEYOND THE BASIC STUFF WITH PYTHON
Best Practices for Writing Clean Code
BY AL SWEIGART
384 PP., $34.99
ISBN 978-1-59327-966-0

OBJECT-ORIENTED PYTHON
Master OOP by Building Games and GUIs
BY IRV KALB
416 PP., $44.99
ISBN 978-1-71850-206-2

REAL WORLD PYTHON
A Hacker's Guide to Solving Problems with Code
BY LEE VAUGHAN
360 PP., $34.95
ISBN 978-1-71850-062-4

PYTHON ONE-LINERS
Write Concise, Eloquent Python Like a Professional
BY CHRISTIAN MAYER
216 PP., $39.95
ISBN 978-1-71850-050-1

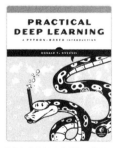

PRACTICAL DEEP LEARNING
A Python-Based Introduction
BY RONALD T. KNEUSEL
464 PP., $59.95
ISBN 978-1-71850-074-7

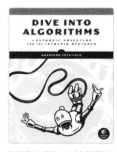

DIVE INTO ALGORITHMS
A Pythonic Adventure for the Intrepid Beginner
BY BRADFORD TUCKFIELD
248 PP., $39.95
ISBN 978-1-71850-068-6

PHONE:
800.420.7240 OR
415.863.9900

EMAIL:
SALES@NOSTARCH.COM
WEB:
WWW.NOSTARCH.COM